Reactions to The Warrior's Table from the SOF Community & Beyond

"I've always been a believer in food's incredible power to bring people together. The brilliance of *The Warrior's Table* is how it focuses that power on those who need it most. After all, it is not just the individuals in uniform who serve our nation; the whole family serves, and those families make incalculable sacrifices, spending more time apart than should be asked of anyone. A book of this nature isn't just long overdue, its excellence is a perfect tribute to those it honors."

— Chef Robert Irvine, Host of Restaurant: *Impossible*

"I spent my career rarely at home and when I was home from a deployment, I had every excuse why I wouldn't be home in time for dinner. Work was my priority and my family time suffered for it. Even though I spent my childhood having to be home at dinner and at dark, I didn't fully realize the impact and importance of gathering around the table to share a meal until we began making it our priority and then a rule. All phones are turned off and left in the living room and we all pitch in to make and clean up. The impact has been significant, we are more in tune with what's going on in each other's lives, and we are stronger and more connected because of it. Make family dinner a priority before it's too late, that time is precious and you don't get a do over."

— CSM (Ret.) Tom Satterly, Co-Founder of All Secure Foundation and author of *All Secure: A Special Operations Soldier's Fight to Survive on the Battlefield and the Homefront*

"I really love it. I wish I and (other operators) were issued this when I first got to SOF. It is something I could have referenced from time to time."

— Retired Army special operations service member

"This book is so powerful! It encourages SOF families and friends to embrace the lifestyle; establish norms (when there really isn't a norm); and keep their family traditions strong. *The Warrior's Table* provides families with bits of wisdom about how to find stability and comfort in this way of life. I hope all who read it gain confidence in this special operations lifestyle and all its moments of joy, happiness, connection, and sadness, and most of all gain a sense of pride and appreciation in the enduring capabilities of our community."

— Cher Powers, Army special operations spouse of 22 years

A Special Note from Dr. Anne Fishel

Family dinner is the canvas on which Special Operations Forces (SOF) family life takes place amidst deployments and reunions, the ordinary travails of raising children, and the extraordinary challenges of unpredictability and sacrifice. The Cast Iron Crew, living in a community that runs on uncertainty, have embraced the magic of creating meaningful family dinner practices, which serve as a checkpoint for the health and nourishment of their family members. This wise, engaging, mouth-watering book offers us a two-layer confection: One layer is composed of family stories, games to play at the table, and user-friendly recipes gleaned from deployments across the country and the globe. The second layer offers a vivid portrait of SOF family life, including photos of private and public moments, military history, the language of the SOF and its customs. If you are part of this community, the stories will resonate. If you are a civilian, you will come away greatly enriched and awed by the creativity and resilience of this community.

As the Executive Director of The Family Dinner Project, I was honored to offer some consultation on the book: I have been inspired by the stories of celebration and heartache, delighted by the photos of military balls and Fire Pit Fridays, and energized by the conversation starters (eg. think of a time when you were ready for a challenge, when you were prepared or not?) This is a book to have at the ready, to refer to repeatedly for ideas that will nourish the minds, bodies, and spirits of your family.

Dr. Fishel is Director of the Massachusetts General Hospital (MGH) Family and Couples Therapy Program, and Executive Director and co-founder of The Family Dinner Project in the MGH Psychiatry Academy. Learn more about Dr. Fishel's work on pages 421-422.

A Letter from a Retired Senior Leader Reflecting on the Importance of The Warrior's Table

Over the course of a long career in U.S. Special Operations, I had the privilege of endorsing and supporting a large number of important activities and missions that went on to have positive and lasting impacts. Yet, until now, no one ever asked me to endorse a recipe book. Nonetheless, when I was first asked, I quickly realized that *The Warrior's Table* may be among the most important efforts I've ever had the privilege to advocate for.

This work serves as a powerful reminder that the preparation, serving, and consumption of meals remains one humanity's most important practices. This tradition not only ensured our species' physical survival, the practice of meal-making and meal-taking has been foundational for how families and other human groups created and nourished the person-to-person relationships that ultimately define a successful society, and thereby sets the conditions that determine how likely any individual is to find happiness, fulfillment, and genuine joy in their lifetime.

Over the centuries, such a society could have been a small prehistoric tribe. It could have been a once thriving city-state during the Bronze Age in the ancient Fertile Crescent. Today, it would be any community, large or small, rural or urban, in modern America. No matter where one goes, the tradition of preparing, serving, and consuming a meal as groups or families has been one of the most important "binding agents" that weaves together the social fabric. And without that social fabric, there is no reliable backdrop or foundation for the happiness of the people of that society . . . either as individuals or as groups.

More specific to *The Warrior's Table*, this project also vividly portrays other powerful elements that directly relate to SOF veterans, and their loved ones, and the recipes within this work offer a familiar and comforting platform for celebrating these elements.

It reminds us of the powerful connection between our service to the Nation, and service we did in raising, nourishing, and serving our Families. It creates a familiar platform through which can be shared the experiences, joys, sorrows, adventures, and misadventures of what it means to be a SOF family and community. It gives us the chance to renew our appreciation for the multi-faceted and varied backgrounds, cultures, beliefs, origins, and practices of the SOF Family, and how that familiarity makes the entire community stronger and more resilient.

It creates an opportunity to remember and honor the extraordinary history and heroic deeds of the SOF community, both at home and abroad. . . . whether in combat, in humanitarian relief efforts, or otherwise helping ensure the safety and security of populations from the predations of evil-doers.

And, perhaps most importantly of all, this work can provide almost limitless opportunities for all of us . . . service member and family member alike, comrade-to-comrade, spouse-to-spouse, parent-to-child, servicemember to civilian, old to young . . . to cherish each other, to recall that we need each other, and that we love and respect each other, and that . . . come what may . . . we will always BE THERE for each other.

With gratitude and respect,

Michael K. Nagata, LTG (Ret.), Former Commander of U.S. Special Operations Command Central

★ ★ ★ THE ★ ★ ★
WARRIOR'S TABLE

MILITARY
SPECIAL OPERATIONS
FAMILY COLLABORATIVE

THE WARRIOR'S TABLE

★ ★ ★

Recipes that Cultivate Connection through War, Change, and Uncertainty

By the Cast Iron Crew, a Military Special Operations Family Collaborative

program in partnership with The Family Dinner Project

Ballast Books, LLC
www.ballastbooks.com

ISBN: 978-1-955026-72-7
Library of Congress Catalog Number: 2022923257

Printed in the United States of America

Front cover art/photo courtesy of Julianne Ziebell
Cover and book design by Mayfly Design

Published by Ballast Books
www.ballastbooks.com

For more information, bulk orders, appearances, or speaking requests,
please email: info@ballastbooks.com

Contents

★ ★ ★

Special Thanks

★ ★ ★

THANK YOU TO EVERYONE WHO CONTRIBUTED to the journey of writing this book and telling the story of special operations' life at home. Our core family dinner team spent well over two years teasing out what it meant to live as a special operations family. We could not have even begun the book if not for our steadfast, insightful, and brilliant partner, Dr. Anne Fishel and The Family Dinner Project (TFDP). TFDP helped us shape the concept and outline, and they stayed with our team through several military moves, baby additions, and of course the pandemic of 2020.

Thank you to the fellow spouses who began the book with us. Mary Duffy, Katie Miller, and April Reddy, you shaped the book and recipes within, and we could not have finished had you not started with us. To our dedicated interns, Bridget Orr, Maisie Paulson, and Gina Rudine, you added extra creativity and commitment and helped write and complete critical aspects of the book. Dr. Christi Luby, our MSOFC team member, for her steadfast heart and commitment to our work and the families in special operations. Thank you!!

Last but not least, thank you to the many community members who shared their recipes, photos, experiences, and wisdom with our team. Without your generosity, thoughtfulness, and insights, this book would not be what it is today. We hope you see your feedback fingerprints in the pages and chapters ahead. Finally, we owe extraordinary thanks to Cher Powers, Jodi Lynch, Erick Miyares, Shayla Hayward-Lundy, Hilary Peters, Elizabeth Persaud, Alexis Moore, and the many others who took part in reviewing *The Warrior's Table*. Your feedback changed chapters and shaped sections, and made our family dinner book what it is. Thank you!

A Note to All Readers

★ ★ ★

THE WARRIOR'S TABLE WAS CREATED from the direct experiences and story-telling of special operations spouses. The Military Special Operations Family Collaborative's Family Dinner Team wrote this book through the lens of special operations spouses *for* special operations spouses, families, extended families, and friends.

A primary goal in writing this book was to elevate the lived experience of the individual special operations family to the broader community level. The history, customs, and other relevant, open-source information about special operations forces (SOF) included in *The Warrior's Table* is for the benefit of the SOF community's well-being. Unit history, customs, and basic language use (even slang) are necessary knowledge for confidence and meaningful connection at home and within our community. Regardless of skill set, mission set, location, or service branch, there are universal truths and experiences within the special operations community that help us connect and thrive in the day-to-day and in the long-term.

The Warrior's Table is really two books in one. It can be read cover to cover as a deep dive in the SOF lifestyle or you can target one recipe, tidbit, or story at a time. This is a book about how to thrive in the SOF community. Imagine you are sitting with our Cast Iron Crew just chatting over coffee. The recipes, stories, and culture woven together in this book are akin to 'experience fingerprints' of hundreds of families. While an effort was made to be technically correct and accurate, the priority in writing was to storytell the special operations lifestyle in a way that any spouse connected to a SOF unit could recognize this book was written for them. For this reason, we use a variety of relevant terms to describe our service members—operator, service member, enabler, service support, warrior, soldier, sailor, airmen, etc.

Each SOF service member and their family play a critical role in safeguarding the defense of our great nation. The men, women, and children within the special operations community of the past and present are the best our country has to offer. They are the epitome of what makes our nation truly great in the eyes of the rest of the world. The life and spirit of each individual and family within our community make it extraordinary.

NOTE: MSOFC considers the special operations community to be composed of any past or present service member and their immediate family members, who served in, or attached to, a special operations unit or legacy unit. Special operations units are any military units in the United States Army, Air Force, Marine Corps, or Navy that fall under the Title 10 authorities of U.S. Special Operations Command.

DISCLAIMER: *The Warrior's Table* was not written in formal collaboration with any military unit and it does not represent the views of the U.S. Department of Defense, U.S. Special Operations Command or any special operations or military unit.

Preface

A Book for the Special Operations Community on the Importance of Shared Mealtime

THE MILITARY SPECIAL OPERATIONS FAMILY COLLABORATIVE (MSOFC) is a nonprofit public health initiative for the special operations community, dedicated to enabling the sustained success of America's special operations warriors and families through collaborative health and well-being research and programs. The shared qualities and ethos of our special operations community propel our elite service members to overcome tremendous challenges—but over time the persistent stressors can present unique hardships to long-term health, performance, and success.

One study found that special operations service members delay care for visible or invisible wounds of war for as much as 13 years and 3 months.[1] By the time special operators decide to seek care, their bodies and relationships are often in dire straits. That collateral fallout often first appears on the homefront, as the service member's spouse and children witness and feel the impact of prolonged uncertainty. It shapes their day-to-day lives and challenges their well-being. The persistent stress also impacts mission performance, leadership quality and potential, and unit and family legacy.

In 2018, MSOFC research identified eight common coping mechanisms that military families may engage in for short-term stress relief. Yet these coping mechanisms threaten special operations service member health, performance, and family well-being when they become long-term habits or family norms. When these eight habits persist for two years or more, families struggle to support one another and feel connected. We call these the SOF Common Pitfalls. They can create conflict and negative outcomes for family well-being. However when the pitfalls are flipped, they become powerful *Healthy Checkpoints* for SOF families.

---

1. Searcey, Dionne. (2016). A General's New Mission: Leading a Charge Against PTSD. *New York Times*. Retrieved from https://nyti.ms/2dElkYT

FLIP THE STRATEGY

...from common but unhealthy & unsustainable coping mechanisms to healthy checkpoints that help special ops families thrive!

COMMON PITFALLS	HEALTHY CHECKPOINTS
Prolonged, unpredictable family routine	Gain control by building routines & norms where possible (start small)
Ceasing family celebrations	Celebrate notable accomplishments, people, & moments
No/few practiced family traditions	Practice meaningful traditions
Skipping family vacation or working on leave	Schedule opportunities to connect with people you care about
Regularly skipping/avoiding family dinner	Prioritize shared mealtime
Avoidance of important conversation	Engage in meaningful conversation with key people in your life
Limited awareness of invisible wounds	Recognize & address chronic stress and invisible wounds
Pessimism regarding military service & tradition	Be proud of your service to own your legacy

Flip the strategy from Common Pitfalls to Healthy Checkpoints to thrive in the special ops lifestyle.

Limited awareness and the breakdown of simple habits chip away the healthy foundation necessary to endure and overcome challenges that inevitably arise in a special operations family, but it doesn't have to be this way. Mealtime can be a family and community ritual that reinforces healthy routines and positive habits. When mealtime becomes a community Healthy Checkpoint, it is a practice akin to the family gym or operations center where well-being essentials take root.

Shared mealtime is not about being tied to an oven or the dinner table; it's about fundamentally caring for the minds, bodies, and hearts of those closest to you. 'Family Dinner' can take many forms—breakfast, coffee, brunch, lunch, snacktime, or supper. It is simply a shared, essential human need that can and should be fertile soil for creativity, energy, compassion, and human connection. Family dinner is ultimately about cultivating a sense of belonging within a family, a community, and a meaningful life.

Recognizing this opportunity, the Military Special Operations Family Collaborative sought out the expertise of Dr. Anne Fishel and the nonprofit initiative, The Family Dinner Project. Then, we formed our own special operations-specific family dinner team—the Cast Iron Crew—to write *The Warrior's Table*. In the pages that follow, the Cast Iron Crew tells the story of seasoned special ops families who learned to prioritize mealtime through decades of military service, countless deployments, and much more. *The Warrior's Table* is a canvas for acknowledging the rewards that accompany the energy drain and the day-to-day realities of life in special operations. It is a tribute to the heart and compassion of our families and an opportunity to motivate and energize those who are tired. There is so much in the special operations legacy of which to be proud.

An Introduction to Our Military Family

★ ★ ★

STRONG BONDS ARE FORGED between people who serve together. This is true of any type of service, but it is especially true for military service. The Military Family is made up of . . .

Universal Ingredients

Whatever the service branch or military expertise—Army, Navy, Air Force, Marine Corps, Space Force, Reserve, or National Guard—we are collectively one military family. Yes, there are differences and rivalries between units, branches, jobs, expertise, and roles. Did you pound the ground, fly through the skies, or sail the seas? These days maybe you launched drones, dropped bombs, or secretly fought terror from a computer desk far away. But regardless of how you served, military service requires you to do hard things that are necessary because of a commitment to our nation's values and service values. Each military life experience requires you to conform to particular ways of living—wearing a uniform, cutting your hair, attending a school, practicing certain fitness regimens, relocating, saying good-bye or welcome home, and the list goes on. These are the *universal ingredients* to military service.

Packing up for a Permanent Change of Station (PCS) move is a common experience for military families. *(Photo courtesy of Lynnsy Snook)*

Another look at a PCS move.
(Photo courtesy of KaLea Lehman)

Duty makes demands of you and, in turn, it makes demands of your family. The demands and meaning are deeply intertwined. There is shared sacrifice among service members and those who love them. Special dates and holidays get missed. Events are planned around training, deployment, and military schedules packed with ceremonies and social events. Service members and their families rely on each other, share tips and tricks, and help each other thrive through countless permanent change of station (PCS) moves and challenges from military duty.

All service families have their own military-shaped story. You moved your wedding date, eloped, or you got lucky and your special day went off without a hitch. Maybe you had a baby alone or your spouse just barely made it back in time. Maybe your family is blended or you entered the service with kids in tow. Then, there is the first move away from family, overseas moves, moves where half your household furniture is broken, and now there are moves colored by the ever-changing complexities of the COVID-19 pandemic. There are tales of how your family manages military training and deployment. Did you write letters, rely on email, call home old school style, use video, or the latest encrypted app? Maybe your communication changed because the Morale, Welfare and Recreation (MWR) tent downrange

An Air Force special operations couple marry. *(Photo courtesy of Jennifer Byrne)*

had a never-ending line or possibly a sandstorm disrupted all connections. Did you spend days crafting care packages or has the care package ship sailed? Quite possibly, Walmart or Amazon came to your rescue and simplified the care package trek to the post office.

Chow Hall food in Honduras (*Photo courtesy of Hilary Peters*)

Part of living the military life is *the table*. There are unit picnics, barbecues, community potlucks, Meals Ready to Eat (MRE), and the chow hall. Downrange on deployment there is a whole other set of crazy stories about food. Maybe service members ate well and enjoyed lobster and ice cream in Iraq. Maybe they relied on MREs for ages or pleaded for care packages with canned goods because they chose hunger over the contracted chow that gave them food poisoning. These are the shared experiences—the good, the bad, and the unbelievable—that connect families and units to each other and the mission.

Maybe you met your battle buddy at a unit Hail and Farewell or you simply bonded because you couldn't stop laughing at the retelling of how energy drinks or coffee kept the tanks "rolling along" (a nod to the official Army song). Or, your service member deployed to train a partner force and getting anywhere with the mission meant drinking tea (more sugar than tea) with the local leader. There is so much truth to the old saying, "you are what you eat." Food is your culture on display—whether it is the food choice of your unit, food from a deployment, or the delicacies served at your own dinner table.

These aspects of military service are passed down from generation to generation. Ancient military tales of battle like Sophocles' *Ajax* still resonate with modern warriors because much of the setting, characters, and the emotions that bond them are universal and timeless. In this way, service and family dinner are alike. Military service connects you through shared experience and hardship, and shared mealtime sets the table for connection and belonging.

Special Operations on the Side

The U.S. special operations community is a blend of small, specialized units from major service branches—Army, Navy, Marine Corps, Air Force, and Reserve forces. These elite units are committed to missions that demand extra training and expertise. The Army Special Forces, Navy SEALs, Marine Raiders, Air Force PJs and many other units are generally called "special operations" or casually

An ODA gone training *(Photo courtesy of KaLea Lehman)*

"spec ops." These warriors are a *well-seasoned side* with different and specialized military missions from their brothers and sisters in arms.

Missions in special operations are unique from one another. Some missions take special operations forces (SOF) to the front of a conflict and others play key supporting roles. Each warrior serving in special operations shares a few unique characteristics. Warriors don't quit, and they thrive in the unknown, navigating uncertainty. They believe in their country, and they believe service is their duty. They train and deploy and deploy again in small teams, to remote deserts, jungles, and mountain tops to do our nation's bidding. Many times their missions are peaceful and involve training or other special activities, but sometimes they are called upon to eliminate the masterminds of terror.

Warriors share in the universal stories all service members know, but there is no certainty to their *menu. Their meat is often served tough and seconds are uncertain.* Their service is one of repeated separation, adventure, loyalty, triumph, and sometimes heartbreak. They value the challenges that accompany the journey, and their families learn to live and love this lifestyle, too. The warrior's military family has a unique culture that tends the table through the changing demands of service. Their necessary support demands grit, a deep respect for the warrior ethos, and a humble heart.

Salt can cleanse and restore a cast iron pan and work loose the grease and grime that builds up dish after dish. It can preserve meat, season it, or, if a curious toddler decides to help in the kitchen, salt will simply ruin the meal. How we process the emotions that naturally accompany our journey in special operations is very much the same. *Living well and thriving in the special operations community is similar to success in the kitchen—both demand proper seasoning.*

Now, we leave the retelling to ladies who've set and cleared the warrior's table through it all.

Our Cast Iron Crew

The Cast Iron Crew is a team of women who are so relaxed it can be unsettling, and yet they are simultaneously sprinkled with intensity brewed by experience. Our Crew is tough, creative, flexible, dependable, and stoic. We have great love for our special operations community. We know the heart behind the missions. We learned to appreciate the secret spice that can help restore a scorched pan when properly seasoned.

In the pages ahead, we attempt to confront our saltiness and acknowledge the experiences that we learned to let go of. We reflect on the people and values that helped us persevere over Murphy's Law and share our story of life in the special operations forces (SOF) community. We have been new spouses ready for adventure, tasted exotic recipes, been burnt by deployment, toasted from distraction, and scrubbed clean with salt. We are scrappy, flexible, and adaptable. We focus on our people and acknowledge our imperfections—which, at times, were humiliating moments we were forced to embrace.

Our Cast Iron Crew knows the tales of those who have repeatedly gone to war and returned home only to go back again, because we've witnessed the home and away routines for decades and dozens of deployments. Each of us found our way as a "new spouse" (at some point in the special operations journey between selection and life post service) or helped another hold the pieces together. We have pictures of homecomings, no pictures from forgotten temporary duty trips, and occasionally saved an unbelievable screenshot. Cumulatively, our dinner team chose not to count the deployments, quick trips, training missions, or time spent away from home. Being "away" is simply a special ops reality. Uncertainty is a fact you learn to embrace. Grit is a secret spice that is necessary to swallow those moments that can be too sweet, bland, or at times very bitter.

We learned how to say no because we had to shore-up our homefront or pause our calendar to be present for a friend. We found a rhythm and respect for the

Spouses on the high ropes course (*Photo courtesy of Mary Duffy*)

life we know and that few consider taking on. We are greased with experience, seasoned with shared sacrifice, and ready to pass on family recipes that helped us through the moments which formed our *Warrior's Table*.

Each of our crew have paused to reflect on what it means to Never Forget. We've attended funerals, memorials, and grave sites. We've witnessed "shots" for the fallen and sometimes shared in them. We know the varying and mixed emotions that accompany 9/11, Veterans Day, Independence Day, and above all, Memorial Day.

None of the military qualifications, years of service, rank, moves, or even service branch matter at home. These are not our centerpieces. Scuba, airborne, freefall, sniper . . . Army Ranger, Air Force Special Tactics, Navy SEAL, Army Special Forces, Marine Raider . . . These accomplishments start out impressive and exciting, but after a few trips, trainings, deployments, or family days they become lifestyle characteristics that merely shape how we cook. We can all tell stories of proud moments like the day our spouse earned the Green Beret, experienced an underwater demolition, or endured a hard landing, but those moments are a flash in the pan. It is the simple moments that hold meaning and make our table strong.

Our family dinner team knows the military special operations lifestyle. We take pride in the sacrifice, triumph, adventure, and misadventures that detail our journey. We have a shared respect for this life because we have seen the good, endured the worst, and remained witness to our community—the SOF community—standard. We fight for the weak and oppressed and have no tolerance for terror. We demand honor, integrity, excellence, creativity, and an allegiance to American values. Our Crew knows peace and security are not privileges. They are

The moment they had been waiting months for—picking up Dad.
(Photo courtesy of Angie McLaughlin)

hard won realities that should be appreciated and must be protected. *Our warriors are witness to the fact that terror can reign when there is an absence of shared values, respect, or law and order.*

So, from West Coast beaches to the sweet Southern states; amid European exploration and Middle Eastern misadventures; over mountains in Asia and back again to unit hubs; the Cast Iron Crew story tells how we kept the warrior's table set. Whether you are on day one in the SOF community or a long-time legacy member, our family dinner team highlights the incredible heart of our community and walks you through how to rally your brood, recognize those who are struggling, show up for friends, rally together as a team, and embrace this community for the long haul. This book of recipes has roots in stories of endurance, honesty, service, belonging, and a commitment to excellence. *The Warrior's Table* is a recipe book for finding belonging in this rough and tumble community of warriors. Ultimately, this book is about building family and community bonds to outlast the shared hardships and transitions that accompany service in special operations units.

Marine couple video chat over a deployment. *(Photo courtesy of Laura Nicholson)*

Enjoying summer fruits with friends.
(Photo courtesy of Andrea Geraldi)

Let's Stew on Family Dinner

★ ★ ★

WHEN FAMILIES ARE STRONG, EVERYBODY WINS. Decades of research show that family dinner is good for the body, brain, and spirit.[2] It is the foundation for winning hearts and minds. It is the thread that holds a family parachute together, the canvas for traditions and celebrations. It is a bowl to concoct future trips, adventures, and accomplishments.

Family dinner leads to healthy bodies and minds.[3] Of all the research on the many positive impacts of family dinner, this one is almost a "well duh" research take-away. The truth is many people know this, but they do not practice it with intention. Cooking intimidates many, and this is often the case for those who did not grow up around the kitchen cooking. Learning to cook when you are young and learning how your community lives impacts the routines you carry into adulthood.[4] That crazy cranberry salad on the Thanksgiving table was more than a dish, it was an opportunity to hand down a family story and holiday tradition. The memory of "putting-up" garden goods for the off season is an important childhood memory and harvest ritual. The milestones and accomplishments we celebrated and how we went about it are often family traditions that get passed on. How you planned your birthday celebration as a kid impacts how you think about it today. What you cooked or helped to cook immediately fed your mind and body, but it also shaped how you do life—the habits, values, and traditions you practice.[5] Healthy meals have a multifaceted, positive ripple effect on many parts of your family life.

Strong families prioritize family dinner. Family dinner boosts vocabulary, improves storytelling skills, and promotes literacy in children.[6] These dinner facts are both intriguing and surprising. At first you might question how family meal time could

2. The Family Dinner Project. 2019. Eat, Laugh, Talk: The Family Dinner Playbook. Familius LLC.
3. The Family Dinner Project. 2019. Eat, Laugh, Talk: The Family Dinner Playbook. Familius LLC.
4. Utter J, Larson N, Laska MN, Winkler M, Neumark-Sztainer D. Self-Perceived Cooking Skills in Emerging Adulthood Predict Better Dietary Behaviors and Intake 10 Years Later: A Longitudinal Study. J Nutr Educ Behav. 2018 May;50(5):494-500. doi: 10.1016/j.jneb.2018.01.021. Epub 2018 Mar 7. PMID: 29525525; PMCID: PMC6086120.
5. Duke, M.P. Lazarus, A., & Fivush, R. 2008. Knowledge of family history as a clinically useful index of psychological well-being and prognosis: a brief report. Psychotherapy Theory, Research Pracie, Training, 45:268-272.
6. The Family Dinner Project Team. Research Shows Family Dinner Improves Literacy. Blog Post August 31, 2020. Accessed from https://thefamilydinnerproject.org/blog/research-shows-family-dinner-improves-literacy/

A special family dinner out. *(Photo courtesy of Samantha Gomolka)*

possibly be tied to literacy and vocabulary. How can it be even more impactful than the nightly book you read to your littles?[7] The answer is there are many more words said over family meal time when families connect, talk about their day, and share their thoughts and emotions.[8] Comfortable and supportive family conversations pass on facts, words, and family values that contribute to success well into adulthood.

Sharing mealtime with others is also associated with better mental and physical health for adults.[9] It can contribute to enhanced team performance.[10] Those pregame, calorie-packed meals that high school sports teams share together, or the church potluck lunch, provide far more than a simple opportunity to eat. They enhance teams, strengthen communities, set the circumstances for friendships to form, and for people to find their place.

7. Snow, C.E., Beals, D.E. 2006 Mealtime talk that supports literacy development. New Directions in Child and Adolescent Behavior, 111:51-66.

8. The Family Dinner Project Team. Research Shows Family Dinner Improves Literacy. Blog Post August 31, 2020. Accessed from https://thefamilydinnerproject.org/blog/research-shows-family-dinner-improves-literacy/

9. Fishel, Anne.. The Benefits of Family Dinner for Adults. Blog Post May 11, 2021. Accessed from https://thefamilydinnerproject.org/food-for-thought/benefits-family-dinner-adults/

10. Kevin M. Kniffin, Brian Wansink, Carol M. Devine & Jeffery Sobal (2015) Eating Together at the Firehouse: How Workplace Commensality Relates to the Performance of Firefighters, Human Performance, 28:4, 281-306, DOI: 10.1080/08959285.2015.1021049

Meals shared within a community foster support in times of stress and need.[11] For our special operations community this translates into safety in life or death situations and critical friendships before, during, and after deployments. Families and communities share challenges, success stories, and bond around food.[12] These are essential ingredients at every point in your family journey through military service and beyond. Whether it is a simple campfire with hotdogs and s'mores or a large, catered reception, gathering for a meal—any meal—nurtures the body, energizes the soul, fosters connection with others, and paves the way for a life well-lived.

Too Meaty to Chew

Family dinner sounds simple. Everyone has to eat. Calories are critical for survival, so why is "family dinner" so hard to chew? Why is it one of the first rituals to disappear when things at home are scattered or stressed? For starters, food takes time, money, and energy. Time to shop. Time to plan. Time to find recipes. Time to cook. Throw in family conflict, small kid chaos, special diets or complicated schedules, and it is tempting to take an "easy out" of family mealtime.

The Family Dinner Project's book *Eat, Laugh, Talk* tackles five common mealtime challenges. They found regardless of who you are or where you come from people everywhere struggle to prioritize family dinner because:

1. Picky eaters
2. Too busy/no time
3. Too much work
4. We're too distracted, mostly by tech
5. Conflict and tension

Today, most of us live busy and fast-paced lives. Often there isn't much time or energy left in our weekly schedule, so finding time to plan and prioritize a whole-family meal can get complicated. Taking on this shared mealtime challenge becomes even less enticing when you add in strained emotions. These emotional hurdles can be tied to all sorts of sources—an adolescent or family member's attitude, health and wellness challenges, or an oh so common relationship spat. In their book *Eat, Laugh, Talk*, The Family Dinner Project reviews evidence-based benefits of shared mealtime, addresses these common and complicated family factors, and offers creative ideas and recipes to baby step over each struggle for

11. Fishel, Anne.. The Benefits of Family Dinner for Adults. Blog Post May 11, 2021. Accessed from https://thefamilydinnerproject.org/food-for-thought/benefits-family-dinner-adults/
12. Mayo Clinic Health System. March 22, 2019. Family Meals: Building Relationships. Speaking of Health blog. Accessed from https://www.mayoclinichealthsystem.org/hometown-health/speaking-of-health/family-meals-building-relationships

the sake of individual and family success. The multitude of benefits are worth the effort.

The Special Operations Flavor

The special operations lifestyle poses unique challenges to the family plate in addition to the 5 discussed above. Our day to day life can feel much like the dishes that fill our table. Some recipes are bitter, sweet, or too spicy, and many times the main dish seems too tough to chew. Special operations families learn to cook with these realities as they set the warrior's table and master two more lifestyle-driven, mealtime challenges:

6. Constant change and uncertainty
7. Intensity around the table

Special operations families learn if their service member is home or away, there are certain variables constantly at play. Change happens nearly by the minute as the service member is consistently wrestling with uncertainty. Just when you think you might get to vacation, the Islamic State is sure to topple a key city, the Syrian government will "cross a red line," the Russians will light up your air space, or the Iranians or Chinese may play in your waters. National headlines won't spur attention from most Americans, but they are sure to mess up your birthday plans, summer vacation, or PCS move. And often there is not a simple, safe, or accepted way to talk about it. Few Americans stand ready and are trained to be the eyes, ears, or scope on the ground. So, uncertainty rules as a mealtime expectation. *This means our families have to be adaptable, flexible, creative, and incredibly intentional. They must be careful to hold fast to a few lifestyle staples, or they risk untethering important family bonds by practicing SOF common pitfalls instead of hitting SOF healthy checkpoints (Revisit page xii for more on SOF Common Pitfalls and Healthy Checkpoints).*

The next obstacle special operations families learn to maneuver around is intensity and the tension it can spur. When each day is somewhat unpredictable, we all stress. Often, we don't recognize the stress in ourselves. Seasoned special operations family *chefs* adapt ingredients and build rapport around a table loaded with tension. This is a tough table challenge

Street food in Uganda (*Photo courtesy of Paul Schmidt*)

A solo mission (*Photo courtesy of Erick Miyares*)

because it is rooted in many legitimate needs, such as mission safety and success, leadership demands, physical health challenges, compounding family demands and dynamics, evolving needs, and so much more. These are real and important tensions, but it doesn't change the fact that powder keg level tension can shut down conversation, intimidate little voices, and generally kill the fun of mealtime connection.

Military families know there are many times the mission comes first. It is often tough to complain, express concern, and mention a need when lives are legitimately on the line. The tensions at play can silence growing kids from expressing concerns or asking for help. They may act out or lean toward risky behavior when family awareness or support is lacking. Families may feel guilty for feeling lonely, tired, or frustrated, and needs may go unsaid or unaddressed.[13] Learning how to "train-up" a special operations family demands compassion, courage, a keen eye, a lot of patience, and the wisdom to know when to push a family priority or to keep subtly "setting the conditions."

---

13. Collins, E. (2015, May 6). *Experts explain mental state of military children*. www.army.mil. Accessed from https://www.army.mil/article/147786/experts_explain_mental_state_of_military_children

Sending Dad off *(Photo courtesy of Samantha Gomolka)*

It does not matter which meal you take aim at, or if family dinner time flip-flops.[14] Breakfast, second breakfast, lunch, dinner, or dessert—the only ingredients that really must be intentionally stirred together are: people, words, and something digestible. Quite possibly it is as basic as a morning coffee, afternoon tea, or a shared "shot" for the fallen.

Family mealtime, any mealtime, is an anchor in the lives of thriving individuals and strong families. MSOFC's Cast Iron Crew knows these challenges. In collaboration with The Family Dinner Project, *The Warrior's Table* storytells how we:

- Learned to recognize stress in our day to day
- Give ourselves and our family permission to feel
- Recognize emotions are signposts to our values and goals
- Share evidence and experience-based ideas to motivate families to prioritize family mealtime
- Suggest practical strategies and tactics to encourage Healthy Checkpoints in SOF family life

There is great meaning in SOF service amid the everyday challenges that accompany war, change, and sustained uncertainty. Part of what makes SOF life extraordinary are the treasures and trials that shape us into who we become. None of us can predict what the future will hold, but we can choose how to find our place and make it worth the ride.

Setting the Warrior's Table

New warrior, old warrior, or friend of a warrior, it doesn't matter. Maybe you are a new family, a kid free family, or a family with a packed house and many mouths to feed. These characteristics make for different dynamics, but various dynamics and diverse backgrounds keep our SOF community interesting, exciting, supportive, and creative. Regardless of who you are—SEAL, Green Beret, Special Aviator, or . . . oops . . . we won't say what you are—dinner dynamics will shift throughout years of training, deployments, and life, but there are some predictable fixin's for the warrior's table.

---

14. Fishel, Anne. 2022. FAQ. The Family Dinner Project. Accessed from https://thefamilydinnerproject.org/resources/faq/

Special Forces Dad works out with his crew. (*Photo courtesy of Andrew Marr*)

If you aren't in the habit of sharing a regular mealtime (anytime), it's okay. Don't get discouraged if you hit a dinner dynamic rut. Meet mealtime uncertainty with flexibility and creativity. Figure out how to make mealtime work with some trial and error. Be a mealtime ambassador. Family meal, mission success must-haves are people and conversation. The challenging part is getting those ingredients to mix together with some certainty. This may sound like a low bar for elite military service member families, but it isn't. It's a REAL bar that sets the whole family up for lasting success.

Rolling out the dough. (*Photo courtesy of Sara Maybouer*)

Little hands bring unique laughter and motion to the table.
(Photo courtesy of Julianne Ziebell)

* * *

TALES FROM THE TABLE

* * *

The Warrior's Table is a joint compilation of stories, games, conversation starters, military history, heritage, and go-to recipes. So when your toddler son climbs the tallest counter, stands up straight, and declares, "My daddy jumps out of airplanes, and I jump off mommy's counters." We don't gasp at the fact that the young, wobbly fella just climbed a high surface. We smile because he admires his daddy who has been "away" most of his days, and we laugh off the event over a chocolate dessert. Likewise, when your little princess writes stories of riding on a flying carpet over the Middle Eastern desert, we are proud because we know the "brave prince" that is the root of her inspiration and the strong momma who laid the groundwork for her fairytale daydream.

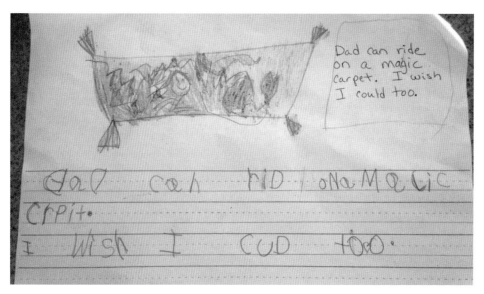

"Dad can ride on a magic carpet. I wish I could too." *(Photo courtesy of KaLea Lehman)*

However, there are a few tips you should know before you join us. To hear and appreciate our tales of how we gather, *The Warrior's Table* has some ground rules:

- **SET A DINNER BASELINE**—Just one shared meal a week[15] at breakfast, lunch or dinner will make a huge and lasting impact on the strength and health of your family. Cut cooking corners if it sets the conditions for connection and belonging.

- **CULTIVATE SELF AND SITUATIONAL AWARENESS**—Be mindful of how you and your family feel and why you do what you do. Get specific with feelings and emotions. It is impossible to be flexible if you don't realize when you are stuck in a rut.

- **TRAIN PATIENCE WITH THE BASICS**—In our fast-paced life, patience is essential. Take a deep breath and work out your frustration. Every frustration is more palatable when you slow down the fast pace by focusing on the basics: sleep, get moving, eat well, and learn to manage the stress of the moment.

- **PRACTICE THOUGHTFUL COMMUNICATION**—This is an important life skill that can take root at the table. Healthy, predictable meals help establish family norms and minimize anxiety that can accompany the unknowns common in a spec ops life.[16] Military special operations units take on the complex

15. The Family Dinner Project. 2019. Eat, Laugh, Talk: The Family Dinner Playbook. Familius LLC.
16. WebMD Editorial Contributors. (n.d.). *Psychological Benefits of Routines*. WebMD. Accessed from https://www.webmd.com/mental-health/psychological-benefits-of-routine

missions that people may or may not know anything about. Your own kids or step kids might not know much about their SOF parent or the military. A great place to start is with the conversation starters and other tools in this book.

- **GET EVERYONE INVOLVED**—Encourage littles to take on small mealtime responsibilities, like lighting a candle or setting the table. Playing a key role in making mealtime work will help them channel their excitement and energy and give you an opportunity to recognize they played a part in making the meal happen.[17]

- **BUILD COMMUNITY**—Make the effort to go beyond the basic, "hello, my name is . . ." This takes intentional effort and compassion because—let's be real—no one in our community is on the same "trip" schedule for long. You will need real friends who have the ability to show up for you and the energy to return their support.

- **DON'T BE A HERO**—We all tend to "show our strength" and sometimes we (unintentionally) make moments harder than they need to be. Dinner doesn't have to be perfect. Life is not perfect. Humble moments will happen, so be honest with yourself, vulnerable with others, and lean on your circle of support. Learning when to reach out and where to access resources is what it means to "be seasoned."

- **SEIZE THE DAY**—Nothing is impossible. Prioritize creating memories with those you love. Overseas, on the fly, R&R meet up, or a once in a lifetime concert. Make an effort to say "yes" to good opportunities. Then do the work to make them happen. Many of these opportunities come with a shared meal opportunity.

- **EMBRACE THE BEAUTIFUL**—A little beauty goes a long way. A beautiful bouquet of your favorite flowers or the sunset on a beach. Seeing or experiencing beauty or nature can be life giving. Sometimes it is all you need to connect with a friend or family member. When we notice the beautiful, we acknowledge what we appreciate. We share a piece of ourselves and we get a taste of how belonging feels. Take a moment to slow down and notice the beauty in your path and sprinkle your surroundings with a shared coffee, s'mores, or an on-the-go picnic.

- **BE UNCONVENTIONAL**—Stretch the idea of dinner to meet the physical or emotional needs of the moment. Unconventional opportunities may require you to seize the moment, be prepared for an outdoor adventure, or simply buffer your energy bank with extra dessert or a beautiful flower centerpiece.

17. The Family Dinner Project. 2019. Eat, Laugh, Talk: The Family Dinner Playbook. Familius LLC.

- **MAKE & MARK THE MOMENTS**—Make a goal to create and document the special moments. Take pictures and hang them up! Each day is filled with the probability of the unpredictable. If you aren't intentional, days will turn into years without you realizing it. Cherish accomplishments, sweet times, and meaningful moments.

- **NEVER QUIT**—Some days and years are hard. It can be tough to craft a good meal when you are short on every staple, but commit to never quit. You might need a moment and a deep breath but try and try again. When you have no energy left to pull it together, call a friend and borrow energy from your support system.

Whether it is a truck bed, a beach, a stroller, or a real dinner table, our meals are flexible and adaptable. We try to be flexible and adaptable, too.

The Ingredients Within

The Warrior's Table tells the story of SOF family life over the course of a full career of service in the special operations community. In the chapters that follow, we begin each chapter describing truths experienced by the SOF family regardless of when or how you became a SOF family. While the chapters don't flow in chronological order, each addresses the unique aspects, phases, and feelings shared by nearly all special operations families. Our common experiences are too rarely

Smile! Good things ahead. (*Photo courtesy of KaLea Lehman*)

shared, acknowledged, or talked about—which increases the burden on families to navigate the unique aspects of SOF culture and the stressors that often shape it.

Through years of coffee chats, our Cast Iron Crew gained an appreciation for the history, heritage, and customs of special operations. We learned to lean on these trusted tactics for connection; and we reveal it in our stories. We start at Day One in the special operations community and continue our storytelling into our lives following military service. We speak of the realities and feelings most are too intimidated to say aloud. To unpack the universal special operations family experience, each chapter covers several connected experiences, personal SOF Stories, Tactical Topics (conversation starters), War Games (fun games to play and spark more discussion), Customs and Camaraderie (SOF history, tradition, tributes to the fallen, and fun facts), and of course, recipes coupled with "SOF Easter eggs" (commonly used or heard words). If you happen upon a word or phrase that is unfamiliar, you can check the glossary to learn more (revisit the Preface for more on Healthy Checkpoints).

Here is a quick glance at some of the features you'll find nested within the chapters ahead:

RECIPES	Feasible food options to match the moment.
SOF STORIES	Personal stories from real SOF spouses about how they managed mealtime intensity and uncertainty. Some names and other identifiable characteristics may have been changed for privacy reasons.
TACTICAL TOPICS	Open-ended conversation starters to get conversation flowing.
WAR GAMES	Playful challenges for mealtime to engage everyone at the table and break the tension.
CUSTOMS & CAMARADERIE	Heritage facts and stories to illustrate how our history is a key part of the SOF culture and legacy.

And at the end of the book, you'll find a few guides to help you better understand the Special Operations community:

- **Translation Please: A Glossary Guide for the Warrior's Table:** A guide to decode SOF terms and "Easter eggs" and better understand SOF life lingo.

- **A Simple Resource List:** A short list of resources, cultivated for SOF families, that address topics covered in the chapters.

The Warrior's Table will ignite your senses, affirm your feelings, and help energize your table. Come join us on our journey—because it is your journey, too.

Harvesting cabbage on the farm.
(Photo courtesy of KaLea Lehman)

1. Our Roots

★ ★ ★

WE EACH COME FROM A DIFFERENT PART OF THE COUNTRY—hills of Texas, flyover states, California coast, Deep South, or the stomping grounds of the Eastern elite. Our roots are unique from one another and our journey in special operations has been just as diverse. Our differences in hometowns, backgrounds, and family heritage flavor what it means to be part of this service oriented, warfighting community. These differences liven up hard and mundane times. A Cuban, Swedish, or Filipino side can lead to stories for hours, and a properly spiced and cooked California tri-tip can cut the grump out of any Green Beret.

Our backgrounds and stories are unique, but we've learned how this tribe welcomes and retains connections to support what matters. Each of us have been shaped by interactions with spouses, service members, kiddos, friends, and extended family. Often the only shared similarity began with an appreciation for

An ODA navigating a driving course as part of a training exercise. *(Photo courtesy of Christine Trax)*

Welcome home daddy. *(Photo courtesy of Angie McLaughlin)*

service and a reverence for the sacrifice that accompanies the profession of arms.

Our roots are tied to our family recipes, which help us tell our story, show up for friends, and meet the basic nutritional needs of those who serve long, hard days and can pack in the calories! Learning how to embrace belonging in the special operations community begins with valuing where we come from and how it connects to our life in SOF.

Initially when we first joined this unpredictable and often intense community, our admiration and curiosity helped carry us through the confusing and often intimidating moments. Getting through and learning the ropes takes time—more time than you would expect. Then, one day we were suddenly the seasoned ones. It just sneaks up on you. Somewhere in the wild ride of this life we were newbies who woke-up one day realizing we had to process it all because it was now on us to welcome new families and hopefully help them thrive as part of our community, too.

Marine returns home from deployment and meets his new daughter. *(Photo courtesy of Laura Nicholson)*

Born in Service

- -

IT CAN FEEL LIKE MOST AMERICANS DON'T UNDERSTAND the military or military life. Less than 10% of adults in our country are veterans.[18] Many people don't know the difference between the Army and the Marine Corps, and when it comes to special operations they understand even less. Many come into this special operations life unaware of the military lifestyle, and some of us grew up in the military. Some call us "military brats" but that is a misnomer. We were not brats. We never floated aimlessly. Our family moved with intention and made the best of every situation because we knew why we were there, and we had to support one another.

As kids, we did not care about rank, status, unit, or service branch. We watched airborne jumps, climbed on boats, trucks, and other equipment, hid in fox holes, and the military obstacle course was our playground. We just wanted to play. All we have known is military moves, ceremonies, and standing at attention for the national anthem or the 5 p.m. bugle retreat. Very few of us were raised singing "The Ballad of the Green Beret" or the songs of sister units, but our lives were shaped by a devotion to something greater than ourselves.

Proud daughter of a Green Beret (*Photo courtesy of Sara Maybouer*)

At times growing up in the military was hard, but the challenges showed us we were strong. As a family, we held tight to service values and learned to appreciate supper staples, slow cooked meals, and the tastes of each new duty station. With every new unit we PCS'd to we found new friends, learned new routines, and re-established how our family would live. It was a childhood unlike most in the U.S.

---

18. Schaeffer, K. (2021, April 5). *The changing face of America's veteran population*. Pew Research Center. Accessed from https://www.pewresearch.org/fact-tank/2021/04/05/the-changing-face-of-americas-veteran-population/

Christmas in Germany **Jägerschnitzel**

TIME: 5 MIN (PREP), 30 MIN (COOK)
MAKES: 4 SERVINGS

- -

Ingredients

Jägerschnitzel Sauce
(Bacon Mushroom Gravy)

3 slices bacon (thick cut - chopped into
  small pieces)
2 tablespoons butter
½ cup onion, diced
1 pound mushrooms, sliced (chanterelle,
  button mushrooms, or portabella)
1 tablespoon tomato paste
1 teaspoon Worcestershire sauce
1 tablespoon paprika
1/2 teaspoon salt to taste
1/2 teaspoon pepper to taste
2 cups beef broth

Schnitzel (Breaded Fried Pork Cutlet)

½ cup all-purpose flour
½ teaspoon salt
½ teaspoon pepper
2 large eggs, beaten
¾ cup plain breadcrumbs
4 pork steaks (or 2 thick cut pork chops cut
  into half-thickness, butterflied fully)
Oil for frying
Parsley, fresh, chopped (optional garnish)

Steps

Jägerschnitzel Sauce
(Bacon Mushroom Gravy)

1. Fry the chopped bacon over
   medium-high heat until browning and
   the fat has been rendered.
2. Add butter and melt with the bacon.
3. Add the onion and mushrooms, sauté
   for about 5 minutes or until the mushrooms are tender and the onion is
   translucent.

4. Add the tomato paste, Worcestershire
   sauce, paprika, salt, pepper, and beef
   broth.
5. Whisk to combine and bring to a low
   boil. Reduce heat and simmer for 5-10
   minutes.
6. The gravy should thicken while simmering. If it does not combine 1 tablespoon
   cornstarch with 1 tablespoon cold water
   to make a slurry. Whisk the cornstarch
   slurry into the gravy to thicken if
   needed. If your gravy is too thick, add 1
   tablespoon of water at a time until your
   desired consistency is reached.

Schnitzel (Breaded Fried Pork Cutlet)

1. Using three shallow dishes, make a
   dredging station. Combine all-purpose
   flour with salt and pepper in the first,
   the large eggs in the second, and breadcrumbs in the third.
2. Move each piece of pork individually
   through the three dredging dishes. Start
   with coating the pork in flour, shaking
   off excess flour before moving to the
   next step.
3. Coat the flour-coated pork thoroughly
   with the eggs. Allow excess egg to drain
   off pork before moving to the next step.
4. Bread the egg-coated pork with the
   breadcrumbs. Press the breadcrumb into
   the pork gently, patting it onto the sides
   and all surfaces as needed.
5. In a deep skillet or frying pan, pour
   enough oil so that the heated oil comes
   up a bit over halfway on the sides of the
   pork cuts.
6. Pan-fry the breaded pork over
   medium-high heat. Cook for approximately 3 minutes per side.

7. Transfer the fried schnitzels to a paper towel-lined plate and repeat for each pork chop or pork steak. Schnitzels can be kept in a warmed oven while the remaining pork is fried.

8. Heat the gravy if needed before serving, then serve each schnitzel with a generous amount of gravy and parsley to garnish for a wonderful jägerschnitzel dinner.

TIP: If your pork cuts ended up being a bit over ¼ inch in thickness, they can be transferred to a parchment paper-lined baking sheet. Cook at 350°F (175°C) for 5-10 minutes, or until they have an internal temperature of 145°F (63°C) as read by a digital meat thermometer.

VARIATION: Use 1 tablespoon of dried minced onion instead of ½ cup fresh onion

SOF STORIES
Military Brat — Christine

Growing up a "military brat" usually comes with a negative connotation, which is why many special operations families opt for another term. I was an only child who moved around every few years, mostly overseas. To me, it was a glorious adventure surrounded by a perfect backdrop full of love from the military family that grew as we moved. One powerful memory was at Christmas time. Not being able to return to our family state-side, we would gather our military family—friends I now lovingly call Aunt and Uncle who have children I was raised around for the last 30 years.

We would head to the Dolomites in Northern Italy for the week surrounding Christmas and stay in a Gasthaus. Our days were spent skiing and the nights jumping from the hot tubs to the piles of deep snow. Christmas Eve dinner was perfection. A kind German family operated the Gasthaus. They would sing Christmas Carols in German, and then we would do the same in English. Dinner was a simple fare but delicious. Jagerschnitzel, pork with mushroom sauce served over spaetzle, and, my favorite Italian dessert of all time, tartufo—a cocoa-dusted chocolate and hazelnut ice cream bomb. We all laughed and played, skied, and ate together for a week. While we missed our family at home, the family built through military life was strong. Every Christmas, I still talk with my "Aunts and Uncles" and we remember the times we had and the dozens more that followed.

Boys having ice cream while stationed in Germany *(Photo courtesy of Angie McLaughlin)*

Chief's **Meatballs**

TIME: 10 MIN (PREP), 1 HOUR (COOK)

MAKES: 6 SERVINGS

Ingredients

3 pounds of lean ground beef
12oz can of evaporated milk
1½ cup of quick oats
½ teaspoon garlic powder
2 teaspoons of chili powder
2 beaten eggs
½ diced onion
2 teaspoons salt
½ teaspoon pepper
BBQ sauce

Steps

1. Mix all the ingredients together.
2. Roll into balls and place on a pan.
3. Bake meatballs at 350 degrees for 45 minutes and then cover with your favorite BBQ sauce.
4. Bake for another 15 minutes.

VARIATION: Make your own sauce by mixing 2 cups ketchup, 1 cup brown sugar, ¼ cup diced onion, ½ teaspoon liquid smoke, ½ teaspoon garlic powder.

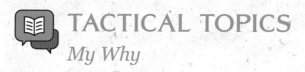

TACTICAL TOPICS
My Why

How did your family come to live a life of service? Service members, what led you to serve? Spouses, what drew you to your spouse and led you to say, "yes?" Kids, what activity or dream excites you the most?

A moment of reflection in the shadow of Freedom Tower. *(Photo courtesy of Fran Racioppi)*

Customs and Courtesies **Honeyed Carrots**

TIME: 10 MIN (PREP), 10 MIN (COOK)
MAKES: 6 SERVINGS

Ingredients

6-8 carrots, peeled, sliced and quartered
3 tablespoons olive oil
3 tablespoons salted butter
2 tablespoons of honey
1 tablespoon lemon juice
Pepper to taste

Steps

1. Add carrots to a warm skillet with olive oil.
2. Cook carrots for about 5 minutes.
3. Add the remaining ingredients until butter is melted.
4. Cook for an additional 4-5 minutes.

VARIATION: Swap out carrots for 16 ounces of baby carrots.

CUSTOMS AND CAMARADERIE
Stop, Pause, and Face the Flag

Did You Know? Regardless of who you are or your affiliation with the military, there are three specific times of each day that deserve your attention and awareness. If you hear the bugle call, you should stop, pause, face toward the American flag, and reflect for a moment. These times are: Reveille at 7 a.m., Retreat at 5 p.m., and Taps at 9 p.m.

These ceremonial calls are keystones of military tradition. Reveille was a bugle call used to muster troops dating back to 1812. Now, it remains as a moment to honor the American flag and the shared values of our country. Retreat marks the end of the day. It is a moment to reflect on what we Americans believe is worth fighting for. These values are mirrored in the values of each service branch and upheld by the U.S. Constitution. Finally, Taps is played daily to honor those who fought and never came home. Each of these calls are worthy of your momentary pause and reflection.[19]

19. Defense Logistics Agency. (n.d.). *Reveille, retreat, and Taps - Defense Logistics Agency.* Accessed from https://www.dla.mil/Portals/104/Documents/Distribution/Reveille.pdf

(Photo courtesy of Wendy Jo Peterson)

Patriot **Potato Salad**

TIME: 5 MIN (PREP), 15 MIN (COOK)
MAKES: 6 SERVINGS

Ingredients

6 Idaho or Russet Potatoes, diced
1½ teaspoons salt
1 small or medium onion, diced
½ cup dill pickles or dill relish, diced
½ cup mayonnaise
2½ teaspoons yellow mustard
Paprika to garnish (optional)

Steps

1. Boil diced potatoes in a large pot of salted water for about 8 minutes.

2. Drain the water off the potatoes and let them cool.

3. When cool, mix in diced onion and pickle.

4. In a separate bowl, combine the mayonnaise with yellow mustard.

5. When mixed, stir this into the potato mixture.

6. Keep chilled until ready to serve. Garnish with paprika.

VARIATION: If you want the salad to have added texture or protein, add 4 cool, diced hard boiled eggs and ½ cup of diced celery.

FOR a creamier texture, add another ⅛ cup mayonnaise and ½ teaspoon mustard.

SOF STORIES
Special Ops Babies and Genius Friends — Emily

Our family has a fire team of kids. We were bringing home number five, and I returned home to find a friend had set us up with a huge pot of chili. It was the gift that kept giving because it fed us for days. At the time, the simple gesture felt like a miracle because this new babe was a tough cookie.

Tired from soothing our newborn, I was totally unaware that she transferred her chili into one of my own pots. It wasn't until after I attempted to return the pot, I realized her thoughtful and genius trick! I was clueless, and in the laughter of that moment, I was touched by her thoughtfulness. She took multiple meals off my plate and attempted to remove the task of returning any dishes on the tail end, too. It was a moment where no words were needed, the gesture alone said it all . . . And we all got a chuckle out of my confusion!

Proud American **Bean Soup**

TIME: 5 MIN (PREP), 2-3 HOURS (COOK)
MAKES: 6 SERVINGS

- -

Ingredients

1 tablespoon vegetable oil

1 medium onion, chopped

½ teaspoon dried thyme

1 (15-ounce) can white beans, drained and rinsed

1 (15-ounce) can chickpeas, drained and rinsed

1 (15-ounce) can kidney beans, drained and rinsed

1 (15-ounce) can crushed tomatoes

4 cups chicken, vegetable, or beef broth

2 cups 100% vegetable juice, such as V8

2 bay leaves

1 teaspoon sea salt

½ teaspoon ground black pepper

1 (15-ounce) can refried beans

2 tablespoons chopped fresh cilantro or italian (flat-leaf) parsley (optional)

Steps

1. Heat oil in a medium skillet over medium heat. Add onion and thyme to sauté until barely tender, about 3 minutes.

2. Transfer to a 5 to 6-quart slow cooker. Add white beans, chickpeas, kidney beans, tomatoes, broth, vegetable juice, bay leaves, salt, and pepper.

3. Stir to combine. Cover the cooker and cook for 3-4 hours on high or 4-8 hours on low, until the flavors are well blended.

4. If the cooker is on low, raise the temperature to high.

5. In a small bowl, mix the refried beans and a few ladles of soup until it reaches a thick cream consistency.

6. Return to the cooker and cook on high for 20 minutes or until the soup is slightly thickened.

7. Stir in cilantro or parsley if using. Remove bay leaves before serving.

VARIATION: If you don't have V8, add 1 cup each of finely chopped carrot and celery when sautéing the onion. Then add ½ cup tomato juice or an additional ½ cup canned crushed tomatoes with the beans.

YOU can also add 4 garlic cloves, 1 carrot, and 1 celery rib, ½ inch diced when you add the onions.

INSTEAD of sautéing the onions in oil, finely chop 4 strips of bacon, cook crisp and use the rendered fat to sauté the onions and thyme. Serve soup with hot sauce, shredded cheddar, and a dollop of sour cream.

Mandatory Fun **Fudge**

TIME: 5 MIN (PREP), 15 MIN (COOK)
MAKES: 48 SERVINGS

Ingredients

Butter to coat pan
1 (12-ounce) can evaporated milk
4½ cups sugar
1 (18-ounce) package semi-sweet chocolate
  chips
2 sticks of butter or margarine, sliced thin
1 cup nuts (optional)

Steps

1. Butter a 9 inch x 13 inch pan
2. In a large saucepan, thoroughly stir
   evaporated milk and sugar.
3. Cook over medium-high heat, continually
   stirring until mixture comes to a full boil.
4. Continue to stir and cook for another
   6 minutes or until soft ball stage
   (235-245°F using a candy thermometer).
5. Remove from heat and immediately add
   chocolate chips, butter or margarine,
   and nuts.
6. Stir until completely mixed and pour into
   the buttered 9 inch x 13 inch pan.
7. Set at room temperature until firm. The
   longer it sits, the smoother it will be.
8. Once set, remove fudge from pan and
   cut into desired size pieces

(Photo courtesy of KaLea Lehman)

Big City Living

NO ONE'S ROOTS ARE THE SAME as another. There is a certain spirit, humor, and sense of adventure that we all share, but everyone has a story. You don't have to look far to meet the spec ops guy that came from the towering buildings of bustling city streets.

City life prepared some to think on their feet while it taught others to become chameleons and blend-in with the surroundings. Some of us became pros on the subway. We knew the city block by block. Others of us frequented the art museums and cultural hotspots featuring pho, the perfect pizza, or the best Thai in town. We rarely experienced camping and certainly not hunting wild game. But we cultivated a sense of adventure exploring city sites and uncovering the treasures within.

Trust comes with service and not where you are from. We were all drawn together on a hard path because we share a hope for the good, an appetite for adventure, and pride in accomplishing hard things. We know that without a wolf guarding the gate, those we love most are vulnerable. So we come together from the inner city and learn to appreciate the stories that each person brings to our table.

Looking out over a Middle Eastern city while away for joint training. *(Photo courtesy of KaLea Lehman)*

Urban Movement Chicken Milanese, p.38 *(Photo courtesy of Wendy Jo Peterson)*

Urban Movement **Chicken Milanese**

TIME: 20 MIN (PREP), 10 MIN (COOK)
MAKES: 4 SERVINGS

Ingredients

4 boneless, skinless chicken breasts
Kosher salt
Freshly ground black pepper
½ cup all-purpose flour
3 large eggs
1½ cups seasoned dry bread crumbs
1 tablespoon butter
1 tablespoon olive oil
1 lemon, cut into wedges

Steps

1. Place one piece of chicken between 2 sheets of wax paper and use the flat side of a meat mallet or bottom of a small heavy-bottomed skillet to pound until about ¼ inch thick.
2. Repeat with remaining chicken cutlets.
3. Season chicken all over with salt and pepper.
4. On a plate, combine flour and ¼ teaspoon each of salt and pepper.
5. Beat eggs in a wide, shallow bowl.
6. Place bread crumbs and ¼ teaspoon of salt in another wide, shallow bowl. Stir to combine.
7. Working with 1 piece of chicken at a time, dredge in the flour mixture, then the eggs, and finally the bread crumb mixture, gently pressing the bread crumbs into the chicken so they stick. Place on a large plate or baking sheet.
8. Heat butter and olive oil in a large pan and cook 2 chicken breasts on medium-low heat for 2-3 minutes on each side, until cooked through.
9. Once cooked, remove and place on a wire rack or plate lined with paper towels.
10. Add more butter and oil if needed and then cook the rest of the chicken.
11. Serve with lemon wedges.

 ## TACTICAL TOPICS
Planes, Trains, and Automobiles!

Name a city you have visited, or you would like to visit. What did you travel there for or what would you travel there to do? How did/would you get around town and surrounding area?

AFSOC family travels for a family mission trip. *(Photo courtesy of Jennifer Caldwell)*

City Slickers **Cozy Chowder**

TIME: 15 MIN (PREP), 35 MIN (COOK)
MAKES: 6 SERVINGS

Ingredients

2 stalks of celery, diced
1 yellow onion, diced
4 tablespoons butter
6 potatoes, diced
5 cups chicken broth
2 (7-ounce) cans minced clam
1 (8-ounce) bottle of clam juice (may substitute with milk or broth)
3 teaspoons salt
pepper to taste
1 cup heavy cream
1 cup milk
4-6 tablespoons cornstarch
4 teaspoons lemon juice
1 tablespoon chopped parsley (optional)

Steps

1. Sauté celery and onion in a pan with butter.
2. Add potatoes and chicken broth.
3. Boil potatoes until tender, about 20 minutes.
4. Add clams, clam juice, salt, pepper, heavy cream, and milk.
5. To thicken chowder, remove ½ cup of the broth from the pan, and mix in cornstarch, 2 tablespoons at a time.
6. Once the cornstarch is mixed in the broth, stir it into the soup and let simmer to thicken. Repeat until you reach desired consistency.
7. Drizzle with lemon juice and garnish with parsley.

WAR GAMES
Big City, Big Teams!

Take turns naming a sports team and see who can name the city they play in.

Or, name a city and see how many sports teams you can name that play there. What's your favorite sport to play or watch? Why is it your favorite sport?

Enjoying a soccer game in DC (*Photo courtesy of Lynnsy Snook*)

Advanced Skills **Mushroom Risotto**

TIME: 10 MIN (PREP), 30 MIN (COOK)
MAKES: 6 SERVINGS

- -

Ingredients

8 cups chicken broth, low sodium

3 tablespoons olive oil, divided

1 onion, chopped, divided

2 garlic cloves, minced, divided

1 pound fresh portobello and crimini
   mushrooms, sliced

2 tablespoons butter

Salt and pepper

2 cups Arborio rice

½ cup dry white wine

½ cup fresh Parmesan cheese, grated

Steps

1. Heat the chicken broth in a medium saucepan and keep warm over low heat.
2. Heat 1 tablespoon of oil in a large saucepan over medium heat.
3. Add ½ of the onion and 1 garlic clove, cook, stirring until translucent, about 5 minutes.
4. Add the fresh mushrooms and butter. Sauté for 3 to 5 minutes until lightly browned.
5. Season mushrooms with salt and pepper and put them into a bowl and for later.
6. Add the remaining 2 tablespoons of oil to the saucepan. Sauté the remaining ½ onion and garlic clove.
7. Add the rice and stir quickly until it is well-coated and opaque, about 1 minute. This step cooks the starchy coating and prevents the grains from sticking.
8. Stir in wine and cook until it is nearly all evaporated.
9. Add 1 cup of the warm broth and cook, stirring, until the rice has absorbed the liquid.
10. Add the remaining broth, 1 cup at a time. Continue to cook and stir, allowing the rice to absorb each addition of broth before adding more. The risotto should be slightly firm and creamy, not mushy.
11. Transfer and mix the mushrooms to the rice mixture.
12. Stir in Parmesan cheese, cook briefly until melted.

Air Surveillance **Pepperoni Pasta**

TIME: 15 MIN (PREP), 20 MINS (COOK)
MAKES: 4-5 SERVINGS

Ingredients

1 tablespoon olive oil
1 red bell pepper, diced
2 tablespoons tomato paste
1 (14-16-ounce) jar of pizza sauce
1 ¾ cups water
1 ½ teaspoons dried oregano
⅛ teaspoon crushed red pepper
1 (8-ounce) box of bowtie pasta
½ cup sliced pepperoni
1 cup shredded mozzarella cheese
1 cup shredded provolone cheese
1/4 cup grated Parmesan cheese

Steps

1. Preheat oven to 400°F.

2. In a dutch oven or large pan, add olive oil and bell pepper. Cook over medium heat for about 3-5 minutes.

3. Stir in tomato paste, pizza sauce, water, oregano, and crush red pepper and bring the sauce to a boil.

4. Reduce the heat to medium-low and add in the bowtie pasta.

5. Allow the sauce and pasta to simmer for 15 minutes or until the pasta is cooked al dente.

6. Remove from heat and fold in the pepperoni and mozzarella and provolone cheeses.

7. If necessary, transfer to an oven safe casserole dish and sprinkle with Parmesan cheese and additional pepperoni.

8. Bake for 10 minutes in the oven at 400°F.

TACTICAL TOPICS
Walk a Mile in My Shoes

How would you tell a new friend what it is like to be in a military family? What is the best part of military life? What is one aspect of military life you would like to change? What has been your favorite duty station, school, or hang out spot?

Being a military family, especially in the special operations community, can be extremely difficult; yet talking about what is challenging and rewarding as a family can strengthen bonds and shine a light on what makes the lifestyle meaningful.

Circumstances, people, and the shoes they wear are unique. Always. *(Photos courtesy of KaLea Lehman)*

Bravo **Buttered Asparagus**

TIME: 10 MIN (PREP), 10 MIN (COOK)

MAKES: 6 SERVINGS

Ingredients

1 bundle (about 1 pound) of asparagus
2 tablespoons olive oil
2 tablespoons salted butter
¼ teaspoon salt
2 tablespoons Parmesan cheese
Pepper to taste

Steps

1. Rinse the asparagus and break off the ends. It can be prepared whole length or broken into 2-3 shorter segments.
2. Heat olive oil and butter in a skillet.
3. Add asparagus.
4. Sauté for about 5-7 minutes over medium to high heat.
5. Add remaining ingredients just before serving.

CUSTOMS AND CAMARADERIE
Where are the SOCs?

Did You Know? Each service branch has its own special operations units. Regardless of their skills and assets, each branch has a "home base." Can you guess which Special Operations Command (SOC) belongs where?

1. Air Force Special Operations Command (AFSOC)
2. U.S. Army Special Operations Command (USASOC)
3. Naval Special Warfare Command (NSW)
4. Marine Forces Special Operations Command (MARSOC)
5. Joint Special Operations Command (JSOC)
6. United States Special Operations Command (USSOCOM)

A. NAB Coronado, CA
B. Ft. Bragg, NC (soon to be Ft. Liberty)
C. Ft. Bragg, NC (soon to be Ft. Liberty)
D. Hurlburt Field, FL
E. Camp Lejeune, NC
F. MacDill AFB, Tampa, FL

1:D, 2:B, 3:A, 4:E, 5:C, 6:F

USTAZIONI - 338 4070625

Living the NSW kid life right (*Photo courtesy of Andrea Geraldi*)

Tactics, Techniques, and Procedures **Tartufo**

TIME: 10 MIN (PREP), 4 HOURS (COOK)
MAKES: 6 SERVINGS

Ingredients

3 cups chocolate ice cream

1 cup frozen, pitted cherries, thawed,
  chopped or fresh cherries, pitted

15 chocolate sandwich cookies, crushed

2 cups semi sweet chocolate chips

4 teaspoons oil

Steps

1. Thaw ice cream until soft but not
   melted.
2. Mix chopped cherries into ice cream.
3. Scoop ice cream mixture into 6 balls
   using ice cream scoop.
4. Roll in crushed cookies. Place on a
   waxed paper lined baking sheet and
   freeze until firm, about 3 hours.
5. In a small saucepan, melt chocolate
   chips with oil, stir until smooth, cool.
6. Place ice cream balls on a wire rack over
   a baking sheet or waxed paper.
7. Spoon melted chocolate over each ball,
   coating tops and sides.
8. Freeze again until firm, at least 1 hour.
9. Remove from the freezer about 10 minutes before serving.

TIP: Experiment with different flavors of ice cream and add ins, such as pistachio ice cream with maraschino cherries, chocolate ice cream with toasted hazelnuts, or coffee ice cream with crushed biscotti

Going Coastal

EAST COAST, WEST COAST, GULF COAST, it doesn't matter. We join together from coast to coast to roast and toast. We blow in like a beach breeze, quickly get our footing, then fall in-line with the needs of the moment.

The California Coast (*Photo courtesy of KaLea Lehman*)

A little humor, a dose of vitamin D, and a deep breath of coastal breeze is all we need to recharge. Some of us were raised on rich New England chowder and others on tempting California fish tacos or spicy Louisiana gumbo. Whether we lived on one coast or all three, we know the value of living close to the water. There are always new happenings to explore as a family. Somehow the waves seep into your soul and bring a sense of calm and flexibility.

Sailboat at sunset in the Atlantic North East (*Photo courtesy of KaLea Lehman*)

(Recipe photos courtesy of Taylor and Kacie Lehman)

Trident **Tri-Tip** with Coronado **Sautéed Mushrooms**

TIME: 10 MIN (PREP), 40 MIN (COOK)
MAKES: 6-8 SERVINGS

- -

Ingredients

2½ pounds tri-tip roast
3 tablespoons butter or extra virgin olive oil

Marinade

1½ teaspoons garlic salt
1½ tablespoons salt
1 teaspoon pepper
1 teaspoon onion powder
2 teaspoons minced garlic
1 teaspoons oregano
1 teaspoon rosemary
¼ cup extra virgin olive oil
1 teaspoon liquid smoke (optional)

Sautéed Mushrooms

8 ounces Baby Bella Mushrooms, sliced
1 medium onion, sliced
½ teaspoon of salt
4 tablespoons olive oil or salted butter
pepper to taste

Steps

1. Mix together all spices with the olive oil and rub over the roast. Allow to marinate in the refrigerator for 1 hour to 2 days.
2. Preheat the oven to 400°F.
3. Remove the roast from the refrigerator, and sear the roast in olive oil or butter in a large frying pan. You want both sides of the roast to have a golden brown crisp.
4. Move to a baking sheet and place it in the oven for approximately 20-30 minutes. Aim for 10 minutes per pound of roast.
5. In a separate frying pan, melt the 4 tablespoons of salted butter.
6. Add the sliced mushrooms, onion, and salt to the melted butter.
7. Sauté over medium-high heat for 7-10 minutes.
8. Remove the tri-tip from the oven. Dribble the juice left from the oven pan over the tri-tip after cutting. Top with sautéed mushrooms and serve.

TIP: Serve with seasoned white rice or mashed potatoes, a vegetable side, and summer fruits!

VARIATION: If the Tri-Tip cut is challenging to find, you can substitute a similar size brisket.

SOF STORIES
Exploring Food — Andrea

Growing up, my father was the cook in our house. He was great at serving us comfort food that was always delicious and predictable. When I went to college in Vermont, I was exposed to new foods, with an emphasis on "local." This was the '90s, so there weren't any signs at the Farmers Market or the restaurants—this was just how you ate. That's when food became more exotic and interesting to me and got me into cooking. As I've moved with my husband during his military career, I've continued to pick up new flavors, methods, and recipes from assignment to assignment. A fancy restaurant might call this "fusion cuisine" but I just call it eating well.

A moment of peace in small, rural Vermont cottage. *(Photo courtesy of KaLea Lehman)*

Southern Shores Sharpness **Jambalaya**

TIME: 15 MIN (PREP), 50 MIN (COOK)
MAKES: 6-8 SERVINGS

Ingredients

1 cup celery, diced
1 yellow onion, diced
1 tablespoon garlic, minced
4 tablespoons butter
3 tablespoons cajun seasoning
1 pound andouille or polish sausage, sliced
1 pound ham steak, diced
2 cups uncooked rice
½ teaspoon salt
2 cups salted chicken broth
1 green bell pepper, diced
1 (15-ounce) can crushed or sliced
   tomatoes
1 (6-ounce) can tomato paste
2 teaspoons Worcestershire sauce
1 teaspoons thyme
4 bay leaves

4 boneless skinless chicken thighs
½ teaspoon hot sauce of choice

Steps

1. In a large pot, sauté celery, onion, and garlic in butter and cajun seasoning until the onion begins to brown and caramelize.
2. Add in sausage and ham and cook until both are warm.
3. Add the rice and brown it.
4. Then add salt, chicken broth, bell pepper, tomatoes, tomato paste, Worcestershire sauce, thyme, and bay leaves.
5. Stir well and add in the chicken. Cover the pan and cook on medium-low heat for about 40 minutes, stirring occasionally.

TIP: Cook the chicken thighs in advance or you can substitute for leftover chicken.

VARIATION: You can substitute ham for raw, shelled medium shrimp. Add the shrimp to the pot in the last 5-10 minutes of cooking.

WAR GAMES
Food Detective

Help your child explore new foods by becoming a food detective! Ask your detective to investigate the food on their plate and record their answers in a notebook. What color is the food? How big is it? What does it smell like? How would you describe the texture? Then you can share the answers with a family member and see if they can guess what food you were investigating.

Coronado **Tamale Pie**

TIME: 15 MIN (PREP), 1 HOUR (COOK)
MAKES: 4-6 SERVINGS

Ingredients

1 box Jiffy corn mix
1 (4.5 ounce) can diced green chiles
1 can of corn or creamed corn
½ yellow onion
1 pound ground beef
1 teaspoon cumin
1 teaspoon chili powder
¼ teaspoon salt
¼ teaspoon pepper
1¼ cups enchilada sauce
2 cups of shredded cheese
Cilantro (optional

Steps

1. Preheat the oven to 400°F.
2. Prepare cornbread according to box directions.
3. Gently fold in chilies and corn. Pour into a greased baking pan or cast iron skillet.
4. Bake until set, about 20-25 minutes. A toothpick should come out clean.
5. While cornbread is baking, sauté onions in a skillet.
6. Add beef with spices and sauté over medium heat until fully cooked, about 10 minutes.
7. Add half of the enchilada sauce.
8. Once cornbread is done baking, reduce the oven to 350°F. Poke holes in the cornbread with a fork and pour remaining enchilada sauce over it.
9. Top with ground beef and shredded cheese. Cover with aluminum foil and bake in the oven for 20 minutes.
10. Remove foil and bake until cheese begins to brown, about 5-10 minutes.
11. Let cool for 10-15 minutes before serving with desired toppings.

TIP: Top with guacamole, sour cream, and lime. To prepare ahead of time, prepare cornbread up to step three and freeze in a freezer-safe baking dish. Thaw and pick up at step four.

VARIATION: Use whatever ground meat you prefer. For an extra kick, add 1 teaspoon of ancho chile powder when cooking meat.

TACTICAL TOPICS
Friend for All Times

Who is your oldest friend? Who has been your friend the longest?

(Opposite) (Photo courtesy of Lynnsy Snook)

Coastal Range **Roast Cauliflower** with Route 1 **Tahini Sauce**

TIME: 10 MIN (PREP), 30 MIN (COOK)
MAKES: 4-6 SERVINGS

Ingredients

1/4 cup extra-virgin olive oil
4 teaspoons salt
2 heads cauliflower, cored and cut into
  1½-inch florets
Freshly ground black pepper, to taste

Dipping Sauce

½ cup tahini
½ cup water
3 garlic cloves, smashed and minced into a
  paste
Juice of 1 lemon

Steps

1. Preheat the oven to 500°F.
2. In a large bowl, toss together oil, cauliflower, salt, and pepper.
3. Transfer to 2 rimmed baking sheets, spread out evenly.

Coastal Range Roast Cauliflower with Route 1 Tahini Sauce, p.52 *(Photo courtesy of KaLea Lehman)*

4. Bake, rotating pans from top to bottom and front to back, until cauliflower is browned and tender, about 25-30 minutes.
5. Meanwhile, combine tahini, garlic, lemon juice, and ½ cup water in a small bowl and season with salt.
6. Serve cauliflower hot or at room temperature with tahini sauce.

CUSTOMS AND CAMARADERIE
Office of Strategic Services

Historic Highlight. President Franklin D. Roosevelt (FDR) established the Office of Strategic Services on July 11, 1941 to ensure intelligence efforts took a more strategic role in national security and defense efforts ahead of World War II. FDR placed "Wild" Bill Donovan at the helm. The OSS-led operations in counterintelligence, guerrilla warfare, sabotage, and psychological warfare are the roots of today's Central Intelligence Agency and many military special operations units. The OSS "Jedburgh" teams that jumped into the European Theater to join the French Resistance against Germany are often referenced among our Army Special Forces units.[20]

20. Warner, M. (2000, May). *Office of Strategic Services - Central Intelligence Agency.* Accessed from https://www.cia.gov/static/7851e16f9e100b6f9cc4ef002028ce2f/Office-of-Strategic-Services.pdf

Stone Bay **Brownies**

TIME: 5 MIN (PREP), 45 MIN (COOK)
MAKES: 16 SERVINGS

Ingredients

1 cup sugar
½ cup butter, softened
2 eggs
¼ cup cocoa
1 cup flour, plus extra to coat pan
¼ cup milk
½ cup walnuts or pecans chopped (optional)
Cooking oil spray

Steps

1. Preheat the oven to 350°F.
2. Mix all the ingredients in a bowl.
3. Spray square pan with cooking oil spray and lightly coat with flour.
4. Bake brownies until they pull away from the sides of the pan or until a toothpick comes out clean, about 30-45 minutes.
5. Cool completely before slicing.

(Photo courtesy of Wendy Jo Peterson)

TACTICAL TOPICS
Family Favorite

What is your favorite family food? Who cooks it best? What are some memories you have that are attached to that meal? What is your favorite part about the dish— smell, taste, look, texture, or the people connected to the meal memory?

A SEAL kid meal memory that will last a lifetime *(Photo courtesy of Andrea Geraldi)*

Sprouting from the Heartland

THE "FLYOVER STATES" ARE THE STOMPING GROUNDS for many of us. Born to single stop-light small towns where Friday night football games and annual hometown events were mandatory. We grew up knowing money didn't grow on trees and freedom isn't free. We watched our World War II veteran grandparents proudly march in the local parades. By listening to them talk about their experiences on the beaches of Normandy or hitchhiking home from airborne school, we witnessed the pride that comes with service.

The grouchy old farmers met every Tuesday night for fried fish and poker, and the whole town knew if you didn't storm a beach, you just better not enter that room. Their wartime experiences forged an unbreakable bond that everyone could see but not imagine. We learned their grit the same way we learned their smile. Today we aren't in that same small town, but we are proud to pass on the heartland traditions and classic American values along with a plate of meat, potatoes, and pie.

Classic scenes from the heartland.
Photos courtesy of KaLea Lehman

Nothing But Roots **Ground Beef and Cabbage**

TIME: 5 MIN (PREP), 50 MIN (COOK)
MAKES: 6 SERVINGS

- -

Ingredients

1 large cabbage

1 (14.5-ounce) can diced tomatoes, with juice

2 teaspoons salt

1 teaspoon pepper

2 tablespoons butter

½ cup water

1 pound lean ground beef

1 onion, sliced thinly

2 teaspoons minced garlic

Steps

1. Slice the cabbage into quarters, cut off and discard the tough root ends, and chop roughly into 2-inch pieces.

2. Combine cabbage, salt, pepper, butter, and water in a large pot over medium heat.

3. Bring to a simmer, cover, and steam until cabbage begins to soften. If the edges of the cabbage turn golden, the flavor will be better.

4. In a separate pan, brown ground beef over medium high heat.

5. Add garlic and sliced onion to the ground beef and cook for 7 minutes or until onions are translucent.

6. Add ground beef mixture and tomatoes to pot with cabbage and allow to simmer over medium heat.

7. Cover and cook until cabbage is tender, about 25 minutes, stirring occasionally.

TIP: Do not drain your meat, as most of the taste will leave with the fat. I use 90/10 ground beef for this recipe. Perfect!

(Opposite) (Photo courtesy of Lynnsy Snook)

SOF STORIES
An Ozark Memory — Melissa

My mother was a country cook, plain and simple. But as I have traveled and worked and experienced foods from around the world, I look back and realize that many of the dishes she prepared, while simple, were perfect for that moment. Sometimes we have to put emotion and love in a dish to make it extra-special. This Ground Beef and Cabbage dish is one like that—simple and easy, yet full of love and goodness. My mother used to serve this with corn on the cob and cornbread. Very inexpensive and very good as well. Enjoy an Ozark memory . . .

The Ozarks *(Photo courtesy of KaLea Lehman)*

Ranch Goes with Everything
Broccoli and Cauliflower Salad

TIME: 10 MIN (PREP), 1 HOUR (COOK)
MAKES: 6 SERVINGS

Ingredients

3 cups broccoli, chopped
3 cups cauliflower, chopped
⅓ cup diced red onion (optional)
⅓ cup thinly sliced radish (optional)
1 pouch of ranch dip mix
1 cup sour cream
1 cup mayo
3-5 slices bacon, cooked and crumbled
½ cup shredded cheddar cheese

Steps

1. Mix the broccoli and cauliflower in a large bowl.
2. Add in onion and radishes, if desired.
3. In a separate bowl, mix the Ranch packet with sour cream and mayo.
4. Stir in a desired amount of the Ranch mixture into the vegetables.
5. Top salad with bacon and cheese.
6. Serve immediately for more crunch, or refrigerate several hours or overnight for a softer texture and more ranch flavor.

 TACTICAL TOPICS
A Season to Remember

Tell a story about your favorite seasonal festival, such as a fall pumpkin patch, Oktoberfest, or strawberry festival. Go around the table and let everyone share a story about their favorite seasonal festival and why they like it so much!

Picking strawberries with dad (*Photo courtesy of Samantha Gomolka*)

Sunday Dinner **Quick Beef Stroganoff**

TIME: 5 MIN (PREP), 30 MIN (COOK)
MAKES: 6 SERVINGS

Ingredients

1 pound ground beef
1 medium onion
1½ cups of beef broth (made with bouillon or broth)
8 ounces bella mushrooms, sliced
1 tablespoon Worcestershire sauce
2 cups sour cream
3 tablespoons flour
Salt and pepper to taste

Paprika (optional)

Steps

1. Brown the ground beef.
2. Add onion and cook until translucent.
3. Add broth and stir in mushrooms and remaining ingredients.
4. Cook until ingredients are tender and desired consistency is reached.
5. Serve over noodles or rice.

VARIATION: Substitute diced or shredded leftover roast beef for ground beef.

TACTICAL TOPICS
Our Way

What is your favorite family tradition? What makes it so special to you? How did you keep traditions going in your family growing up? What traditions are you passing on to your family today, or plan to pass on to your future family? How has life in the special operations community affected the traditions you've kept?

Mom's **Meatloaf**

TIME: 15 MIN (PREP), 1 HR AND 15 MINS (COOK)
MAKES: 6 SERVINGS

- -

Ingredients

Meatloaf

1 ½ pounds ground beef

2 eggs

¾ cup tomato sauce or ketchup

⅔ cup oats

½ teaspoon dried sage

1 tablespoon salt

2 tablespoons dried onion or ½ diced onion

Sauce

¼ cup ketchup

1 teaspoon dry mustard

2 tablespoons brown sugar

¼ teaspoon nutmeg

Steps

1. Preheat oven to 350°F.
2. Combine all ingredients for the meatloaf in a mixing bowl.
3. Mix well by hand or countertop mixer, then move to a loaf pan.
4. Bake for 1 hour at 350°F
5. In a separate bowl, combine all the ingredients for the sauce.
6. Spread sauce over the top of the cooked meatloaf.
7. Bake for 15 more minutes.
8. Let rest for 10 minutes, slice, and serve with mashed potatoes and green beans for a classic American meal.

VARIATION: The sauce can be made of ⅛ cup ketchup and ⅛ cup barbeque sauce of choice. You can also substitute the oats for crushed ritz crackers or cooked rice.

Grandma's Secret Recipe **Mashed Potatoes**

TIME: 5 MIN (PREP), 25 MIN (COOK)
MAKES: 8 SERVINGS

Ingredients

10 large potatoes
1 cup sour cream
4 tablespoons butter
1 (8-ounce) package cream cheese
2 tablespoons chives
1 tablespoon salt or salt to taste
½ cup milk

Steps

1. Boil potatoes until they are fork tender.
2. Drain the water and mash the potatoes.
3. Stir in sour cream, butter, salt, milk, and cream cheese.
4. Place in a buttered 9x13 dish and bake at 350°F for 30 minutes.
5. Top with chives. Serve and enjoy!

VARIATION: For cheesy seconds, sprinkle 1 cup of shredded colby-jack cheese over the potato mixture freshly pressed into a buttered, glass casserole dish. Bake in a 400°F oven for approximately 15 minutes.

WAR GAMES
'Tis the Season

Go around the table and one person at a time names a season of the year. Then, everyone takes turns naming a fruit or vegetable that grows in that season. Whoever can name a recipe that includes their fruit or vegetable gets extra points! Who thought of the most out of the box food or recipe?

(Photo courtesy of Andrea Geraldi)

Down Home **Peanut Butter & Chocolate Pie**

TIME: 15 MIN (PREP), 0 MIN (COOK)
MAKES: 8 SERVINGS

Ingredients

1 (3.4-ounce) package instant chocolate
  pudding
1½ cup milk, separated
1 (12-ounce) container of Cool Whip, separated
1 (3.4 ounce) package instant vanilla pudding
½ cup peanut butter
1 (9-inch) pie shell, baked

Steps

1. Beat chocolate pudding and 1 cup milk
   with a mixer or whisk until thickened.

Fold in ½ of the Cool Whip and pour
mixture in the pie shell.

2. Beat vanilla pudding and the rest of the
   milk until thickened. Then fold in the
   remaining half of the Cool Whip and the
   peanut butter. Spoon over the chocolate
   layer, piling high.

3. Swirl the top of the peanut butter layer
   and/or add some chocolate chips or
   sprinkles to decorate the pie. Freeze the
   pie overnight or for up to 2-3 months.

TIP: The pie will be very tall. Cutting into it frozen is important.

SOF STORIES
Small Town Festival Favorite — KaLea

I grew up in a small town too tiny for a stop light. It was a safe little farming community, so we grew up walking all over town, playing in fields, climbing trees, and looking forward to the annual fall festival which started with the harvest season. Back then, everyone contributed to making the festival spectacular. The men of the community gathered to put up the big blue tent. Others decorated the square to match the festival theme, and the carnival came to town.

For four days the county fair lit up the town, and people came from near and far to enjoy "ranch burgers" with a side of good American, homemade pie. My mom made pies for days and probably took 50 up to the town square to help feed the masses. Of all the pies she made each year, it was her beautiful peanut butter and chocolate pie that stood out from the common fruit pies. They were gone as fast as she took them. As a young kid, I went for funnel cakes and cotton candy, but those home made pies left a more permanent mark in my memory of those small town days before military life. In many ways our unit reunions have a similar sweetness—but typically with barbecue and less pie.

An ODA explores sites in Jordan while deployed.
(Photo courtesy of Christine Trax)

2. Where in the World

Map of Theater Special Operations Command areas of responsibility (*Image courtesy of Keith Snook*)

FOOD HAS A WAY OF BRINGING BACK A MEMORY and reminding you of the highs, lows, easy coasting, and just plain hards of the journey. Embracing the SOF life is about embracing the whole ride. It's a commitment to a just, honorable, and free society; and often it means our warriors are away laying the groundwork to sustain peace. In our nation's time of need, our table typically responds first (often before it even hits the news cycle), leads the way in, and remains long after the conflict leaves the headlines and America's conscience. Oftentimes our units work in the shadows, and those of us at home quietly bottle up the possibilities of what may happen. We do our best to put on a strong face, navigate the awkward dynamics demanded by operational security norms, and go about our normal day. Regardless of the theater (region of the world) or the special operations unit we are part of, our families proudly keep the family table together. Our service member's energy and commitment to service is a defining ethos that trains a stoicism in us all.

Hellicopter landing on an aircraft carrier at sea *(Photo courtesy of Fran Racioppi)*

This chapter is a glimpse into the regional tastes and tasks of our spec ops community at work around the world. Special operations units are actively deployed in over 100 countries at any given time, but their missions and what they do are most often determined and overseen by a Theater Special Operations Command (TSOC). Each TSOC has expertise in a particular world region and tasks units with missions based on national defense priorities. Each demands language and cultural competency in addition to unique military capabilities. Most often our service members launch from their home unit, but may move to a TSOC headquarters toward the end of a SOF career.

Between our explorations, overseas moves, and countless deployments, we've collected an assortment of flavors to spice up your palate and table storytelling. These are the stomping grounds of the special operations community both at home and away doing the nation's bidding.

Special Operations Command North (SOCNORTH)—The North American Theater

A SPECIAL OPERATIONS FAMILY COOKBOOK can't leave out the literal homefront! The mission of Special Operations Command North (SOCNORTH) is to plan, coordinate, and execute special operations to defend the United States and its interests. Practically speaking, this entails working with partner SOF from Canada, Mexico, and the Northern Caribbean region to defend the U.S. homeland from terrorism, weapons of mass destruction, and transnational organized crime.

SOCNORTH is located in the Colorado mountains, which is a military family favorite location.[21] The mountains are like a beacon for adventure and exploration. This TSOC keeps operators closer to home, and busy with unique missions. They stay busy collaborating with our interagency brothers and sisters whose days are filled with countering organized crime. Each assignment brings new friends and new stories to the family table, and this region in particular often welcomes close friendships as the language and cultural barrier isn't quite as high as it is in other TSOC regions.

CV-22 flight over the Grand Canyon (*Photo courtesy of Keith Snook*)

---

21. Special Operations Command North. (n.d.). *Special Operations Command North (SOCNORTH).* Accessed from https://www.socom.mil/socnorth/Pages/default.aspx

G-Force **Grilled Garlic Artichokes**

TIME: 15 MIN (PREP), 30 MIN (COOK)
MAKES: 4 SERVINGS

- -

Ingredients

1 lemon, quartered

2 large artichokes

¾ cup olive oil

4 garlic cloves, chopped

1 teaspoon salt

½ teaspoon ground black pepper

Steps

1. Fill a large bowl with cold water. Squeeze the juice from one lemon wedge into the water.

2. Trim the tops from the artichokes, then cut in half lengthwise, and place halves into the bowl of lemon water to prevent them from turning brown.

3. Bring a large pot of water to a boil. Meanwhile, preheat an outdoor grill for medium-high heat.

4. Simmer artichoke halves for about 15 minutes, then drain.

5. Squeeze the remaining lemon wedges into a medium bowl. Stir in the olive oil and garlic, and season with salt and pepper.

6. Brush the artichokes with a coating of the garlic dip, and place them on the preheated grill.

7. Grill the artichokes for 5 to 10 minutes, basting with dip and turning frequently, until the tips are a little charred.

8. Serve immediately with the remaining dip.

VARIATION: Trim and cut artichokes into 6 wedges, coat in lemon water, and microwave for 5 minutes. Proceed with marinade, then thread on skewers and grill until lightly charred.

(Opposite) Artichokes—not yet picked. *(Photo courtesy of KaLea Lehman)*

SOF STORIES
Monterey Artichoke — Robyn

Early in our marriage, we moved to Monterey, California, for language school. It was one of those quick PCS moves where there is time to explore but not time for much else. I didn't have many friends and we didn't have any kids, which meant I was free to adventure. Every day while my husband was deep in language immersion training, I was in an immersion training of my own. I would hop in my car and drive down Highway 1. Big Sur had fun little stands, five artichokes for a dollar. I would grab some locally grown fruit and find a "pull-off" along the way and sit on the beach. I would close my eyes and listen to the symphony of sea lions, with the occasional solo soprano from the seal. I would watch the ballet of otters jumping out of the waves and then float with a crustacean on their bellies. When it was time to head home, I would be just in time to meet my husband for dinner. We would wander down to the fresh market on Tuesdays and grab a roasted chicken and potatoes, and pick our favorite seasonal vegetable to complement it. And, of course, we never left without a bottle of local wine.

Big Sur on the California Coast. (*Photo courtesy of KaLea Lehman*)

Peterson SFB **Roast Beef**

TIME: 10 MIN (PREP), 4-5 HOURS (COOK)
MAKES: 6-8 SERVINGS

- -

Ingredients

3 tablespoons butter

1 large bottom round roast or rump roast

1 teaspoon smoked paprika

1 teaspoon salt

1 teaspoon garlic powder

1 teaspoon onion powder

4 cups beef broth or water

1 teaspoon Worcestershire sauce

Steps

1. Melt the butter in a large skillet and brown both sides of the roast for 3-5 minutes. Both sides should be golden brown.
2. When browned, transfer the roast to a slow cooker.
3. In a separate bowl, mix the spices and spread over the roast. Add the water or broth and Worcestershire sauce to the area around the roast.
4. Cook at 260 degrees for 4-5 hours. If you cook it in a slow cooker, the roast may need to be cut into smaller pieces.
5. Serve warm.

TIP: You can serve simple sides by adding sliced white or red potatoes, sweet potatoes, carrots, and mushrooms to the cooker in the last 2 hours of cook time.

(Photo courtesy of KaLea Lehman)

NAB "I see Mexico" Tostadas

TIME: 45 MIN (PREP), 40 MIN (COOK)
MAKES: 6 SERVINGS

- -

Ingredients

Crispy Tortillas

Vegetable oil for frying
6 white or yellow corn tortillas
Kosher salt for sprinkling

Chicken

3 cups cooked shredded chicken
⅓ cup freshly squeezed lime juice
¼ cup olive oil
¼ cup fresh cilantro, chopped
Kosher salt and freshly ground black pepper

Refried Beans

2 tablespoons olive oil
¼ medium onion, finely chopped
1 teaspoon ground coriander
1 teaspoon ground cumin
4 garlic cloves, minced
1 (15-ounce) can pinto beans (with liquid),
  mashed
¼ teaspoon kosher salt
Freshly ground black pepper

Salsa Cruda

2 ripe tomatoes or 4 plum tomatoes, cored
  and roughly chopped
¼ medium onion, finely chopped
¼ jalapeno, seeded and minced
2 tablespoons fresh cilantro, chopped
1 teaspoon kosher salt
Freshly ground black pepper

Tostadas

Refried beans, warm
3 ounces Monterey Jack cheese, shredded
  (about ½ cup)
½ head iceberg lettuce, cored and shredded
1 Hass avocado, thinly sliced
2 cups salsa cruda

½ cup sour cream
1 scallion, thinly sliced
12 fresh cilantro leaves

Steps

1. To make the tortillas, pour the oil for frying into a large heavy-bottomed pot to a depth of about 2 inches. Place over medium heat and heat to 375°F.

2. Add the tortillas, one at a time, and fry until golden brown and crispy, about 1½ minutes. Using tongs, transfer to a paper towel lined pan and sprinkle with salt. Set aside.

3. To make the chicken, in a small bowl, mix together the chicken, lime juice, oil, coriander, and salt and season with pepper to taste. Cover with plastic wrap and set aside.

4. To make the refried beans, heat the oil in a large skillet over medium-high heat. Add the onion, coriander, and cumin and cook, stirring, until lightly browned, about 2 minutes.

5. Add the garlic and cook, until lightly browned, about 1 minute more. Add the beans and cook, stirring frequently, until thick and amber brown in color, about 4 minutes. Stir in the salt and season with pepper to taste.

6. To make the salsa cruda, in a small bowl, mix together the tomatoes, onion, jalapeno, coriander, salt, and season with pepper to taste. Cover with plastic wrap and set aside.

7. To assemble the tostadas, preheat the broiler. Spread the refried beans evenly over one side of each tortilla and sprinkle with some of the cheese. Transfer to a baking sheet and broil until the cheese is lightly browned and melted, about 30 seconds.

(Photo courtesy of Wendy Jo Peterson)

8. Divide the tortillas among 6 plates. Evenly mound the chicken on each tostada and top with lettuce, avocado, salsa, and a dollop of sour cream.

9. Sprinkle with the scallion and garnish with the cilantro leaves. Serve immediately.

TIP: The tortillas must be fried until very crispy, otherwise they may become rubbery, making them difficult to cut with a knife and fork. Alternatively, buy tostada shells at the store, or break taco shells in half. Substitute canned refried beans and premade salsa to save time.

Bragworthy **Beer Cake**

TIME: 30 MIN (PREP), 1 HOUR (COOK)
MAKES: 12 SERVINGS

Ingredients

Cake

1 cup Guinness Extra Stout
17 tablespoons unsalted butter
¾ cup unsweetened cocoa
2 cups superfine sugar
⅔ cup sour cream
2 large eggs
1 tablespoon vanilla extract
2 cups all-purpose flour
2½ teaspoons baking soda

Topping (optional)

8 ounces cream cheese
1¼ cups confectioners' sugar
2 teaspoons cornstarch
½ cup heavy cream

Steps

1. Preheat the oven to 350°F.
2. Butter and line a 9 inch springform tin.
3. Pour the Guinness into a large wide saucepan. Add the butter - in spoons or slices - and heat until the butter is melted.
4. Whisk in the cocoa and sugar.
5. Beat the sour cream with the eggs and vanilla and then pour into the brown, buttery, beery pan.
6. Finally, whisk in the flour and baking soda.
7. Pour the cake batter into the greased and lined tin and bake for 45 minutes to an hour.
8. Leave to cool completely in the tin on a cooling rack, as it is quite a damp cake.
9. When the cake's cold, sit it on a flat platter or cake stand.
10. To make the topping, lightly whip the cream cheese until smooth, sieve over the confectioners' sugar and cornstarch and then beat to combine.
11. If using heavy cream, add it and beat until you have a spreadable consistency.
12. Ice the top of the black cake so that it resembles the frothy top of the famous pint.

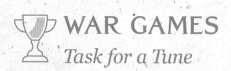

WAR GAMES
Task for a Tune

Pick a song and prepare for dinner as you sing along. How many dinner preparation tasks can you finish before the song ends? Whoever finishes first gets to pick the next tune!

Bragworthy Beer Cake
(Photo courtesy of Andrea Geraldi)

Green Platoon **Chipotle Lime Rice**

TIME: 5 MIN (PREP), 45 MIN (COOK)
MAKES: 4 SERVINGS

Ingredients

2 cups long grain white or brown rice
½ cup fresh cilantro, chopped
¼ cup fresh squeezed lime juice
2 garlic cloves, minced
Pinch of salt

Steps

1. Cook rice per package directions, or in rice cooker.
2. Chop cilantro and juice the limes, set aside.
3. When rice is done, fluff with a fork and stir in cilantro, lime juice, garlic, and salt.
4. Serve warm.

TACTICAL TOPICS
Adventure at Home

What is your favorite National Landmark or National Park? Name a park or landmark you still want to explore, and describe why you want to make the trip to see it.

Mount Rushmore National Memorial. *(Photo courtesy of KaLea Lehman)*

Special Operations Command South (SOCSOUTH)—The South American Theater

SPECIAL OPERATIONS COMMAND SOUTH is hopping with activity at their home footprint in Miami and in the 31 South American countries and 16 sovereign areas in which it operates. Drawing on special operations forces based in Florida, Virginia, California, and other areas, SOCSOUTH missions "find and fix threats and enable the Interagency."[22] Their missions are essential to counter threats to U.S. interests and help ensure the region remains as stable as possible.

Field kitchen in Colombia (*Photo courtesy of Hilary Peters*)

---

22. Special Operations Command South. (n.d.). *Special Operations Command South (SOCSOUTH)*. Accessed from https://www.socom.mil/socsouth.

The special operations units who routinely fulfill the SOCSOUTH mission are always busy working with partners and the Interagency in and around South America. Much like the people and geography of the region, the cultures are full of personalities and flavors that complement the tempo, which is anything but dull. Luckily for the families who hold down the homefront as the SOCSOUTH mission keeps steady, most of the installations serving this TSOC are near a beach and plenty of beach front and family friendly options to keep them busy between trips and deployment rotations.

A get together on the beach. Who doesn't love a special treat drink? *(Photo courtesy of Jennifer Caldwell)*

(Opposite) SOF kid fishing catch *(Photo courtesy of Jennifer Caldwell)*

SEAL Ceviche de Colón

TIME: 10 MIN (PREP), 1 HOUR (COOK)
MAKES: 4-6 SERVINGS

Ingredients

¾ pound sole filet, cut into ½-inch strips
¾ cup fresh lime juice
1 garlic clove, minced
¼ cup olive oil
3 tablespoons cilantro, chopped
2 tablespoons green onion, chopped
1 tablespoon green chili, diced
¾ teaspoon salt
¼ teaspoon pepper
Dash of hot sauce

Steps

1. Marinate the fish for 1 hour in the fresh lime juice.
2. While the fish marinates, combine the remaining ingredients.
3. Drain the fish and then toss in the combined ingredients.
4. Let stand for 30 minutes.
5. Serve with saltine crackers.

SOF STORIES

Ceviche, Ice Cream, and our Friend — Amber

SEAL daughter enjoying ice cream. *(Photo courtesy of Andrea Geraldi)*

While stationed in Panama with 7th Group, one of our favorite activities was going to the swimming pool at a country club in Colón. The club allowed visitors to purchase a single-day membership for a small fee. Our initial visit to the country club was for the beautiful swimming pool, but eventually we went for the kindness of our attendee Amos, the Ceviche, and the ice cream. Our lunch at the club was always several orders of Ceviche, as our two preschool aged boys loved scooping up the fish with the endless supply of saltine crackers Amos provided. I marveled at their acquired taste! Amos was a gem. We still remember his smile, affection for our children, and his kind gesture of bringing them a dish of ice cream after gorging on Ceviche. "They need something sweet after all that fish," he said. Amos made us all smile, and every time we enjoy this recipe, we remember our friend.

The Bridge Between
Sweet and Spicy Fried Plantain

TIME: 10 MIN (PREP), 10 MIN (COOK)
MAKES: 4 SERVINGS

Ingredients

2 ripe plantains, peeled and sliced (with black spots or can be totally black)
1 teaspoon ginger powder
½ teaspoon onion powder
1 teaspoon chili powder
½ teaspoon sugar
Salt to taste
Vegetable oil for frying

Steps

1. Put sliced plantains in a bowl or container with a tight fitting lid.
2. Add ginger, onion powder, chili powder, and sugar to the container.
3. Mix to ensure that plantains are evenly coated.
4. Add salt as needed and let the mixture sit for 5 mins.
5. Heat oil in a frying pan.
6. Fry plantains till golden brown.

 TACTICAL TOPICS
Learning New Languages

What language would you like to learn and why? Is this something you would start tomorrow or is it just a fun idea to think about?

Colombian **Corn and Avocado Salsa**

TIME: 10 MIN (PREP), 5 MIN (COOK)
MAKES: 4-6 SERVINGS

Ingredients

2 ears corn, husk and silk removed
16 cherry tomatoes, halved
1 ripe avocado, chopped
½ small red onion, finely diced
1 garlic clove, finely chopped
1 jalapeño pepper, seeded and finely
  chopped
¼ cup chopped cilantro or basil
2 tablespoons oil
¼ cup fresh lime juice
½ teaspoon salt
¼ teaspoon pepper

Steps

1. Cook corn in boiling salted water for 1 minute.
2. Drain ears of corn and remove the kernels.
3. Place the corn kernels in a medium bowl along with the remaining ingredients, and stir together well.
4. The salsa will keep covered and refrigerated, for up to 1 day.

TIP: You can roast corn at 400°F for 15 minutes or grill corn for a deeper flavor.

(Photo courtesy of Hilary Peters)

 # CUSTOMS AND CAMARADERIE
Grenada: Operation Urgent Fury

We Honor in Remembrance. In October 1983, following a deadly coup in Grenada that put hundreds of American and allied lives in danger, the U.S. launched Operation Urgent Fury. The operation was among the first joint special operations efforts and included forces from Navy SEALs, Army Rangers, Air Force Special Operations, Marines, elements of what is now 160th Army Special Operations Aviation, and other special operations units. When the mission was complete, 599 Americans and 121 others were evacuated. Nineteen American service members were killed and 116 injured, but the operation was a success. It highlighted the stunning capabilities special operations units possess together as well as areas needing improvement. Ultimately, the operation in Grenada gave cause for major legislation (Goldwater-Nichols Act) to improve joint military operations and build the case for what would authorize and form the U.S. Special Operations Command (USSOCOM).[23]

23. Markowitz, M. (2013, June 3). *Urgent fury: U.S. Special Operations Forces in Grenada, 1983.* Defense Media Network. Accessed from https://www.defensemedianetwork.com/stories/urgent-fury-u-s-special-operations-forces-in-grenada-1983/

Special Operations Command Europe (SOCEUR) — The European Theater

SPECIAL OPERATIONS COMMAND EUROPE (SOCEUR) is one of the far off assignments our families get to enjoy and gallivant around Europe on four day weekends. Consisting of 51 independent nations, SOCEUR is home to our nation's oldest allies and 27 of 29 North Atlantic Treaty Organization (NATO) members. Geographically, the theater encompasses the area from Greenland east through the European continent, all of Russia, and south to include the Mediterranean Sea and Caucasus region. Gastronomically, the region is a foodie's heaven, with a cultural focus on seasonal and local cuisines that can vary not just by country, but even by village and valley.

A little family fun while stationed at SOCEUR *(Photo of Angie McLaughlin)*

The majority of allied and partner special operations forces that deploy alongside U.S. SOF to combat and peacekeeping operations in the Middle East and Africa are from European nations, which means our operators spend a lot of time in training exercises with these partners. Trading food and stories about life in their home countries creates strong bonds between practicing SOF tactics and communications procedures.

Often these stories of service with partner forces make it home and are retold when the right flavors ignite the storytelling. These memories become attached to recipes that we adopt and adapt for our own families.

I Love Italy **Zucchini Fritters**

TIME: 20 MIN (PREP), 15 MIN (COOK)
MAKES: 12 SERVINGS

Ingredients

2 medium zucchini, coarsely grated (2 packed
    cups after squeezing all the liquid out)
2 tablespoons onion, grated
⅓ cup whole wheat or all-purpose flour
½ teaspoon kosher salt
Freshly cracked black pepper
1 large egg, lightly beaten
1 lemon, finely zested
Small handful of fresh mint leaves, chopped
    (or any other fresh herbs you have on
    hand)
¼ cup olive oil for frying
Maldon sea salt, for serving (optional)
Lemon wedges, for serving (optional)

Steps

1. Grate the zucchini into a fine mesh sieve over the sink, and use your hands to squeeze out as much liquid as possible.
2. Place the zucchini and the grated onion in a clean dish towel and wrap up into a ball, wringing out any excess liquid.
3. Add the flour, salt, pepper, egg and zest in a large mixing bowl and combine. Then add mint and the zucchini-onion mixture and stir to combine.
4. Over medium heat, pour in enough oil to cover the bottom of a cast iron skillet.
5. When the oil shimmers, spoon a heaping tablespoon of batter into the pan for each fritter. Don't crowd the skillet.
6. Cook for 2 minutes on each side or until golden and crisp.
7. Place the fritters on paper towels or a wire rack, and season with salt.
8. Repeat until all the batter is cooked, adding more oil as needed between batches.
9. Serve immediately, or keep fritters warm in a 200°F oven.

TIP: Don't let the batter sit around; the zucchini will release more liquid and make the batter too wet.

SOF STORIES

Italian Roots — Andrea

Before we had kids, we spent two and a half years stationed in Italy while my husband did an exchange tour with the Italian Incusori (Navy SOF) near La Spezia. I learned the language, we traveled all over, and more importantly, I learned to cook Italian the Italian way. My favorite meals to make have Italian roots and bring back the most amazing memories, to include which wine to pair it with! It was there that I learned to shop daily for our meals, and where I started incorporating more vegetables into our diet. The fritter is the easiest way to use up scraps in the crisper. My favorite will always be the zucchini fritter. I love to make these and let my mind drift back to bustling food markets and a slower pace of life.

Root vegetables at market in Europe *(Photo courtesy of Angie McLaughlin)*

Civil Affairs **Greek Salad**

TIME: 15 MIN (PREP)
MAKES: 6 SERVINGS

Ingredients

Dressing

6 tablespoons extra virgin olive oil
2 tablespoons fresh lemon juice
½ teaspoon garlic, chopped
1 teaspoon red wine vinegar
½ teaspoon dried oregano or 1 teaspoon
   chopped fresh oregano
½ teaspoon dried dill or 1 teaspoon chopped
   fresh dill
Salt and freshly ground black pepper

Salad

3 large plum tomatoes, seeded and coarsely
   chopped
¾ cucumber, peeled, seeded, and coarsely
   chopped
½ red onion, chopped
1 bell pepper, seeded and coarsely chopped
½ cup pitted black olives (preferably
   brine-cured), coarsely chopped
½ cup crumbled feta cheese

Steps

1. To make the dressing, whisk the olive oil,
   lemon juice, garlic, vinegar, oregano, and
   dill together until blended. Season to
   taste with salt and freshly ground black
   pepper.
2. Next combine salad ingredients. Combine the tomatoes, cucumber, onion,
   bell pepper, and olives in a bowl.
3. Toss with dressing.
4. Sprinkle with cheese and serve.

TIP: The dressing can be prepared 3 hours ahead. Let stand at room temperature. Re-whisk before using. To take some of the bite away from the onions, after you chop them, soak them in a little vinegar or lemon juice.

Black Hawk **Prosciutto and Melon**

TIME: 10 MIN (PREP), 10 MIN (COOK)
MAKES: 12 SERVINGS

Ingredients

1 cantaloupe
4-5 ounces Prosciutto di Parma, thinly sliced
2 tablespoons honey or balsamic glaze,
   more to your liking
Basil leaves for garnish, optional

Steps

1. Cut the cantaloupe in half. Using a spoon, remove and discard the seeds. Then cut each half into wedges and peel them.
2. Wrap the prosciutto around the cantaloupe wedges and arrange them on a serving platter
3. Drizzle a little bit of balsamic glaze or quality honey (or both, if you like) .
4. If using, arrange a few basil leaves on the platter.
5. Serve immediately or chill for a few hours until ready to serve.

VARIATION: You can try the same idea with other fruit such as ripe figs, pears or sweet apples.

TACTICAL TOPICS
A Deliberate Moment of Gratitude

Talk about two things you felt thankful or grateful for today.

Black Hawk Prosciutto and Melon *(Photo courtesy of Andrea Geraldi)*

Swedish Pancake Cake

TIME: 15 MIN (PREP), 20 MIN (COOK)
MAKES: 20 SERVINGS

Ingredients

8 eggs
4 cups milk
½ cup melted butter or vegetable oil
2 cups flour
½ cup sugar
2 teaspoons salt
2 teaspoons extract or cinnamon (optional)

Filling

3 cups heavy whipping cream
¾ cup powdered sugar
1 teaspoon vanilla extract (or flavor of
  choice)
8 ounces mascarpone cheese (optional)

Toppings

6 ounces blackberries
6 ounces raspberries
6 ounces blueberries
6 ounces strawberries
1 tablespoon powdered sugar

Steps

1. Mix the eggs, milk, and melted butter or oil.
2. Then stir in the flour, sugar, and salt.
3. Add vanilla extract or cinnamon, if desired.
4. Mix well by hand or with a stand mixer until thoroughly combined.
5. Pour approximately ¾ cup batter on a pan or griddle at medium heat in an 8-10 in. circle.
6. Flip when it begins to bubble slightly, just like a pancake. Each side should have a slightly golden color.
7. Repeat until the batter is gone, stacking the pancakes on a plate or sheet pan.
8. To make the filling, add all ingredients to a mixing bowl and begin to mix at a lower speed.
9. Once it begins to thicken, increase the stirring speed slowly to whip.
10. Whip all ingredients together until firm peaks form.
11. Spread ¼ cup of the icing on each pancake as you stack them.
12. Repeat until you achieve the desired height.
13. On the top of the cake, place a thick layer of cream. Decorate with berries and sprinkle with powdered sugar.

VARIATION: This recipe will make a tall pancake cake. If you want a smaller cake, halve the recipe or save the extra pancakes for later.

(Photo courtesy of KaLea Lehman)

TACTICAL TOPICS
All Aboard the Orient Express

In many places, especially in Europe, you can quickly get nearly anywhere on a train. What would your itinerary look like? What stops would you schedule and how long would your trip be? What would your final destination be and why?

Special Operations Command Africa (SOCAFRICA)— The African Theater

SPECIAL OPERATIONS COMMAND AFRICA (SOCAFRICA) IS a bustling command hub nestled in Germany alongside SOCEUR. While our special operations forces are no stranger to the African continent, SOCAFRICA is the newest theater special operations command, established in 2008. Families living on the TSOC footprint in Germany often explore Europe and the nearby regions, and special operations units operate at full capacity across the African continent.

Joint training in the African Theater *(Photo courtesy of Fran Racioppi)*

Like other TSOCs, the special operations units tasked with SOCAFRICA missions are often based at several military installations around the world (such as the east coast of the U.S.). These special operations warriors stay incredibly busy working with partner forces and countering violent extremism on the African continent. Their missions can span any of the special capabilities that special operations forces have, but the demands in the region for the past few decades have been tied to countering terror.[24] Each return from the SOCAFRICA region is ripe with stories of wildlife and wild and wooly adventures of all sorts.

---

24. U.S. Special Operations Command Africa. (n.d.). *Welcome*. Accessed from https://www.socom.mil/socaf/

Traditional Moroccan Tea on TDY (*Photo courtesy of Paul Schmidt*)

Hostage Rescue **Chicken Suya**

TIME: 15 MIN (PREP), 20 MIN (COOK)
MAKES: 6 SERVINGS

Ingredients

1 tablespoon garlic powder

1 tablespoon onion powder

1 tablespoon smoked paprika

1 tablespoon pepper

½ tablespoon cayenne pepper

4 tablespoons peanut butter

1 tablespoon chicken or vegetable bouillon powder or paste

Wood skewers, soaked in water 15 min

3 pounds of chicken tenderloins or thinly sliced chicken thighs

3 tablespoon vegetable oil

Steps

1. Preheat the grill or oven to 450°F.
2. In a bowl, mix the garlic and onion powders, paprika, pepper, cayenne, peanut butter, and bouillon. If you do not like much spice, use less cayenne pepper in this mixture.
3. Add chicken to the wood skewers and cover as much of the skewer as possible.
4. Brush the spice mixture over the skewer of chicken, and place them on a greased baking sheet.
5. Drizzle the chicken skewers with the vegetable oil.
6. Grill or bake until the juices run clear, flipping halfway through.
7. Serve with pepper sauce or if you need to cool it down a bit, serve with ranch or blue cheese dressing.

(Photo courtesy of Andrea Orr)

SOF STORIES

Across the Pond yet Far from the Theater — Jenny

My husband's orders were SOCAFRICA, but all I heard was, "we're going to Germany!" While I should've paid more attention to the job details, I've learned over the years to tune him out. Everything changes so why focus on what he's supposed to be doing? But once we got to Germany, and I heard talk of Africa, I started to pay attention.

When my husband went on his first trip, I didn't think much of it. When he returned I asked, "how was Africa?" I don't know—maybe I'm numb after all these years, but some part of me thought it would be a cool traveling experience. My husband laughed and said, "How was Africa? . . . Shitty!" His response was an abrupt reminder he's not going on safaris or buying cool pottery or spices in Morocco. He's trying to calm things down in a country most of us only know about from tragic military movies.

Like most military spouses I've known, we made the best of it. The kids and I would make pottery on Kelley Barracks to send to family back in the U.S. for Christmas. Or we'd take a little drive to the indoor skate park, which entertained all my kids for hours. We'd stop at the bakery on our way home to get delicious pretzels and Apfelschorle, a common drink in Germany that is basically sparkling apple juice, all the while wondering if he was in Djibouti or Chad. I always wished for Kenya—it sounded exotic!

Quiet Professional **Peri Peri Sauce**

TIME: 15 MIN (PREP), 10 MIN (COOK)
MAKES: 8 SERVINGS

Ingredients

2 tablespoons vegetable oil

½ red onion, diced

4 garlic cloves, crushed or 4 teaspoons
   minced garlic

2 tablespoons sweet paprika

2 red peppers

6 Thai red chilis

¼ cup red wine vinegar

3 tablespoons lemon juice

Lemon zest

2 teaspoons brown sugar

4 teaspoons oregano

1½ teaspoons salt

1 teaspoon pepper

Steps

1. Peel and seed the red peppers. Roast them in the oven at 400°F until soft.

2. Sauté the red onion with the vegetable oil in a saucepan until the onion begins to soften. Add the minced garlic and paprika, and sauté for 1 minute.

3. Place the sauteed mixture in a blender and add all remaining ingredients. Blend until smooth.

VARIATION: If you would like the Peri Peri sauce to be extra spicy, then you can add extra Thai red peppers or blend the peppers with the seeds included. If fresh peppers are not available, substitute jarred fire roasted peppers but make sure to drain the liquid from the peppers.

 WAR GAMES
Going on Safari

If you were on an African safari, what animal are you most afraid to see? What animal would you hope to see? If you have young kids, have them make the animal sounds and guess the animals they are thinking of. What do these animals eat? This game is sure to bring some quick table laughs.

Camels in Africa (*Photo Courtesy of Fran Racioppi*)

(Opposite) Tandoori Chicken on TDY in Morocco (*Photo courtesy of Paul Schmidt*)

Moroccan **Lentil Soup**

TIME: 10 MIN (PREP), 25 MIN (COOK)
MAKES: 6 SERVINGS

Ingredients

3 tablespoons extra virgin olive oil
1 large onion, chopped
1 celery stalk, chopped
1 carrot, chopped
2 jalapeño peppers, diced
3 garlic cloves, chopped
2 tablespoons Garam Masala
1 teaspoon ground cumin
1 teaspoon ground turmeric
½ teaspoon paprika
½ teaspoon sea salt
Dash of pepper
8 cups vegetable broth, low sodium if
   possible
2 cups red lentils, rinsed until water runs
   clean
1 lemon, juiced
1 tablespoon fresh cilantro, chopped

Steps

1. Heat olive oil in a Dutch oven or large pot over medium-high heat.
2. Add the onions, celery, carrots, and peppers. Sauté until tender (about 3-4 minutes).
3. Add the garlic and all of the spices. Continue cooking for another 2-3 minutes stirring the whole time.
4. Add the broth and lentils. Stir well and heat to a boil. Then simmer uncovered on low heat for about 20-25 minutes (until the lentils are tender), stirring occasionally.
5. Stir in the lemon juice and cilantro, cover and cook for 10 minutes.
6. Serve hot with warm pita bread or bread of your choice. Garnish with extra cilantro if you desire.

VARIATION: Use a sweet pepper in place of jalapenos if you don't want it to be spicy.

WAR GAMES
Map Games

The beloved game of JCET ping-pong. It's training while on a deployment trip. Where will they go? Who will they go with? Where will they stay? An adventure awaits them, a story awaits us. It is always interesting, and the places they go always have a good history lesson attached, and a good meal with it.

- Pull out a map, throw a ping-pong ball or a dart,
- Guess where in the world it hit.
- What do you know about that region?
- If you could visit, what would you hope to see?
- If you could return home with a treasure, what would you bring?

(Photo courtesy of KaLea Lehman)

Gothic Serpent **Tikel Gomen**

TIME: 10 MIN (PREP), 30 MIN (COOK)
MAKES: 6 SERVINGS

Ingredients

⅓ cup olive oil
4 carrots, peeled and sliced
1 onion, diced
1 teaspoon salt
¼ teaspoon pepper
1 teaspoon cumin
1 teaspoon turmeric
½ teaspoon ground ginger
1 head of cabbage, chopped
6 red potatoes, diced

Steps

1. Sauté the carrots and onion in the olive oil over medium heat in a large stockpot.
2. Stir in all seasonings, then add in the cabbage and potatoes.
3. Stir all ingredients to combine, then cover the pot and cook on medium to low heat until the potatoes and cabbage are soft and tender. The smaller the potatoes are diced, the faster it will cook.

TIP: If you do not want to dice a head of cabbage, you can use a 20 oz bag of cabbage slaw mixture.

(Photo courtesy of KaLea Lehman)

CUSTOMS AND CAMARADERIE
Battle of Mogadishu

We Honor in Remembrance. In a United Nations effort to feed starving Somalis, the United States launched a special operations raid called Operation Gothic Serpent. Operators from several special operations units including Rangers targeted the warlord General Aideed in Mogadishu on October 3-4, 1993. The mission was a strategic loss, but it drove many changes in how special operations units plan, train, and execute missions. Two Black Hawk helicopters were shot-down, 18 service members were killed, and 84 more were wounded. Those who fought in the battle inspired many with their courage and bravery. The Battle of Mogadishu is more commonly known as Black Hawk Down today.[25]

Photographs from before and after the Battle of Mogadishu. *(Photos courtesy of Tom Satterly)*

25. South, T. (2018, October 2). *The battle of mogadishu 25 years later: How The fateful fight changed combat operations.* Accessed from https://www.armytimes.com/news/your-army/2018/10/02/the-battle-of-mogadishu-25-years-later-how-the-fateful-fight-changed-combat-operations/

Just a JCET in the Levant (*Photo courtesy of KaLea Lehman*)

Special Operations Command Central (SOCCENT)—The Middle East Theater

SPECIAL OPERATIONS COMMAND CENTRAL (SOCCENT) OVERSEES special operations throughout the Middle East and the Horn of Africa, yet its home base rests next to Special Operations Command and Central Command at MacDill Air Force Base in Tampa, Florida. Families here can enjoy the warm sunshine and explore the Gulf waters. Many units that support SOCCENT are sprinkled around the country at installations in Kentucky, North Carolina, and Virginia.

There is no shortage of missions or needs in this region. The wars in Afghanistan, Iraq, and Syria have defined service in this region for over 20 years now.[26] The terrain and the partners are rough. Regional demands are diverse and change with each news cycle. One moment the task is just a quick Joint Combined Exchange Training (JCET), but with any change in region dynamics, it can quickly become a new set of long, repeating, rugged deployments to a desert or the mountains of the Middle East. The demand and the hardness of the missions leave a mark on the force and the families that routinely experience them. Nearly every operator and special ops family has at least one story to tell from a deployment to this region.

Tasty favorite in the SOCCENT area of operations (*Photo courtesy of KaLea Lehman*)

---

26. U.S. Special Operations Command Central . (n.d.). *Welcome*. Accessed from https://www.socom.mil/soccent/Pages/Home.aspx

Ghostrider Shakshuka Eggs in Tomato Sauce

TIME: 10 MIN (PREP), 20 MIN (COOK)
MAKES: 6 SERVINGS

- -

Ingredients

1 medium onion, diced

1 red bell pepper, seeded and diced

4 garlic cloves, finely chopped

2 teaspoons paprika

1 teaspoon cumin

¼ teaspoon chili powder

1 (28-ounce) can whole peeled tomatoes

6 large eggs

Salt and pepper, to taste

½ cup fresh cilantro, chopped

½ cup fresh parsley, chopped

Steps

1. Heat olive oil in a large sauté pan on medium heat. Add the chopped bell pepper and onion, and cook for 5 minutes or until the onion becomes translucent.

2. Add the garlic and spices and stir for another minute until they're nice and fragrant.

3. Pour in tomatoes and juice into the pan and break up the tomatoes using a large spoon. Season with salt and pepper and bring the sauce to a simmer.

4. Use your large spoon to make small wells in the sauce for the eggs, then crack an egg into each well.

5. Reduce the heat to low, cover the pan and cook for another 5-8 minutes or until the eggs are done to your liking.

6. Before serving, season the eggs with salt and garnish with parsley and cilantro.

SOF STORIES
A Dish from an Israeli Trip – Liz

(Photo courtesy of Lynnsy Snook)

Shakshuka is my favorite because my husband came home from a temporary duty in Israel and raved about the most amazing tomato sauce he'd ever had with a poached egg for breakfast. He made sure to have it daily while deployed, and he just couldn't stop talking about the tomato and egg dish. Eventually, I Googled it to find out what it was and made it for our family. Then, I realized that it was something my mom, who is from Morocco, used to make when I was a kid. Every time I make it, we reminisce about his time in Israel and how my mom would make it when I was a kid. Our kids enjoy the meal and the story mashup of dad's deployment and my childhood retellings.

One Man, One Pan **Chicken and Rice**

TIME: 20 MIN (PREP), 1 HOUR (COOK)
MAKES: 6 SERVINGS

- -

Ingredients

Chicken

1 pound chicken thighs, boneless, skinless
1 tablespoon Garam Masala
1 lemon, juiced
1 teaspoon salt
½ teaspoon pepper
1 tablespoon olive oil

Rice

2 tablespoons butter, unsalted
½ cup white or yellow onion, diced
4 garlic cloves, minced
1 cup Jasmine or basmati white rice
2 cups chicken broth, low sodium
½ teaspoon turmeric
½ teaspoon cumin
½ cup fresh parsley, for garnish

Steps

1. Preheat the oven to 350°F.
2. In a medium sized bowl, mix chicken thighs with Garam Masala, lemon juice, salt and pepper.
3. Heat cast iron skillet over medium heat. Add in olive oil, then brown chicken for about 3-4 minutes on each side.
4. Remove the chicken from the cast iron and set side on a plate.
5. Keep the cast iron on medium heat, melt the butter and add in diced onion. Cook for about 2-3 minutes and then stir in garlic.
6. Add in the uncooked rice and stir for 30 seconds. Stir in the chicken broth, turmeric, and cumin. Place chicken back in the pan on top of the uncooked rice.
7. Cover with lid or foil and bake in the oven for 40-45 minutes or until the chicken reaches an internal temperature of 165°F and rice is cooked.
8. Garnish with parsley.

TIP: Garam Masala is a spice blend of coriander, black pepper, cumin, cardamom, and cinnamon. If you can't find it, try curry powder, Jamaican Jerk rub, or your own favorite spice blend.

VARIATION: You can use skin-on chicken thighs. If using bone-in chicken thighs, cooking time will need to be increased.

DOL Dolma

TIME: 15 MIN (PREP), 1 HOUR, 30 MIN (COOK)
MAKES: 25 SERVINGS

Ingredients

3 tablespoons olive oil

1 garlic clove, minced

1 small yellow onion, minced

½ cup long-grain rice

½ teaspoon minced fresh thyme

Kosher salt and freshly ground black pepper to taste

3 cups chicken stock

1 ounce dried Turkish apricots, minced

½ cup minced cilantro

⅓ cup minced parsley

¼ cup golden raisins

¼ cup pine nuts

2 tablespoons minced mint

2 tablespoons red currant jelly

⅛ teaspoon cayenne pepper

1 tablespoon fresh lemon juice, plus the zest of 1 lemon

25 grape leaves packed in brine, rinsed and pat dry

1 lemon, thinly sliced

Steps

1. Heat oil in a 4 quart. saucepan over medium-high heat.
2. Add garlic and onions; cook, stirring, until soft, 3-5 minutes. Add rice, thyme, salt, and pepper and cook for 2 minutes.
3. Add 1 cup stock and bring to a boil. Reduce heat to low and cook, covered, until rice is tender, 22-24 minutes.
4. Stir in apricots, cilantro, parsley, raisins, nuts, mint, jelly, cayenne, lemon juice and zest, salt, and pepper.
5. Preheat the oven to 375°F.
6. Working with one leaf at a time, stuff the grape leaves by laying a grape leaf vein side up with the stem facing you. Put 1 tablespoon of filling in the center of the leaf and fold the right side over the filling.
7. Next, fold the left side of the leaf over the filling, overlapping the other side completely. Squeeze filling on top and bottom to compact it. Fold the bottom of the leaf over the center and roll it forward into a cylinder, tightening as you go.
8. Place stuffed grape leaf seam side down in a single layer in an 8" x 8" baking dish. Repeat for the rest of the leaves.
9. Add remaining stock and distribute lemon slices over grape leaves. Cover the pan with aluminum foil and bake until tender, about 1 hour.
10. Let Dolma cool before serving with tzatziki sauce.

SOF STORIES
Night Catch — Becka

A solitary moment while away from home. *(Photo courtesy of KaLea Lehman)*

My children have always loved looking at the stars. They got that from me. I would look up and find Cassiopeia gazing into her mirror or find Orion running from the Scorpion. Before children, I would ask my husband what stars he would see when he was "traveling" or if he saw Venus or Mars rise with the moon. Stargazing kept us talking (mostly writing back then) about things that were light and engaging, in a way that made him feel as if he was next to me when he was far from home.

When I had our second child, I was given the book *Night Catch* by Brenda Ehrmantraut. My eldest immediately wanted to play catch with the North Star. We would read the book and look out the window at the night sky. My son would show his baby sister the north star and tell her that we would toss it to daddy. My husband would then text the next day to say thanks for throwing it back. The connection between father and son was tangible at that moment.

Joint Training **Tzatziki**

TIME: 10 MIN (PREP)
MAKES: 4-6 SERVINGS

Ingredients

¾ English cucumber, partially peeled (striped) and sliced

1 teaspoon kosher salt, divided

4-5 garlic cloves, finely grated or minced

1 teaspoon white vinegar

1 tablespoon olive oil

2 cups plain Greek yogurt

¼ teaspoon ground white or black pepper

Warm pita bread for serving

Sliced vegetables for serving

Steps

1. Use a box grater to grate the cucumbers or you can use a small food processor to finely chop the cucumbers.

2. Toss the grated cucumbers with ½ teaspoon kosher salt. Spoon the grated cucumber into a cheesecloth or a double thickness napkin and squeeze dry.

3. In one large mixing bowl, place the garlic with remaining ½ teaspoon salt, white vinegar, and extra virgin olive oil. Mix to combine.

4. Add the grated cucumber to the bowl with the garlic mixture.

5. Stir in the yogurt, and a pinch of pepper. Stir to combine well.

Special Forces ODA conducting joint training in Jordan. *(Photo courtesy of KaLea Lehman)*

WAR GAMES

Star Light, Star Bright, Where are the Stars Tonight?

What constellations can you find? And, if your spouse is away, guess what stars and constellations will fill their sky. If deployed or away training, have them take pictures of the night sky and play "guess that constellation" or "find me by the stars."

These are fun and memorable ways to bring them to the table to interact even when not physically there. Practical tip: Download a stargazing app to see what stars/constellations are in the sky anywhere in the world.

A Special Forces daughter drifts off to dreams after finding her favorite constellation of the night. *(Photo courtesy of Christine Trax)*

The Levant **Hummus**

TIME: 10 MIN (PREP)
MAKES: 6 SERVINGS

Ingredients

1 (14.5-ounce) can garbanzo beans, drained
   and liquid reserved
2 tablespoons tahini
1 garlic clove
2 tablespoons extra virgin olive oil
½ lemon, juiced
Salt, to taste

Steps

1. Place drained garbanzo beans, tahini, garlic, olive oil and lemon juice into a food processor.
2. Process for 1 minute.
3. Using the liquid from the canned beans, drizzle in until desired consistency is achieved.
4. Season with salt to taste.

TIP: If you use olive oil instead of the canned liquid, the mixture will become greasy and separate. The trick to creaminess is the liquid from the can.

VARIATION: Optional additions: ¼ cup roasted red bell peppers, ¼ cup kalamata olives, 2 tablespoons sesame seeds, 3 tablespoons toasted pine nuts, 1 teaspoon za'atar seasoning, or top with olive oil, lemon zest, and chopped parsley.

(Photo courtesy of Wendy Jo Peterson)

What are you going to do after service? What draws your interest to that job, activity, or mission? If you could spend free time dedicated to one cause, what would it be? What makes this important to you?

Former SOF Medics work to help SOF veterans find and buy homes and commercial property in TX. *(Photo courtesy of Patrick Brennan and Daniel Bell)*

THE WARRIOR'S TABLE

Jordanian Desert **Chai Tea**

TIME: 2 MIN (PREP), 5 MIN (COOK)
MAKES: 3 SERVINGS

Ingredients

3 cups water

3 bags black tea

½ cup sugar

1 tablespoon sage

Steps

1. Boil water with tea bags.
2. Add sugar and sage, stirring until sugar dissolves.
3. Filter sage out of tea before serving.

(Photo courtesy of Bridget Orr)

CUSTOMS AND CAMARADERIE
Horse Soldiers in Afghanistan

Historic Highlight. Immediately following the attack on September 11, 2001, the U.S. launched Operation Task Force Dagger. Small teams from the Army's 5th Special Forces Group were among the first boots on the ground in Afghanistan. Their mission was to link up with local warlords and other fighters who were part of the Northern Alliance, take-down the Taliban, and eliminate safe havens for al Qaeda in Afghanistan. The

A Special Forces team embedded with elements of the Northern Alliance during Operation Task Force Dagger and later Operation Anaconda. *(Photo courtesy of Perry Blackburn)*

Green Berets of 5th Special Forces Group improvised and adapted and rode into the fight on horseback against Taliban equipped with old Soviet tanks. They liberated Mazar-e-Sharif in an early success of what would become the U.S. war in Afghanistan. The mission and spirit of these Special Forces teams is the basis of the movie, *12 Strong*.[27]

THE WARRIOR'S TABLE

27. Correll, D. (2022, August 18). *How the 'horse soldiers' helped liberate Afghanistan from the Taliban 18 years ago.* Military Times. Accessed from https://www.militarytimes.com/news/your-military/2019/10/18/how-the-horse-soldiers-helped-liberate-afghanistan-from-the-taliban-18-years-ago/

Special Operations Command Korea (SOCKOR)— The Korean Theater

IT IS NOT UNUSUAL FOR MILITARY families or solo service members (better known as geographical bachelors) to do a stint of time in Korea; but when it comes to special operations, it isn't a location that comes up often. Camp Humphrey is the home of Special Operations Command Korea (SOCKOR).

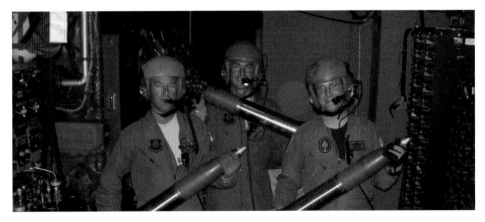

AFSOC AC-130 gunners with 105mm howitzer ammunition. *(Photo courtesy of Greg Smith)*

SOCKOR is tasked with making sure we and our Korean partners are ready to fight and defend the Korean peninsula. The U.S. military has had strong ties to Korea for decades, and the presence of SOCKOR is a testament to that strong commitment. For the families fortunate enough to accompany their servicemember, there is no shortage of food adventures to spice up their palate. Everyone returns with a list of new pantry favorites and tales of Korean BBQ and Kimchi.

Korean Tea *(Photo courtesy of Nicole Spitzack)*

Tower of Power **Kimchi Fried Rice**

TIME: 10 MIN (PREP), 15 MIN (COOK)
MAKES: 2 SERVINGS

- -

Ingredients

4 cups leftover white rice

1 1/2 cups kimchi, sliced and diced

1 cup kimchi juice

Leftover meat and/or vegetables (optional)

1 teaspoon Gochujang (Korean red chili paste; optional if you don't like spiciness)

1 1/2 tablespoons sesame oil

2 eggs

1 teaspoon sesame seeds

Sliced Gim (Korean dried seaweed)

Sliced scallions

Steps

1. Drain juice from the kimchi into a bowl, squeezing as much juice from the kimchi as possible. Stir the gochujang into 1 cup extracted kimchi juice until well blended.

2. Slice kimchi into 1/2" size pieces and fry for 2-3 minutes in a pan on medium high heat, stirring continuously so it doesn't stick.

3. If adding leftover meat or vegetables, reheat gently in a separate pan. Once the kimchi has been sufficiently fried and the meat has been heated up, mix the meat and vegetables into the kimchi pan for about 30 seconds.

4. Add in the cold leftover cooked rice, using a spatula to break up the clumped rice. Pour the kimchi/gochujang juice mixture all over the top, and fold in until the white rice has turned red. Cook for an additional 2-3 minutes to warm the rice up and mix the flavors, making sure to move the ingredients around to prevent burning.

5. Drizzle the sesame oil over the dish, mix together one more time, and remove from heat.

6. In a separate pan, fry the eggs and season to taste.

7. To plate, fill a small bowl with the kimchi fried rice, place a plate on top, and flip the two over so the rice forms a neat mound on the plate. Place a fried egg on top of each mound. Sprinkle sesame seeds, sliced seaweed, and scallions to taste.

VARIATION: Add seasoned meat (light on saltiness) or additional vegetables to the dish during step 2 of the instructions. Seasoned chicken, beef, or pork are all good additions to this dish.

A special operations family living in Korea. *(Photo courtesy of Nicole Spitzack)*

SOF STORIES
Kimchi Bo Kum Bop — Steven and Alissa

Growing up with a Korean-American mom, we always had a full-flavor dinner table. I learned to cook some of my mom's great classics, but Kimchi Bo Kum Bop is our favorite meal to make when the leftovers in the fridge are starting to accumulate. I'm sure that there are folks who will say that fresher ingredients bring out better flavors, but for me there's some level of satisfaction that enhances the flavor of the dish when I simultaneously find a use for food that is just sitting idly in my fridge. Outside of my semi-OCD, there is some logic to using less fresh ingredients for the two stars of the dish—kimchi and rice.

For kimchi, the older it gets the more fermented it becomes. When this happens, its spiciness is superseded by that classic sour flavor that fermented foods have. When you cook it, that sourness is dramatically reduced and a little bit of the spiciness is brought back. For rice, its moisture is slowly extracted when it sits in your fridge, which makes the flavors you add to the stir fry stick to the rice. Fresh rice is full of water moisture that will dilute the rest of the ingredients. Adding leftover meat and/ or vegetables is optional, but go easy on the salt and pepper when cooking it so it doesn't overpower the dish. Another great meat option is spam. Some folks may balk at this, but spam is fan-favorite in our household. If you've never had it, give it a try and you'll see what I mean.

Advise, Support, and Stabilize **Korean Beef**

TIME: 10 MIN (PREP), 10 MIN (COOK)
MAKES: 6 SERVINGS

Ingredients

¼ cup brown sugar, packed

¼ cup reduced sodium soy sauce

2 teaspoons sesame oil

½ teaspoon crushed red-pepper flakes, or
more to taste

¼ teaspoon ground ginger

1 tablespoon vegetable oil

3 garlic cloves, minced

1 pound ground beef

2 green onions, thinly sliced

¼ teaspoon sesame seeds

Steps

1. In a small bowl, whisk together brown sugar, soy sauce, sesame oil, red pepper flakes and ginger.

2. Heat vegetable oil in a large skillet over medium high heat. Add garlic and cook, stirring constantly, until fragrant, about 1 minute.

3. Add ground beef and cook until browned, about 3-5 minutes, making sure to crumble the beef as it cooks. Drain excess fat.

4. Stir in soy sauce mixture and green onions until well combined, allowing to simmer until heated through, about 2 minutes.

5. Serve immediately, garnished with green onion and sesame seeds, if desired.

(Photo courtesy of Wendy Jo Peterson)

CUSTOMS AND CAMARADERIE
Korea: A Need for the Unconventional

Did you know? Many of today's special operations units trace their lineage to heroic missions that highlight World War II history. Despite their success, the special mission units were disbanded following the war, but their unique capabilities were missed in Korea. In great need of unconventional assets, the GHQ Raiders (an Almo Scout-type unit from General Headquarters), Marine Mobile Training Teams, and the Special Operations Group of Amphibious Group One (PhibGruOne) were formed and put to work.

While these ground efforts were notable, the Air Force played many key roles inserting guerrilla forces, collecting intelligence, and waging psychological warfare missions in C-46s, C-47s, C-119s, B-26s, B-29s, UH-19s, and SA-16s over Korea in "Special Air Missions." Two notable air missions were codenamed Operation Aviary and Operation Firefly.[28] Following the Korean War, it was obvious that special mission capabilities would be needed by all branches of service in modern war. Special capabilities were a key strategic, shaping force in war.[29]

28. Briscoe, C. H. (2012, November 1). *Born of Desperation: Early Special Operations in the Korean War*. Accessed from https://arsof-history.org/articles/v6n1_born_of_desperation_page_1.html
29. National Museum of the United States Air Force. (n.d.). *Special Operations: In the Enemy's Backyard*. Accessed from https://www.nationalmuseum.af.mil/Visit/Museum-Exhibits/Fact-Sheets/Display/Article/196083/special-operations-in-the-enemys-backyard/

Korean Kimchi

TIME: 8-12 HOURS (PREP)
MAKES: 2 QUARTS

Ingredients

1 head of napa cabbage, tough end removed and chopped
1 daikon radish, peeled and grated
2 carrots, peeled and grated
¼ cup salt (not iodized)
¼ cup Korean chili powder
10 garlic cloves, peeled
2-inch piece of ginger, peeled
6 green onions
1 teaspoon fish sauce
1 teaspoon yellow miso paste

Steps

1. In a large glass bowl, mix the chopped cabbage, radish, and carrots with salt. Cover the bowl with a towel and let the mixture sit overnight. This draws out the liquid from the vegetables.
2. In a food processor, mix the chili powder, garlic, ginger, green onions, fish sauce, and miso until combined.
3. Add the chili paste mixture to the salted vegetables and stir to combine.
4. Clean 2-3 quart-sized Mason jars and pour boiling water into them. Let the jars sit for 5 minutes then dump the water.
5. Fill jars with the kimchi mixture and pack in with a clean spoon. Each jar should be PACKED.
6. Leave one inch on the top, pressing down to have the liquid cover the surface.
7. Place the lid on the jar, but leave it loosely sealed.
8. Place the jars on a baking sheet to catch spillage (the mixture will bubble and release gasses). Cover the jars with a towel and leave in a cool spot.
9. Each day, use a clean knife to stir and release excess air bubbles, the place lid back on loosely.
10. Do this for 3 days then refrigerate. The kimchi will continue to ferment in the refrigerator and is good for up to 6 months.

TACTICAL TOPICS
Korean BBQ Reimagined

Let's make a menu. What is your dream dinner? What would you make for a family meal? Would it be a one-pot wonder or multiple favorites as you build a plate Korean barbecue style?

(Opposite) **Kimchi on the table in Korea** *(Photo courtesy of Nicole Spitzack)*

Special Operations Command Pacific (SOCPAC)—The Pacific Theater

SPECIAL OPERATIONS COMMAND PACIFIC (SOCPAC) is located in paradise overlooking Pearl Harbor in Hawaii. While families are able to soak in the sun and sight of breathtaking mountain hikes and stunning waterfalls, the service members manning SOCPAC direct operations in four geographic regions: Southeast Asia, South Asia, Northeast Asia, and Oceania.

A classic moment in Okinawa. Bull fighting is a common local activity *(Photo courtesy of Steven Miller)*

Our special operators stay busy deterring aggression, training foreign partners, and responding to crises in the Pacific region,[30] while families explore their base typically along the West Coast of the U.S., in Hawaii, or from a military base in the South Pacific such as Okinawa. SOCPAC is a busy place to work, yet a lovely place to play and adventure. Whether you crave the excitement of the sea or the challenges of tropical mountain hikes, the tastes of the islands have a way of leaving a lasting impression on our families.

---

30. United States Special Operations Pacific. (n.d.). *Special Operations Command Pacific (SOCPAC).* Accessed from https://www.socom.mil/socpac/

75th Ranger **Ramen**

TIME: 15 MIN (PREP), 50 MIN (COOK)
MAKES: 2 SERVINGS

Ingredients

2 teaspoons sesame oil

1 tablespoon fresh garlic, minced

2 teaspoons fresh ginger, minced

3 tablespoons low-sodium soy sauce

2 tablespoons mirin

4 cups chicken stock

1 ounce dried shiitake mushrooms (or ½ cup fresh)

Kosher salt and freshly-ground black pepper to taste

2 large eggs

2 (3-ounce) packages dried ramen noodles

2 chicken breasts, cooked and sliced

½ cup scallions, sliced

Optional: fresh jalapeño or chili slices for serving

Steps

1. Heat the oil in a large pot over medium heat. Add the garlic and ginger, and cook for a few minutes until softened.
2. Add the soy sauce and mirin, and stir to combine. Cook for another minute.
3. Add the stock, cover, and bring to boil. Remove the lid, and let simmer uncovered for 5 minutes.

VARIATION: You can use any leftover protein in place of the chicken. Use rice vermicelli noodles if needed gluten-free and gluten-free soy sauce.

4. Add the dried mushrooms and simmer gently for another 10 minutes. Season with salt to taste.
5. To make the soft-boiled eggs, fill a pot with enough water to cover the eggs, and bring to a boil. Gently lower the eggs (still cold from the fridge) into the boiling water, and let simmer for 7 minutes (for a slightly-runny yolk) or 8 minutes (for a soft, but set-up yolk).
6. Meanwhile, fill a large bowl with ice water. When the timer finishes, transfer the eggs to the ice bath to stop the cooking process. Wait at least 5 minutes, or until cool enough to handle, then carefully peel away the shell and slice in half, lengthwise. Set aside until ready to serve.
7. When the eggs finish cooking, add the ramen noodles to the boiling water. Cook for 2-3 minutes, until soft, then divide the noodles into two large bowls.
8. Add the sliced chicken and the ramen broth. Top with the fresh scallions, jalapeño and the soft boiled egg. Serve immediately.

(Photo courtesy of KaLea Lehman)

SOF STORIES

Hawaii Self Care — Amy

My husband was deployed for our twins' first birthday; and since they were born in Hawaii, I wanted to go back and celebrate it there amongst our friends who helped us through those crazy first couple of months. Our Hawaii trip also happened to fall on my birthday, making for a sweet escape. My husband arranged for my friends to babysit the twins while I had a massage; but more importantly he got me a gift card to Honolulu Coffee Company. He knew I loved that place and the coffee was key to getting me through solo parenting one-year-old twins!

Cherry blossom season in Japan. (*Photo courtesy of Steven Miller*)

STRAY 59 Beef Bulgogi

TIME: 20 MIN (PREP), 5-10 MIN (COOK)
MAKES: 6 SERVINGS

Ingredients

¾ cup soy sauce
1 garlic clove, diced
2 tablespoons brown sugar
3-4 teaspoons of sesame oil
2 pounds thin sliced beef (bulgogi cut preferred)

Steps

1. Mix marinade and soak the sliced beef for 15-30 minutes.
2. Pan fry the beef and serve with rice and stir-fried vegetables.

CUSTOMS AND CAMARADERIE

Special Forces in the Vietnam War

Historic Highlight. Military Assistance Command, Vietnam, Studies and Operations Group, better known as MACV-SOG, predates the modern structure of special operations. Those who volunteered to serve in the MACV-SOG conducted classified special operations missions to include: Strategic reconnaissance, kill and capture, rescue, and other clandestine activities during the Vietnam War.[31] Many MACV-SOG volunteers hailed from Army Special Forces, Navy SEALs, Air Force, CIA, and Marine Corps Force Reconnaissance units. Their service and success is a powerful legacy piece of many modern special operations units today.[32]

When history comes to life: A MACV SOG veteran helps a Special Forces mom manage a busy toddler. (*Photo courtesy of KaLea Lehman*)

31. HISTORY OF MACV-SOG. (n.d.). *About SOG*. Accessed from https://sogsite.com/about-sog/
32. Seals, R. (2019, January 25). *MACV-SOG history*. Accessed from https://www.army.mil/article/216498/macv_sog_history

Torii Station **Ginger Tea**

TIME: 1 MIN (PREP), 5 MIN (COOK)
MAKES: 1 SERVING

Ingredients

1 cup boiling water
1 black tea bag
½ teaspoon ginger
Sugar and milk to taste

Steps

1. Boil water with a tea bag.
2. Add ginger, sugar and milk.
3. Serve and enjoy!

(Photo courtesy of Bridget Orr)

TACTICAL TOPICS
Star Light, Star Bright

What is your favorite night-time object? Is it the moon, constellation, or a particular star? Why is it your favorite? Have your favorites changed through the years?

TDY **Turkey and Rice**

TIME: 10 MIN (PREP), 30 MIN (COOK)
MAKES: 6 SERVINGS

- -

Ingredients

2 cups Jasmine rice

2 cups water

¼ cup brown sugar, packed

¼ cup reduced sodium soy sauce

2 teaspoons sesame oil

Crushed red pepper to taste

¼ teaspoon ground ginger

1 tablespoon vegetable oil

3 garlic cloves, minced

1 pound ground turkey

2 green onions, thinly sliced

¼ teaspoon sesame seeds

Steps

1. Rinse rice under water until water runs clear.
2. Add rice and water to a pressure cooker or multi-cooker. Secure the lid and turn the valve to seal. Set on manual high pressure for 5 minutes. Allow natural release for 10 minutes.
3. In a small bowl, whisk together brown sugar, soy sauce, sesame oil, red pepper flakes and ginger.
4. Heat vegetable oil in a large skillet over medium high heat. Add garlic and cook, stirring constantly, until fragrant, about 1 minute.
5. Add ground turkey and cook until browned, about 3-5 minutes.
6. Stir in soy sauce mixture and green onions until well combined, allowing to simmer until heated through, about 2 minutes.
7. Serve turkey topped on rice, garnished with green onion, red pepper and sesame seeds, if desired. This pairs well with a side of steamed broccoli and carrots.

(Photo courtesy of Wendy Jo Peterson)

Here come the HALO teams!
(Photo courtesy of KaLea Lehman)

3. Real Life Ruck March

★ ★ ★

WITH EVERY DEPLOYMENT COMES A STORY from afar. Each begins with a service member who is swept off, sent off, carried away, or seemingly goes missing. They reappear a few days later by phone, email, or app with stories from some unique place in the world. One trip the setting is a desert with no end and the next trip it is a jagged mountain top targeted by enemy forces. It takes a few trips to learn to brush off the unique tensions that accompany each place or mission. After a while, they all feel like stories in the making. You learn to wait and hold your breath to get over the bumps and tension.

A virtual note from Dad. (*Photo courtesy of KaLea Lehman*)

As new military spouses, we half expected a knock at the door with the worst possible news. Breaking news alerts come out faster than a casualty notification. Learning to balance fear, pressure, and paranoia demands family routines, personal discipline, and a lot of intentionality. Over time we learned to turn our attention to less fearful places, embrace this way of life, and focus on the circumstances within our span of control. Learning how to live well amid more than a few deployments is a community effort with learned ground rules. We learned how to flow with the constant "home and away" routine about the same time we stopped taking redeployment (welcome home) pictures. Now, we look back at those pictures, which we treasure, and think about how young and new we were during those early trips. Back then, everything was a big deal. Early on in our journey, we helped them pack, knew all the gear, and even chilled in the team room. Deployments used to start and end with a military ceremony, but that changed to solo pick-ups in the airport, then the airport curb late at night. That stopped around baby two . . . or deployment three. The return dates changed a thousand times. Eventually, he figured out how to get home flying solo, and we wrapped-up those quick trips with a surprise "daddy's home" re-entry for the kids. When he would actually return was totally unpredictable, so it took a load off both of us not to share the moment to moment details.

These days, we don't think of the coming and going—at least not as much. We embrace most deployment trips as extra time to get our own things done and pass time by sprinkling the weeks with adventure and our own accomplishments. Often his away time became "my time." We got really good at the coming and going and mastered the unpredictability, but then we realized we needed a family break because we had put-off too many family vacations, celebrations, and important conversations. In fact, we put them off so much we convinced ourselves we didn't need them. But we did. Every one of us can tell you our salty do's and don'ts. Our recipe may be intimidating or even seem harsh at times, but that is because the ingredients came at a cost. It is hard to be soft and serious when you rarely have a chance to decompress.

Some experiences are too tough to share and others are definitely too intense for common conversation. Seasoned families know this. We've seen the wide-eyed look in the eyes of friends or family following conversations we thought were real and normal. The truth is, some of our dishes are too tough for a community plate. There are times you have to learn to trust sage advice with a pinch of patience and grace.

Special operations couple reunites. *(Photo courtesy of Jennifer Bryne)*

SERE Says it All

- -

UNIVERSAL TRAINING FOR ALL SPECIAL OPERATORS is Survival, Evasion, Resistance, and Escape school—better known as SERE school. There operators learn how to avoid capture, live off the land, and how to stay alive if captured. It is physically and psychologically demanding training that many think of as a "stress inoculation," but anyone blessed with a baby who refused to eat or sleep knows that is just wishful thinking. Sleepless nights[33] and bad nutrition take a toll on us all. There is no inoculation for stress or sleep deprivation. You learn to function through both experiences, but the ground truth is you won't be at peak performance.[34]

During SERE they were freezing in a box, and we were home in warm beds but we both endured endless hours of crying babies on radio and real life. They ate worms, roasted a wild rabbit, and brewed nettle tea to survive. We kept the home fires burning and squashed bananas and green peas for infant food. Eventually the training came to an end, and they returned home dirty, tired, skinny and starving, but equipped with a few stories that will forever spark laughter and stunned expressions and fuel awkward but funny moments. Few nonmilitary dads teach their kids what wild things can be eaten or surprise their young son by swallowing the worm he just found in the mud. Each SOF service member has a SERE story, and much like motherhood, sometimes a simple understanding expression says it all.

Water hoist training as seen through night vision goggles. *(Photo courtesy of Paul Schmidt)*

---

33. Ryan, Tom. April 19, 2022. Sleep in the Military. Sleep Foundation. Accessed from https://www.sleepfoundation.org/sleep-in-the-military

34. Yaribeygi H, Panahi Y, Sahraei H, Johnston TP, Sahebkar A. The impact of stress on body function: A review. EXCLI J. 2017 Jul 21;16:1057-1072. doi: 10.17179/excli2017-480. PMID: 28900385; PMCID: PMC5579396.

SERE Recovery **Crab Legs**

TIME: 10 MIN (PREP), 8 MIN (COOK)
MAKES: 4 SERVINGS

Ingredients

8 quarts water

2 tablespoons salt

1 lemon, quartered

4 clusters crab legs, frozen or fresh

For the sauce:

¼ cup extra virgin olive oil

½ cup unsalted butter, melted

3 garlic cloves, minced

1 teaspoon sea salt

1 lemon, zested and cut into wedges for serving

2 tablespoons lemon juice

1 tablespoon dried dill weed

½ cup finely diced green onions

Steps

1. Bring a large pot with water to a rolling boil.
2. Add in salt and lemon wedges and turn down to medium heat.
3. Add in the crab leg clusters, cover with a lid and cook at a low boil for 5 minutes.
4. Pull out crab legs with tongs and place on a serving platter.
5. To make the sauce, in a medium mixing bowl, whisk together olive oil, butter, garlic, sea salt, lemon zest, lemon juice, dill, and green onions.
6. Place the remaining lemon wedges around the crab legs on the serving platter and serve with dipping sauce.

(Photo courtesy of Andrea Geraldi)

SOF STORIES

High-Calorie Recovery — Wendy

Any extensive training period equates to mega-calorie needs for our soldier. I recall sometimes my husband eating over 20,000 calories in a day. These training schools can leave our soldiers at a major calorie deficit, resulting in significant weight loss. One memory I have was my husband having wrapped up SERE (Survival, Evasion, Resistance and Escape) school, where he lost 25 pounds! He looked emaciated. We were young and on a strict budget in those days, and our budget-savvy solution for such times included trips out to any All-You-Can-Eat restaurant, so my husband could recoup at a set fee what was lost at sea.

A Special Forces dive team warrant officer earns his scuba bubble. With some community support, he raises the bar for high performance for all. *(Photo courtesy of Nick Lavery)*

At that time in San Diego there was a restaurant called Dick's Last Resort, and they offered crab legs in their All-You-Can-Eat deal; sides included. A couple guys joined us, and those boys dug in. They were knee deep in crab legs! The folks in the back must have been pretty upset that they were eating so much because suddenly, the crab legs became saltier and saltier. Little did they know that this crew probably needed all that salt. I'm not sure we ever looked at crab legs quite the same after that, and now, we prefer our crab legs cooked at home.

THE WARRIOR'S TABLE

136

Selection **Turtle Soup**

TIME: 15 MIN (PREP), 6-8 HOURS (COOK)
MAKES: 6 SERVINGS

Ingredients

1 pound boneless chicken breasts
2 (32-ounce) boxes of chicken broth,
   preferably low sodium
1 cup diced onions
1 cup diced celery
1 cup sliced carrots
3 garlic cloves, minced
½ teaspoon dried basil
½ teaspoon dried oregano
1 pinch thyme (optional)
salt and pepper to taste
3 zucchini squash, cut into zoodles

Steps

1. In a slow cooker, add chicken, chicken broth, onions, celery, carrots, garlic, basil, oregano, and thyme.
2. Stir, cover and cook on low for 6-8 hours.
3. Remove chicken, shred with a fork, and return to soup.
4. Divide zucchini noodles into 6 bowls.
5. Ladle hot soup mixture over the zoodles and serve

One giant snapping turtle. *(Photo courtesy of Collin Moore)*

TACTICAL TOPICS
Survival of the Fittest

Name three items you could not live without and share why you need them so much. Do you need them for comfort, survival, or perhaps both?

Take a twist on it! If you were stranded on an island, what are three items you would need to survive? What would you need the items for? How long do you think you could last before you were found?

A girl and her gear. *(Photo courtesy of Christine Trax)*

Ghostrider **Grilled Corn**

TIME: 5 MIN (PREP), 20 MIN (COOK)
MAKES: 6 SERVINGS

Ingredients

½ cup chopped cilantro
1 tablespoon ancho chile pepper
2 tablespoons grated lime peel
¼ teaspoon cayenne pepper (optional)
¼ cup melted butter
2 tablespoons mayonnaise
2 tablespoons lime juice
2 tablespoons sour cream
6 ears of corn, shucked

Steps

1. In a small bowl, combine cilantro, ancho pepper, lime peel and cayenne pepper.
2. In a large bowl combine butter, mayonnaise, lime juice, and sour cream.
3. Grill corn ears over medium heat for 15 minutes or until the corn is tender. You will want to turn the corn about every 5 minutes.
4. Remove the corn from the grill and coat the hot ears in the butter mixture.
5. Garnish the ears with the cilantro mixture and salt, then serve hot.

(Photo courtesy of KaLea Lehman)

 TACTICAL TOPICS
Challenge and Triumph

What has been your biggest challenge:

- This week?
- This month?
- This year?

What made it so difficult? How did you overcome it or what is your plan to overcome it?

Rolled in Dirt **Pudding**

TIME: 15 MIN (PREP), 4 HOURS (COOK)
MAKES: 6 SERVINGS

Ingredients

1 (5.9-ounce) package instant chocolate
  pudding
3 cups milk
8 ounces cream cheese, softened
1 cup powdered sugar
8 ounces whipped cream topping
1 (14.3-ounce) package Oreo Cookies,
  crushed in a plastic bag or food processor
Gummy worms (optional)

Steps

1. In a large bowl, whisk together the instant pudding and the milk for 2 minutes
   or until beginning to thicken. Let stand
   for 5 minutes.
2. Beat together the cream cheese and
   powdered sugar with a hand mixer on
   medium speed until light and fluffy,
   about 3 minutes.
3. Using a rubber spatula, fold the cream
   cheese mixture into the chocolate
   pudding.
4. Then fold in the Cool Whip until completely combined.
5. Layer the dessert with alternating layers
   of cookie crumbs and pudding mixture,
   starting and ending with the crushed
   cookies. You can layer the dessert a
   number of ways, such as individual cups,
   a trifle dish, or rectangular baking dish.
6. Refrigerate for 4 hours or overnight
   before serving.
7. Decorate with gummy worms, sprinkles,
   or other toppings before serving, if
   desired.

TIP: Dirt pudding can be made up to 24 hours in advance. Leftovers can be stored covered
in an airtight container in the refrigerator for up to 3 days.

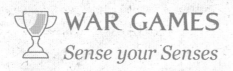

WAR GAMES
Sense your Senses

Describe your dinner using your five senses. Go around the table and take turns
answering the five-senses questions. What does your favorite part of the meal taste
like? What smells are tingling in your nose? What does your plate look like? What
colors do you see? Describe the texture of your most favorite or least favorite part
of the meal. Did you hear any sounds while dinner was cooking?

Real Deal Infil

OUR SERVICE MEMBERS TRAIN FOR EVERYTHING. They are always ready but the opportunity to infiltrate behind enemy lines sort of takes the cool guy cake. Many daydream their whole career for a chance to jump, ruck, swim, fast rope, or ratline to the mission objective. Some units in our community can infiltrate hostile territory basically blind-folded. We've watched them pack their bags. We are familiar with what's in their med kit and go-bag. We've patiently listened to the stories and half dismissed them as a way to cope with the possibilities.

How do you wrap your head around your service member maneuvering behind enemy lines while you go about your day functioning and unfazed? Quiet professionals don't talk much, but the news does. Talking heads often care more about ratings than the safety of the "boots on the ground." Gone are the days of reading simple newspaper headlines. Many spouses get hamstrung checking minute-to-minute updates, emails, apps, and instant messages. Our people are deployed every place that terror reigns, and there is an app to track or follow everything—bombs detonating, suicide bombings, shootings, foreign troop presence—you name it. It sounds like a video game, but it's all real now in our hyper-connected world.

There is a fine line that families have to walk to be engaged at home and stay healthy, functional, and happy in general. There are hardly any breaks for those of us in the special operations community. Few service members have the unique capabilities of our units and even less have their relentless, warrior drive—so the missions keep humming.

Special Forces team shares a meal with their Partner Force in Syria *(Photo courtesy of Britt'n Morrison)*

Carnitas on the Objective

TIME: 10 MIN (PREP), 4-5 HOURS (COOK)
MAKES: 8 SERVINGS

- -

Ingredients

5 pounds pork shoulder

Sea salt

2 tablespoons vegetable or other neutral cooking oil

1 cinnamon stick

2 bay leaves

5 garlic cloves, minced

1 teaspoon chile powder

1 teaspoon ancho chile powder

¼ teaspoon cumin

Steps

1. Preheat oven to 350°F. Cut the meat into 4-5" chunks, removing any excess fat. Season all sides of the chunks well with sea salt.

2. In a large Dutch oven or pot, heat the oil and cook the meat in batches until very well browned on all sides. Once browned, remove from the pot and set aside.

3. Once all the meat is browned and removed from the pot, add 2 cups of water and scrape the bottom of the pot to release all the brown bits.

4. Add the cinnamon stick, bay leaves, garlic, chile powder, ancho chile powder, and cumin. Mix until well combined and then add the meat back in. Add more water (if needed) until the meat is about ⅔ covered.

5. Braise in the oven, uncovered for 3½ hours, turning the pork a few times during braising.

6. Remove the pot from the oven and transfer the meat to a platter. Strain the liquid into a bowl. Reserve any meaty bits and discard any other solids.

7. When the meat is cool enough to handle, shred it up and put it back in the pot.

8. Add the liquid and return the pot back to the oven. Cook until much of the liquid evaporates and the outer edges of the pork become caramelized and crispy. The time will depend on how much liquid you have left and how crispy and crackly you want it.

9. Serve with tortillas, onions, cilantro, salsa, limes. . . . the possibilities are endless!

TIP: Freeze the carnitas with its juices in an airtight container for up to 3 months.

TO reheat, warm the carnitas in a slow cooker on the "WARM" setting until heated through or place the pork with its juices in a saucepan on the stovetop over low heat. Cover and cook, stirring occasionally, just until the meat is warm.

(Opposite) (Photo courtesy of Lynnsy Snook)

SOF STORIES
Russian Hacked — Sarah

There is so much coming and going that deployments can move to the back of your mind and become part of the family routine. Now, it only takes us one or two days to switch between life together and life deployed. We have a cadence and a new way to communicate. I learned how to put inherent risk to the back of my mind. But every blue moon, I still get surprised.

Our last go around was one of those moments. I was in our kitchen scrambling to gather snacks for the kids for our after school events, and I heard my phone ding. It was an encrypted text to switch apps. The Russians hacked the app my husband and I were using and we had to pivot to another option. It wasn't really a big deal, but it was enough to cause a gut check and make me wonder if the life we lived was really real. After talking to some friends rowing a similar boat, I learned I wasn't the only one who felt momentarily jarred. We all know it is really only a normal experience in our community and a few others like ours.

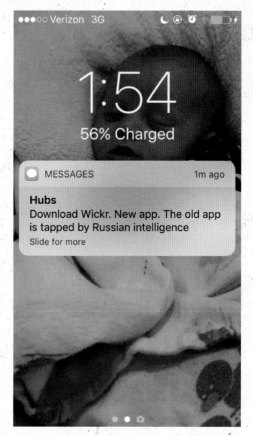

The importance of operational security as it plays out in real time. *(Photo courtesy of KaLea Lehman)*

THE WARRIOR'S TABLE

Close Quarter **Cuban Black Beans**

TIME: 10 MIN (PREP), 25 MIN (COOK)
MAKES: 4 SERVINGS

Ingredients

½ cup diced green pepper
½ cup diced yellow onion
2 garlic cloves, minced
2 (15-ounce) cans black beans
1 cup water
1 tablespoon extra virgin olive oil
1 tablespoon red wine vinegar
2 teaspoons granulated sugar
½ teaspoon salt
½ teaspoon oregano
½ teaspoon cumin
¼ teaspoon black pepper
1 bay leaf

Steps

1. In a saucepan, sauté green pepper, onion, and garlic at medium heat for 5 minutes until softened.
2. Next, add canned black beans with liquid in can, water, olive oil, red wine vinegar, sugar, salt, oregano, cumin, pepper, and bay leaf.
3. Stir to combine and bring to a boil. Place the lid on top and reduce to low heat.
4. Cook, stirring periodically, for 20 minutes until a thick and silky consistency is reached.
5. Taste and adjust seasonings, if needed. Serve on top of white rice or by itself. Enjoy!

VARIATION: You can substitute the canned beans for one 12 ounce bag of dried black beans. Soak the beans overnight in a pot with 3 cups of water. The next day, drain and then add 5 new cups of water to the pot. Bring to a boil and cook for 60 minutes, stirring frequently. Be careful not to let the beans dry out completely. You can add 1 cup of water if they are absorbing the water too quickly. After cooking the beans for 60 minutes, drain and transfer to a bowl. Add these beans as you would in step 2.

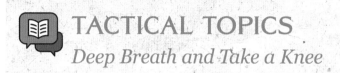

TACTICAL TOPICS
Deep Breath and Take a Knee

Name one action that stresses you out, makes you anxious, or nervous. What do you do to relax and counter the trigger? How did you learn to counter it? Share tips around the table and see if anyone else experiences the same stress.

Learning about what brings us stress can be a way to teach each other what sets us off and how we can better support each other. Go around the table and help each other find creative solutions.

Jumpers ready! (*Photo courtesy of KaLea Lehman*)

Mama **Mojito**

TIME: 5 MIN (PREP)
MAKES: 1 SERVING

Ingredients

5 mint leaves
2 tablespoons simple syrup
2 tablespoons lime juice
¼ cup white rum
⅛ cup sparkling soda water

Steps

1. Place the mint leaves in the bottom of a glass, and add simple syrup and lime juice. You may want to use less mint, depending on the size of the leaves.
2. Add ice and rum, then top with soda water.
3. Serve and enjoy!

SOF STORIES
OIF Answering Machine — Andi

The night before my husband deployed, I remember we were watching a movie and the answering machine picked up a phone call. This was April 2003—the beginning of Operation Iraqi Freedom. The message conveyed that his deployment was about to change. Or not. The unknowns at that time . . . and how I loved Australian Shiraz . . . by the case.

Seasoned Chips for the Go Bag

TIME: 5 MIN (PREP), 16 MIN (COOK)
MAKES: 6 SERVINGS

Ingredients

4 tablespoons extra virgin olive oil

2 tablespoons lime juice

8 corn or flour tortillas

½ teaspoon salt

½ teaspoon cumin

½ teaspoon paprika

½ teaspoon garlic powder

½ cup shredded mozzarella or cheddar
   cheese (optional)

Steps

1. Preheat the oven to 350°F.

2. Combine olive oil and lime juice in a bowl. Brush the mixture on both sides of the tortillas.

3. Combine salt, cumin, paprika, and garlic powder in a bowl.

4. Stack the tortillas on top of each other and cut in strips or quarters. Spread chips on a nonstick baking sheet and sprinkle with the seasoning mix.

5. Bake for 12 mins. Top with cheese, if desired, and bake for 3-4 more minutes.

6. Remove from the oven to cool and serve.

VARIATIONS: If you don't have garlic powder you can add ½ teaspoon of minced garlic to the oil mix in step 2. If you'd rather have sweetened chips, swap the cheese for sugar! If you need seasoned chips fast, grab a bag of plain corn tortilla chips. Place them in a big bowl and apply the seasoning with the same method. Place in the oven for 2-3 minutes, and serve.

(Photo courtesy of Lynnsy Snook)

Raider-ready nacho table *(Photo courtesy of Jessica Doty)*

 **TACTICAL TOPICS**
Our Home, Your Away

What challenge and opportunity do you notice most with the flip from home to away (non-deployed to deployed/gone training)? What is the biggest challenge and opportunity you experience with the return back home?

Please Send Coffee

- -

NOTHING BEATS THE SMELL OF FRESH BREWING COFFEE in the morning. The smell snaking around corners, enticing you out of bed to sit and enjoy that warm hug in a mug. If you are blessed enough to get two cups in before the chaos fires up, you've already had a winning day. Breathing in the rich scent of the brew is basically like breathing in patience.

An ODA deployed to Nangarhar Province, Afghanistan in June 2017. (*Photo courtesy of James Westfall*)

We need coffee at home, and they need coffee downrange. It's a comfort for us, but our guys don't always have access to such delicacies. When their supply gets slim, that's a crisis. For them it is less a cup of peace and more like a cup of red, hot fuel. Coffee is nearly mission essential. It keeps the operations center and missions running. Where there is a will there's a way, and they will brew coffee anywhere—on a field burner deep in the desert or the rear of a tank engine. We all know, when we get the message, "Please send coffee," there are few care packages that can beat a box stuffed to the brim with that ground gold.

Special Forces team deployed to Northern Afghanistan in 2009. *(Photo courtesy of Hilary Peters)*

Just like the comfort of coffee, they look forward to the comfort of their favorite meal. It might be a simple item, but it brings back memories of home. Sometimes that meal is chicken fingers and other times it is a pork roast. The specifics don't matter much, as long as you enjoy it together. Keep those comforts alive and please, send coffee.

For Love of **Coffee**

TIME: 5 MIN (PREP)
MAKES: 6-8 SERVING

Ingredients

1 - 1 ½ cups coffee grounds
1 teaspoon ground cinnamon
1 cup heavy whipping cream
½ teaspoon vanilla
2 tablespoons maple syrup (optional)
1 tablespoon chocolate sauce
1 tablespoon caramel sauce
6 ounces bourbon (optional)

Steps

1. Combine desired coffee grounds and cinnamon. Brew coffee according to preference. If you are really tired, double the coffee grounds for a very strong brew.

2. While the coffee is brewing, whisk heavy cream, vanilla, and maple syrup together until it is a whipped cream consistency.

3. Pour brewed coffee into your favorite mug and top with the amount of whipped topping you need to spur a smile. Drizzle with chocolate and caramel sauce, if desired.

4. For a boozy coffee, add 6 oz of bourbon to the coffee pot before topping with whipped cream.

5. Enjoy! Best served in a silent and peaceful place, but it can also be enjoyed in a chaotic environment.

No better way to start the day than a good brew in a cup with a solid legacy behind it. *(Photo courtesy of Herb Thompson)*

SOF STORIES
Patience Pill — Kay

My morning coffee sets the tone for the rest of my day, and the cup that I sip it from sometimes matters even more. I mark the phases of our military life by my coffee cups. When my girls were really little, I made a cup that said, "Chocolate doesn't ask silly questions. Chocolate understands." Under the quote were pictures of "those oh my goodness mom moments." You can imagine them . . . A toddler in heels, a screaming baby, a powdered sugar explosion.

Coffee is a critical resource for every dive guy. *(Photo courtesy of Calli McGraw)*

My next favorite cup wasn't even a coffee cup. It was a ridiculous fish chowder cup that just made me laugh, and I needed to laugh. Then, it was a black classy cup with a gold, lace-like, dot design. It reminded me of my friend and mentor and inspired me to stay focused on the moment. That cup got me through graduate school. I grabbed it every time I needed some calm and confidence. Everyone has a comforting drink or sweet escape moment that just sings to their soul. Coffee is mine.

Camp Lejeune **Grilled Pizza**

TIME: 20 MIN (PREP), 8 MIN (COOK)
MAKES: 5-8 SERVINGS

Ingredients

1 pound Pizza dough (homemade or store bought)
2 tablespoons olive oil
½-1 cup pizza sauce
Desired Toppings:
½ cup shredded cheddar
½ cup shredded mozzarella cheese
½ cup ham, sliced
⅛ cup olive of choice
1 fresh jalapeno, sliced, or pickled jalapenos from a jar

Steps

1. Grill should be well cleaned and oiled, to prevent the crust from sticking. Preheat it to 425°F (medium-high heat).
2. Divide pizza dough into about 5-8 portions (depending on how big and thick you want your pizza crust). Stretch or roll dough into desired size and thinness and place on a piece of parchment paper.
3. Brush tops of the prepared dough with oil, then lift the parchment the crust is on and carefully flip the crusts onto the grill, oil side down. Peel the parchment paper off.
4. Cover and cook for 2-3 minutes and check for doneness with tongs to see if the bottom side has grill marks and is golden brown.
5. Flip the pizzas onto a plate and add sauce and toppings to the cooked side.
6. Lower the grill heat slightly and slide pizzas back onto the grill to cook the bottom side for another 3-5 minutes, until cheese is melted and bottom crust is golden.

TIP: You can make this a pizza party with a table of different sauces and toppings. Easy to grill the crust and prep ahead.

SOF STORIES
Pizza Party — Amy

Mom is always in demand. *(Photo courtesy of KaLea Lehman)*

One Friday night I was alone with kindergarten-age twins, an exhausting toddler, and my husband "away" from home again. I realized I needed help, and I needed my community. So, I made the dough, and my friends brought the rest of the toppings for a Friday pizza night. Dads rolled in, pizza was grilled, drinks were spilled, knees were bruised, movies were watched, and most importantly, bonds were made. That Friday night was eight years ago, and the community and friendships continue to grow into our "framily."

SOF STORIES

The Chaplain Postal Service — Father Uncle Sam

As a chaplain in a Special Missions Unit, I ran love letters to the Middle East. The letters were part of a secret, surprise morale mission between soldiers I knew personally and their wives. There was no guarantee I would find the Soldier on my deployment. It depended on where my travels took me as I offered mass, confession, prayers, counsel, and DFAC trays at mess tents and makeshift kitchens in former school houses and residential buildings. I'd put the sealed white #10 envelope, pastel greeting card, or folded packet of taped, loose leaf paper into a Ziplock bag in my duffle bag, and the letters went wherever the Army mission led me.

I carried them in case I met the husband of the author somewhere in the Levant. Running love letters from the Middle East back home was much easier. I knew I'd find the Soldiers' wives at church with their children, school pickup/dropoff, or the soccer fields. As an Army chaplain, it's a thrill to bring a deployed Soldier's letter home to his wife. It's a way to bring Soldiers to God and God to Soldiers.

It was especially sweet when a Soldier's wife had no idea that I had encountered her beloved recently on some pile of rocks between home and nowhere. One time I delivered a letter to the bride of a Soldier a day after I came home. Her husband still had a few weeks left in theater, and I found his wife outside the chapel, kids swarming her ankles. "Hey, any chance you recognize this handwriting?" I said, as I offered her a makeshift envelope with her name written on it. "Father! Are you trying to make me cry?" she asked with a grin bigger than the distance I'd just traveled.

In this day and age, with email, FaceTime, texts, and phone calls, soldiers and families can stay better connected than ever, but there's nothing like a handwritten, hand-delivered letter, courtesy of the Chaplain Postal Service.

Simple Sabotage **Broccoli Slaw**

TIME: 10 MIN (PREP)
MAKES: 6 SERVINGS

Ingredients

1 (10-ounce) bag of broccoli slaw
¼ cup sliced almonds
½ cup sliced green apples (optional)
¼ cup dried cranberries or any raisin
  (optional)
2 tablespoons sugar
1½ tablespoon vinegar
½ teaspoon lemon juice
¼ cup mayonnaise or Miracle Whip
2 tablespoons sugar
¼ teaspoon salt (optional)

Steps

1. Mix all salad ingredients together in a medium bowl. Fruit will add sweetness and is optional.
2. In a separate bowl, add the sugar, vinegar and lemon juice and mix to dissolve the sugar. Add in the mayonnaise or Miracle Whip and salt to taste.
3. Once this is mixed well, stir into the salad combination and chill. This slaw is best when mixed close to the meal time.

TACTICAL TOPICS
What's in the Box?

Special Forces kids pack a care package for daddy in Syria. *(Photo courtesy of Britt'n Morrison)*

If you made a care package for someone you love today, what would you put in it? What if you were to make a family care package? Go around the table and take turns naming things you might want in your package—your most delicious comfort food, a favorite item that always helps you feel better, or something else that reminds you of the people you love? On the other hand, is there something you get too much of?

Commander's Curry

TIME: 10 MIN (PREP), 1 HOUR 20 MIN (COOK)
MAKES: 6 SERVINGS

Ingredients

1/2 onion, chopped

2 serrano chiles (remove seeds for a milder curry)

3 garlic cloves

1 tablespoon canola oil

1¾ pounds sirloin tip steak, cut into ¾ inch cubes

½ teaspoon fine sea salt, plus more to taste

1 cinnamon stick

1¼ teaspoons coriander seeds

1¼ teaspoons ground cumin

1 teaspoon ground turmeric

1 (13.5-ounce) can light coconut milk

1 (14.5-ounce) can diced tomatoes, drained

½ teaspoon sugar

1 pound red potatoes, cut into 1 inch pieces

⅓ cup cilantro

Steps

1. In a blender, combine onion, chiles, garlic and ½ cup water and blend until smooth. Set aside.

2. In a large high-sided skillet with a tightly fitting lid, heat oil over high heat.

3. Sprinkle steak with salt. Add half the steak pieces to the skillet and cook, stirring occasionally, until lightly browned. Transfer to a bowl with a slotted spoon; repeat with remaining steak. Set aside.

4. Return the skillet to medium-high heat and add cinnamon, coriander, cumin and turmeric. Stir for 10 seconds and then add the onion and chile mixture.

5. Simmer for 1 minute and then stir in coconut milk, tomatoes, and sugar. Add the beef back in, cover the skillet, and simmer for 40 minutes.

6. Stir in potatoes and continue to simmer until beef and potatoes are very tender, about 20 minutes more.

7. Remove the lid during the last 10 minutes of simmering for a thicker sauce.

8. Remove cinnamon stick; taste curry, and add more salt if desired. Serve garnished with chopped cilantro leaves.

TACTICAL TOPICS
A Tale of the Cup

Name your favorite drink and whether you like it hot or cold! It could be anything from strong, black coffee, a cool, strawberry milkshake, or a cup of warm, frothy chai. What is your favorite drink when you are cold? What is your go-to pick when you are tired and need a break? What drink do you opt for when you treat yourself and celebrate? What makes it a special pick?

(Photo courtesy of Lynnsy Snook)

SOF STORIES
Commander's Curry and Loads of Laundry — Christine

One snowy morning amid another deployment and early in COVID, my washing machine caught fire. I stood in the kitchen with a baby on my hip and two other children asking for breakfast, and just laughed. Of course, this would happen! I immediately went online and ordered a new washing machine, promised to arrive in five days. Nearly a month later, I had no washing machine and a mountain of dirty laundry.

Then, my luck changed following a casual "deployment curse" phone conversation with our commander's wife. She hadn't realized our washing machine was still MIA, and she was absolutely horrified for me! She insisted I pack the dirty laundry and the kids up and immediately come to her home. Our kids played and were thrilled to finally see a face off a screen, and we completed my laundry and folded hers. She made a dinner filled with spices as warm as her hospitality. Her kindness was inspiring. I will forever remember the "Commander's Curry," as a house full of inviting smells, children laughing, and a warm belly.

Cammo **Carrot Cake**

TIME: 15 MIN (PREP), 30 MIN (COOK)
MAKES: 6 SERVINGS

Ingredients

2 eggs
1 cup of sugar
½ teaspoon orange extract or juice
1½ teaspoons cinnamon
½ teaspoon of salt
1 cup flour
1 teaspoon baking soda
¾ cup vegetable oil
1 ½ cups grated/chopped carrots
½ cup shredded coconut
½ cup walnuts (optional)

Frosting Ingredients

2 tablespoons orange juice
3 ounces cream cheese
1½ - 2 cups powdered sugar
Zest of 1 orange (optional)

Steps

1. Preheat the oven to 350°F
2. Mix eggs, sugar, orange flavor, cinnamon, and salt.
3. Then add flour, baking soda, and oil to the mixture.
4. Once stirred in, add remaining ingredients, mix, and pour into a cake pan.
5. Bake for approximately 30 minutes. Set aside to cool.
6. To make the frosting, cream the orange juice and cream cheese in a mixing bowl.
7. Stir in the powdered sugar ½ cup at a time.
8. Add orange zest if desired.
9. Spread frosting evenly over the carrot cake after it is cooled.

SOF STORIES
Homecoming Birthday Cake — Jessica

Homecoming is a funky event. You imagine it as a perfect event where your husband returns in uniform, your kids rush to hug him, and you are overwhelmed with joy. But it rarely, if ever, plays out that way. Reality is a much different picture. Flights change multiple times and complicate everything. Now they are landing at 10 p.m., and you do not want to wake your children, and the dinner you planned is not quite working out. After several returns, I gave up on the big, crazy homecoming. I found it stressful for me and the kids. Homecoming is different every time, but the one consistent detail is that he lands late.

Now I don't make a big meal and the kids are unaware of the upcoming return. Disappointment is just too hard, but their surprise is always fun. Like the year he returned on my son's birthday . . . I woke up the kids, loaded them in jammies, drove an hour to pick up their dad, and we all returned home to enjoy leftover birthday cake. It was the best birthday gift ever. The best part of homecoming is living and relishing the moment.

Wave Jumping to "Rowing"

SEA, AIR, OR LAND, OUR DAREDEVILS LEAVE EVERYTHING TO CHANCE and experience. Iconic images, a boat full of commandos being catapulted over a wave, green men you can barely see deep in the woods, small teams maneuvering in scuba gear in deep, dark waters, or mountain teams geared up for snowy terrain—these are powerful images that display the courage and willpower of everyone who serves in special operations. They were born to rock boats, jump ship, and then do it again. Their fortitude is only matched by that of their families, who mirror their strength and anchor their character.

We know they signed up for the toughest missions that take a high physical toll, but demand even more from the heart and mind. We know our special operators are attracted to adventure, but compelled by an innate desire to free the oppressed and protect the innocent. They have a stomach to endure evil because they want their own children to sleep in peace, able to freely dream. We keep the table lightly set when they are off on adventure, and we keep them grounded with more hearty dishes when they are forced to go against their grain and "row" on a staff.

Our spice racks have unique seasonings collected from duty stations and friends, and our hearty dishes help tame the bull that suddenly finds himself pushing paper or behind a desk. It's part of the job and the changing environment of a leader of any rank or unit. The kitchen tricks we learned on those early deployment repetitions helped us prepare the table for the nights a frustrated operator needs to decompress from a day spent knee deep in spreadsheets and bureaucracy. Duty that wears on the soul of a curious adventurer needs to be coupled with sides that refresh the whole person and family.

A SEAL and Green Beret pause from mission planning. It's time for the most important event, the daddy daughter dance. *(Photo courtesy of KaLea Lehman)*

Pentagon Duty Waldorf **Wheat Bread**

TIME: 1 HOUR(PREP), 40 MIN (COOK)
MAKES: 2 LOAVES

- -

Ingredients

1½ cups boiling water

½ cup honey

1½ cups cold tap water

1½ tablespoons yeast

2 teaspoons salt

2 tablespoons olive oil

6 cups whole wheat flour

1-2 cups rye flour (or whole wheat if preferred)

Steps

1. In a large mixing bowl add the boiling water, honey, cold tap water and yeast, stirring after each.
2. Let sit for five minutes and then stir in the salt and oil.
3. Add and stir in the flour until it is of kneading consistency.
4. Knead for 15 minutes, adding a little more flour if dough is too sticky to handle.
5. Form the dough into a smooth ball, placing the smooth side up in the washed and oiled bowl. Cover and keep warm.
6. After 1½ hours, gently press the dough flat and divide in half.
7. Gently shape into two loaves.
8. Place into two greased loaf pans (or form into loaf shapes on a baking sheet lined with parchment paper). Let rise for 30-45 minutes.
9. Bake in a preheated, 350°F oven for about 40 minutes.

(Photo courtesy of KaLea Lehman)

SOF STORIES
Pentagon Waldorf Bread — Andrea

My Husband was assigned to a supposed 9-to-5 job in the bowels of the Pentagon that quickly turned into insanely long 5-to-9 days. Our three-year-old twins attended a Waldorf School so I could have a needed three-hour break, and they could play outside with other kids. For their snack at school we got in the routine of baking homemade bread, and we still make this today. The smell of fresh bread takes us back to innocent and carefree days while Dad did his thing. That grueling desk job was a big switch-up from his time on the teams, and it wasn't an easy time or adjustment. But baking bread certainly helped occupy our time and filled our stomachs! Now it fills our hearts with memories of days gone by.

Pearl Harbor **Penne with Chicken, Arugula, and Roasted Tomatoes**

TIME: 10 MIN (PREP), 40 MIN (COOK)
MAKES: 4 SERVINGS

- -

Ingredients

3 (12-ounce) packages cherry tomatoes

2 tablespoons olive oil

5 garlic cloves, chopped

¾ teaspoon dried crushed red pepper

2 cups shredded roasted chicken breasts without skin (from purchased roast chicken)

8 ounces penne pasta

6 cups arugula leaves

Steps

1. Preheat oven to 475°F.
2. Mix cherry tomatoes, oil, garlic, and crushed red pepper on a rimmed baking sheet. Sprinkle with salt and pepper.
3. Bake until tomatoes are soft and beginning to brown in spots, stirring occasionally, about 20 minutes.
4. Transfer tomato mixture, including any juices, from sheet to large skillet.
5. Add chicken to the skillet and simmer until heated through, about 5 minutes.
6. Meanwhile, cook pasta in a large pot of boiling salted water until just tender but still firm to bite, stirring occasionally.
7. Ladle out ¼ cup pasta cooking water and reserve. Drain pasta; return to pot.
8. Add tomato mixture, arugula, and reserved pasta water to pasta.
9. Toss over medium heat just until arugula begins to wilt, about 30 seconds.
10. Season to taste with salt and pepper.

VARIATION: Grill or bake 4 chicken breasts and use the arugula/tomato mixture as a topping.

CUSTOMS AND CAMARADERIE
The Naked Warrior to Today's Navy SEALs

Historic Highlight. Special operations units are made of daring, adventurous, and courageous individuals. The story of the "naked warriors" is one of the most fun stories depicting the origins of one of our most recognized special operations units—the Navy SEALs.

Just before the end of World War II, Navy Combat Swimmers Ensign Lewis F. Luehrs and Chief Petty Officer Bill Acheson were on a reconnaissance mission leading up to the assault planned for the Kwajalein atoll. They were not able to complete the recon mission in the standard gear of the time, so they stripped to their underwear to get over the reef surrounding the atoll. A statue commemorating these two early frogmen stands at the Navy SEAL Museum today.[35]

A SEAL family visits the Navy SEAL Museum in Fort Pierce, FL. *(Photo courtesy of Dan and Leslie Luna)*

35. National Navy UDT-SEAL Museum. (n.d.). *The History of the Naked Warrior*. Navy Seal Museum . Accessed from https://www.navysealmuseum.org/nakedwarrior

Tampa **Cheesy Bread**

TIME: 1 HOUR (PREP), 40 MIN (COOK)

MAKES: 6-8 SERVINGS

Ingredients

1 cup whole milk

1½ teaspoons salt

½ cup extra virgin olive oil

2 teaspoons minced garlic or ¼ tsp garlic salt

2 eggs

2 ½ cups tapioca flour

1½ cups Parmesan cheese

Steps

1. Preheat the oven to 375°F.
2. In a mixing bowl, combine the milk, salt, olive oil, eggs, and garlic.
3. Then stir in the tapioca flour until the mixture is well combined and has a smooth consistency.
4. Add in Parmesan cheese and mix.
5. Once well mixed, pour into a mini cupcake pan. This will likely make about 24 small cheese breads. This mixture can also be poured onto a flat baking dish lined with parchment paper.
6. Bake for 15-20 minutes. The bread will be golden brown with a crispy exterior and gooey interior when ready.

VARIATION: This bread can be cooked poured thin (¼ inches deep) on a baking sheet or in a loaf pan (3-4 inches deep). It is always tasty, but the varied ways to bake it change the consistency of the bread from crispy to cheesy-gooey.

TSOC it to You **Chocolate Chip Cookies**

TIME: 15 MIN (PREP), 11 MIN (COOK)
MAKES: 5 DOZEN SMALL COOKIES

- -

Ingredients

2¼ cups flour

1 teaspoon baking soda

1 teaspoon salt

1 cup butter, softened

¾ cup brown sugar

1 teaspoon vanilla

2 eggs

2 cups chocolate chips

1 cup chopped nuts (optional)

Steps

1. Preheat the oven to 375°F.
2. Combine flour, baking soda and salt in a small bowl.
3. Beat butter, granulated sugar, brown sugar and vanilla extract in a large mixing bowl until creamy. Add eggs, one at a time, beating well after each addition.
4. Gradually beat in flour mixture. Stir in chocolate chips and nuts, if using. Drop rounded tablespoons two inches apart onto ungreased baking sheets.
5. Bake for 9 to 11 minutes or until golden brown. Cool on baking sheets for 2 minutes; remove to wire racks to cool completely.

(Photo courtesy of Wendy Jo Peterson)

TACTICAL TOPICS
Moving—Again?!?

What are the three most challenging differences about any new school, job, or location? What makes these challenges for you? What are positive changes that surprise you? How have challenges changed through the years or moves?

Great reads for littles on a cross country PCS drive. *(Photo courtesy of KaLea Lehman)*

Muddy Boots and Parachutes

IT'S A BIRD! IT'S A PLANE! Nope, it's our people falling from the sky. It's exciting to watch an airborne jump. They jump high in the clouds, gliding with the other birds of prey, but quickly make their way to the ground, bracing for impact, set to avoid other 'chutes and trees. Water jumps are the best. The water lessens the impact of their landing; but for us families, water jumps double the adventure. We get to see the trucks, helicopters, flippers, parachutes, and boats all in a day. Depending on the airborne crew when the jump is done, we might even get to embrace some fishing or surfing.

It's a long day of sitting and waiting intermixed with photographic moments. Families don't attend most jumps, but when they do, you can bank on the need for a picnic and imaginary play. Jump days are filled with "hurry up and wait" moments. There is no keeping commando kids from finding the mud puddles, tall grass, or spotting fish in the water. They will lay bored across the lap of their dad with his 'chute on his back ready and waiting to go, find a shaded spot to hide in a giant truck tire, or join in a game of tag or hide and seek with other unit kids. They play, wait, fuss, and take all your energy as you try to get them to appreciate the moment. "Look! helicopter!" "Look! Fighting soldiers "falling from the sky!"

Baby at a water jump. *(Photo courtesy of KaLea Lehman)*

Air Force Special Tactics jumpers and CV-22 Ospreys *(Photo courtesy of Lynnsy Snook)*

Eventually, the day culminates with giant smiles and little hands helping to shake a 'chute. In these moments, kids don't understand that few Americans experience and know muddy boots and parachutes. Later they will look back at the pictures from the day, ask questions, and have an access point to hear and begin to understand stories of jumps and other long days.

Jump Day **Buffalo Chicken Dip & Veggies**

TIME: 10 MIN (PREP)
MAKES: 6 SERVINGS

Ingredients

2 cups cooked shredded chicken

1½ (8-ounce) packages cream cheese, softened

2 cups shredded cheddar

1 cup Frank's hot sauce

1 cup plain Greek yogurt

1½ tablespoons ranch dip mix

Steps

1. Add all ingredients to the food processor and pulse until desired texture.
2. Heat in a slow cooker on low until warmed through.
3. Serve with crunchy fresh veggies like cauliflower florets, carrots, celery, and sweet peppers.

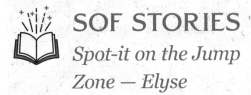

SOF STORIES
Spot-it on the Jump Zone — Elyse

Waiting for the big jump fun to happen. *(Photo courtesy of KaLea Lehman)*

The kids and I have been lucky to score a few strong memories watching their daddy jump. In some ways the day feels like a never ending picnic where you entertain the toddlers with chips and a juice box. The big kids find creative games to occupy themselves for a bit, but eventually everyone ends up with a hotdog trying to spot who's who in the sky. All the service members look the same falling from afar, but kids have eagle eyes. I'll never forget how proud I felt watching our daughter run to meet her daddy as he returned from his landing in a nearby field. Or, the memory of my son entertaining himself in a mud hole while everyone waited to load the Chinooks. The kids powered through the long wait by exploring the training town designed to model a Middle Eastern urban area and momentarily reclining in giant, military truck tires next to dad.

Hurlburt Field **Hot Dogs**

TIME: 20 MIN (PREP)
MAKES: 8 SERVINGS

Ingredients

8 hot dogs
8 hot dog buns
⅓ cup yellow mustard
½ cup sweet onion, chopped

Steps

1. Boil the hot dogs until fully cooked. Once the hot dogs are cooked turn down the heat to simmer—they need to stay hot!

2. While the hot dogs cook, prepare all the buns.

3. Spread yellow mustard across the inside of the buns and then sprinkle with the chopped onions.

4. Using tongs remove one hot dog from the simmering water and place it in a prepared bun.

5. Quickly wrap the hot dog (like a burrito) in one sheet of foil.

6. Place the foil-wrapped hot dog in a Dutch oven so the warm hot dogs steam while in the buns.

TACTICAL TOPICS

The Colors of Your Sunset

What is your favorite color in the sunset and why? Does it make you feel a certain way? Share your favorite part of watching the sunset. Who would you like to watch the sunset with? Has the service member ever seen the sunset while flying or parachuting from a plane or helicopter?

A rural Kentucky drive during a pink sunset.
(Photo courtesy of KaLea Lehman)

Any Place, Any Time, Anywhere
Mediterranean Bean Salad

TIME: 10 MIN (PREP)
MAKES: 6 SERVINGS

Ingredients

2 (15-ounce) cans cannellini beans
1 cup cherry tomatoes, halved
2 small cucumbers or 1 large cucumber, diced
½ red onion, diced
½ cup black olives, sliced
½ cup green olives, sliced
½ cup crumbled feta cheese
½ cup marinated artichoke hearts, diced
½ cup green bell pepper, diced
½ cup red bell pepper, diced
½ cup yellow bell pepper, diced

Dressing

¼ cup olive oil
4 tablespoons red wine or balsamic vinegar
1 teaspoon Italian seasoning
1 garlic clove, minced
Salt and pepper to taste

Steps

1. Drain and rinse the cannellini beans and pour into a large salad bowl.
2. Add in all other salad ingredients once sliced or diced.
3. Combine all dressing ingredients in a separate small bowl and drizzle over salad mixture prior to serving.

VARIATION: Replace the green and/or black olives with kalamata olives, if preferred.

TACTICAL TOPICS
Let's Talk about Lunch

What did you have for lunch today? Where do you eat your lunch? Do you eat with friends? Do you ever see anyone sitting alone? How could you make someone feel included? If you were sitting alone at lunch, what could someone do or say to help you feel more included? What would you like for someone to ask you at lunch?

Junior's **BBQ Kielbasa Sausage**

TIME: 20 MIN (PREP), 4-5 HOURS (COOK)
MAKES: 8 SERVINGS

Ingredients

2 cups ketchup
½ cup light brown sugar
1 tablespoon Worcestershire Sauce
2 teaspoons Creole mustard
1 teaspoon hot sauce
1 onion medium, finely chopped
½ cup Bourbon (optional)
2 pounds kielbasa, cut into ½ inch rounds

Steps

1. Combine all ingredients in the slow cooker.
2. Cover and cook on low for 4-5 hours, until sausage is hot.
3. Serve in a bowl with toothpicks or individually on a plate

TACTICAL TOPICS.
Fun Times

What's one fun thing you hope to do in the next year?

Exploring the outdoors together in Peru. *(Photo courtesy of Chris and Robin VanSant)*

Precision Strike **Pantry Salad**

TIME: 10 MIN (PREP)
MAKES: 6 SERVINGS

Ingredients

2 tablespoons red wine vinegar

3 tablespoons extra virgin olive oil

1 teaspoon prepared mustard

1 teaspoon dried oregano

½ teaspoon garlic powder

1 can roasted red peppers, drained and chopped

1 can garbanzo or kidney beans, drained and rinsed

1 can artichoke hearts, drained

1 jar or can black or green olives, drained and halved

Salt and pepper, to taste

Optional add ins: feta cheese, couscous, chopped salami, fresh chopped parsley

Steps

1. In a serving bowl, whisk together red wine vinegar, olive oil, mustard, oregano, and garlic powder.
2. Add in all remaining ingredients, toss to coat with vinaigrette.
3. Season with salt and pepper, as desired.
4. Serve immediately or salad can be kept in the refrigerator for up to 5 days.

 WAR GAMES
Daredevil Wants To . . .

Name three bucket-list things you want to do.

- What's one daredevil activity you've always wanted to try? Bungee jumping? Diving with sharks? Is there something your SOF service member does that you want to try?
- Name one crazy food item you would be bold enough to try. Would it be fried crickets from a street vendor in Asia? What about alligator meat in Florida?
- Think of the wildest adventure you'd like to go on. Is it climbing Mount Everest, or a space exploration to Mars? Maybe a deep, underwater dive? Who would you bring with you to share the adventure with? Maybe your adventure of choice is more simple. What is on your bucket-list?

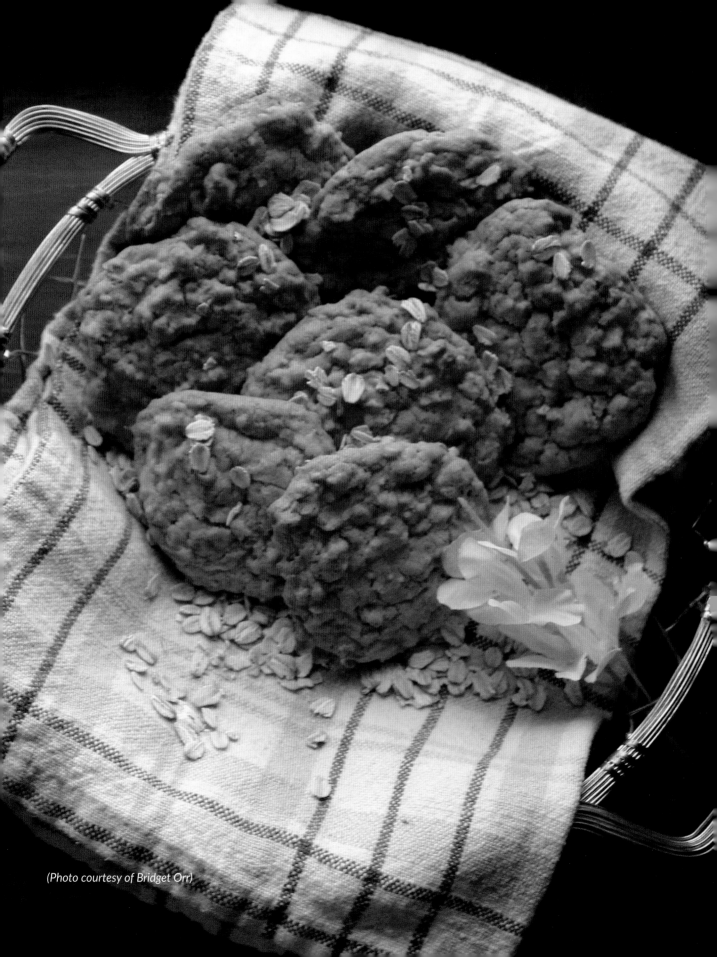

ODA **Oatmeal and Coconut Cookies**

TIME: 10 MIN (PREP), 10 MIN (COOK)
MAKES: 15 SERVINGS

Ingredients

1 cup brown sugar
1 cup white sugar
1 cup crisco or butter
2 eggs
2 cups of flour
1 teaspoon salt
1 teaspoon baking powder
1 teaspoon baking soda
1 cup of rolled oats
2 cups of shredded coconut
2 teaspoons of vanilla

Steps

1. Preheat the oven to 350°F
2. Mix together sugars and the crisco until creamed.
3. Mix in eggs, flour, salt, baking powder, and baking soda.
4. Add the rolled oats, coconut, and vanilla.
5. Drop spoonfuls of batter 2 inches apart on a greased baking sheet.
6. Bake for 10 minutes. Cool on baking sheets for 2 minutes; remove to wire racks to cool completely.

 TACTICAL TOPICS
Quickfire Questions

Go around the table and ask each person a question, any question. Kids really enjoy learning about parents with questions such as: What's your favorite color? Where do you wish you were, right now? Who do you miss most? Who is your got-your-back buddy, right now? or countless other questions.

This quickfire strategy may open topics with teens or kids going through tough times. It can be silly or serious. It is a great way to get to know each other as a family again, especially after a long trip, rough tour of duty, or hard time at home.

(Photo courtesy KaLea Lehman)

A SEAL's son practicing knife skills safely *(Photo courtesy of Andrea Geraldi)*

4. Heart and Soul at Home

★ ★ ★

OVER THE YEARS, WE'VE LEARNED that sugar, salt, and sage have a purpose both in the kitchen and out. Hope and courage accompany sugar, and salt cleans, seasons, and preserves. Sage gets the least use. Hearty family staples or traditional sides benefit from its unique flavor that we savor, but must be called on wisely. These key ingredients came together at our families' tables. They each served a unique role and helped us flourish as individuals, unite as a family, and care for our community. While our partner served, we were the family pillar that made our home stable through all the trips away, back home, and away again.

The demands of the daily household jam can feel endless, and the steady cycle of train-ups, deployment trips, and resets left us fantasizing about a vacation or night out with our closest friends. We all got restless and vented our frustrations. We wanted someone to see and validate our struggle. In those moments we believed unleashing the thoughts and complaints would be cathartic, but we really just needed quality time with people we loved. It took some trial and error, but we learned to let our little Rangers lead the way. We discovered that their bright eyes and hopeful begging began to motivate us to make the effort to connect. With a bit of patience and self-awareness, our kids inspire the best in us. Cooking as a family creates special memories, and it is a golden opportunity to teach kids that family mealtime matters. We pass on family tales, sage wisdom,

Family meal prep the Raider way. (*Photo courtesy of Michael Mason*)

and kitchen "land nav" tactics. It is a timeless opportunity for our kids to open-up and work out what is on their mind, this is especially true of our teens who need security in a safe thought proving ground.

Some meals were too heavy on the salt. They seemed to come with the hard moments that call for a hearty meal that is best once it has seasoned a bit and time makes it better. We remember receiving those dishes and baking them because those dishes mark those rare moments where we journeyed together gently. They were moments so tense there were no words – our clumsy mouth was testament to that. All we had were innate responses of love rooted in a hope that our friend would not feel alone in their most challenging moment. They had to persevere and make sense of it on their own. We could only take pride in being able to walk alongside them, alleviating unnecessary distractions. The process of making meaning of the hard cannot be done without the safeguards of community. Our journey is a long walk that takes training, direction, friends, and old sages to show us the right point on the course. There is no one way to live, but there are some ground rules and Healthy Checkpoints that keep you on the right course, and sometimes the right course needs some sweetening.

Always ready to help in the kitchen (*Photo courtesy of Britt'n Morrison*)

We were left craving sugar and the hope that can spark with a great dessert. Of course the dessert can't be made of hope, but somehow it seems to make everyone smile at least a little. Some experiences don't make sense in the moment, but with perspective and hope we persevered. Staying connected as a special operations family can demand some out of the box tactics. We had to get creative and make sweet moments happen. Though now that we look back, those are some of our most favorite memories sprinkled with sweet recipes.

Dad & Dessert

WHETHER DAD IS HOME OR AWAY, his military demands often create an unpredictable schedule. Oftentimes, making it home in time for a family meal just isn't in the cards. A long day of training, a late return from a trip, or an evening meeting—it doesn't matter the reason. They all contribute to an 8 p.m. meal or a too often missed family dinner. We've all tried to troubleshoot this scenario. We've done the late dinner. We've re-heated his meal and joined him at the table. And we've dropped the dinner plan completely for a fast food meet-up. We get it! As the pillar of family stability, we know that holding off dinner for an unpredictable entry isn't always worth it. This SOF life truth doesn't change the fact that finding ways and time to connect over shared mealtime remains essential.

Our favorite way to make this happen is the Dad and Dessert tactic. Eat before the kids are "hangry," knock out homework, baths, the nightly run around. And when the moment presents itself, we can all rally for a daddy-dessert win. This out of the box opportunity lets you move on with the night routine and save room for a special moment of intentional connection.

Dessert can get skipped for lack of time, energy, or a need for behavior management. Yet it is a timeless treat that creates its own energy. Dessert is a way to quickly connect and set the table with happy faces. If there is time, kids can make the dessert ahead of his arrival as a special surprise, but if there is no time for that, a classic go-to is just as good. The brilliance of dessert is that many favorites can be whipped up quickly, and somehow that sugar seems to cruise through our fingers and ignite a contagious excitement. Even if dad returns smoked from the day, this quick family moment can make a powerful memory.

Special Operations family enjoying popsicles together in Europe—even when they are all grown up. *(Photo courtesy of Jim and Jodi Lynch)*

Hand-to-Hand **Ice Cream Cookie Sandwiches**

TIME: 5 MIN (PREP), 15 MIN (COOK)
MAKES: 24 SERVINGS

Ingredients

Pre-made cookie dough
Ice cream of choice

Steps

1. Prepare cookies per package directions, let cool.
2. Scoop ice cream onto a cookie, then top with another cookie.
3. Enjoy before it melts, especially on nights when the family needs something extra fun.

VARIATION: Roll edges in sprinkles, mini chocolate chips, or chopped nuts

SOF STORIES
Speedy Pickup Express to Dessert — Emma

After a few airport pick-ups, I learned not to psych up the kids too soon. The flight was always delayed. Once the kids and I ended up burning a few hours eating out

Special Forces kids enjoy a special ice cream outing with Dad. *(Photo courtesy of KaLea Lehman)*

at the nearest mall. They had a great, kid-friendly restaurant with a giant aquarium and slow service. We somehow burned a few hours there. We had such a great time, once I finally got to surprise them with a dad-pick-up, we decided to celebrate and stop for a special ice cream spluge. Now every return trip, we take a walk down memory lane and mark the return with an ice cream outing.

(Photo courtesy of Lynnsy Snook)

On Time, On Target
Fruit, Cheese, and Cracker Charcuterie

TIME: 10 MIN (PREP)
MAKES: VARIES

Ingredients

Fruit of choice, peeled and cut into bite sized pieces

Cheese, cut into cracker-sized chunks or slices

Crackers, pretzels, or small slices of bread

Optional: Jelly for smearing on crackers and cheese

Steps

1. Prepare fruit and slice cheese(s).
2. Arrange all ingredients on a board or plate for a quick and easy not-too-sweet after dinner snack.

(Photo courtesy of Lynnsy Snook)

CUSTOMS AND CAMARADERIE
Merrill's Marauders, MARS Task Force, and the 75th Ranger Regiment

Historic Highlight. The Army's Infantry is home to many Rangers whose wartime heroics marked military history even prior to the Revolutionary War, but today only the 75th Ranger Regiment falls under U.S. Special Operations Command. It is the Army's elite, light infantry force, and its roots go back to the China-Burma-India Theater in World War II where they were known as Task Force Galahad. Led by Major General Frank Merrill, these Rangers operated behind enemy lines scouting, raiding, ambushing, and assaulting Japanese forces in an effort to "Lead the Way" for their Chinese allies.

Task Force Galahad later become known as Merrill's Marauders.[36] They are a critical piece of the 75th Ranger Regiment's heritage. In fact, today's 75th Ranger Regiment's unit crest is the same design as the Marauder patch.[37] Merrill's Marauders were disbanded, but many Marauders became part of the MARS Task Force in the 1944 campaign in Burma. MARS Task Force was created to conduct long-range penetration capabilities, and they proved these special capabilities played a powerful shaping role in war.[38]

Snow angels with dad in the dark. (*Photo courtesy of Justine Margaret*)

---

36. Military.com. (n.d.). *The Army Rangers: Missions and History*. Accessed from https://www.military.com/special-operations/army-ranger-missions-and-history.html

37. U.S. Army Rangers. (n.d.). *History & Heritage*. Heritage - United States Army Rangers - The United States Army. Accessed from https://www.army.mil/ranger/heritage.html

38. Sacquety, T. J. (2009, November 4). *Over the Hills and Far Away: The MARS Task Force, the Ultimate Model for Long Range Penetration Warfare*. Accessed from https://arsof-history.org/articles/v5n4_over_the_hills_page_1.html

(Photo courtesy of Lynnsy Snook)

Covert **Chocolate-Dipped Fruit Favorites**

TIME: 10 MIN (PREP), 5 MIN (COOK)
MAKES: 4 SERVINGS

Ingredients

Fruit of your choice (suggestions include berries, sliced bananas, cubed apples, grapes, etc)

1 cup semisweet or milk chocolate chips, or chopped chocolate of your choice

½ cup heavy whipping cream

Steps

1. Rinse/peel the fruit, slice into bite-sized pieces if necessary, and thread onto skewers or toothpicks for easy dipping.
2. Add the chocolate chips to a medium sized bowl and set aside.
3. Add the heavy whipping cream to a microwave safe bowl or measuring cup and heat for about 1 minute, keeping an eye on it. Do not let it bubble over.
4. Pour the warm cream over the chocolate chips and allow to sit for 3-5 minutes.
5. Gently stir the cream and chocolate together until they come together to a smooth consistency. Try not to whisk too vigorously, which can add air bubbles to the ganache. If you prefer the sauce thinner, add more cream until desired consistency is reached.
6. Served cooled ganache with fruit skewers for a fun and delicious dipping treat.

VARIATION: Use this chocolate ganache recipe on cakes, cheesecakes, cupcakes, cookies, etc

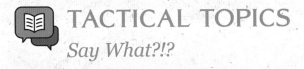 TACTICAL TOPICS
Say What?!?

Who is your favorite social media influencer or YouTuber? What do you like about what they create? Does it inspire you to try anything new?

Ready in a Minute **Rice Krispie Surprise**

TIME: 5 MIN (PREP), 10 MIN (COOK)
MAKES: 15 SERVINGS

Ingredients

6 tablespoons butter

16 ounces mini marshmallows

6 cups Rice Krispies cereal

1 cup surprise topping of choice: M&Ms,
   crumbled Oreos, chopped peanut butter
   cups, sprinkles, or caramel syrup

Steps

1. Melt the butter in a large pot over medium heat.
2. Stir in marshmallows and continue to stir until marshmallows are melted.
3. Remove from heat and stir in Rice Krispies cereal.
4. Dump the mixture into a buttered 9x13 inch pan, spread out evenly, and sprinkle with your surprise topping.
5. Once cool, cut and serve.

Nothing says "Happy Birthday" like a home-made Rice Krispy Cake! *(Photo courtesy of Britt'n Morrison)*

Freeze Time **Fruit Cup**

TIME: 20 MIN (PREP), 12-24 HRS (COOK)
MAKES: 20 SERVINGS

Ingredients

3-4 bananas
16 ounces maraschino cherries
1 can frozen orange juice
1 can frozen lemonade
12 ounces frozen strawberries
8 ounces crushed pineapple
1 cup sugar
1½ cups cold water
20 (7-9-ounce) plastic disposable cups

Steps

1. Slice bananas and cherries.
2. Thaw frozen juices.
3. Mix all ingredients in a large pan, and pour mixture in small plastic cups. The cup should be ¾ full with fruit mix.
4. Freeze at least 12 hours before serving.

Daughter of a Green Beret builds a snowman. *(Photo courtesy of KaLea Lehman)*

SOF STORIES

Battle it Out! – Dad vs Mom

On special nights where dessert needs a little extra fun, we do a Dad vs Mom dessert challenge. We kick-off the challenge seeking out the most random ingredients. Each time we both manage to concoct the most ridiculous dessert. Then, it's a full house taste-test. The kids get to vote who wins the battle. Dad usually wins, but the kids come to me later and say, "you always win mom, we just want to make dad feel good!" The kids know where their bread and butter comes from—ha!

Dad's winning board. *(Photo courtesy of Christine Trax)*

Magic Moment Mashup

A FAMILY RE-FRESH IS PRETTY SWEET when it arrives accompanied by kid-spiration. Keeping the wheels on the figurative family bus can wear you down. Sometimes responding to everyone's needs (outside of your own) is all you can do. In these phases, family mealtime can feel like a herculean lift, but kid-confidence and optimism can be contagious. A little sweetness from quality family time may be just what you need to recharge. Let them take the lead.

"My time to pick, Mom!" *(Photo courtesy of KaLea Lehman)*

Oven on, plates out, where's the knife, mom? Whatever it is, they got it (with just a bit of guidance). Some days feel slow, like the day's end would never come. Others seem to have a deep breath built into them. The normal hustle just wasn't there. We longed for days like this because the rat race of everyone's schedule seemed to pause, and we could be truly present in the moment. Summer day, holiday break, or an easy, no activities weekend—it was prime time to get caught-up on catching-up. Give yourself permission to embrace the chaos, let the kids cook, and roll with it. Make a memorable moment happen and ask, "So what's for dinner?" Their imagination can run wild and it sets the stage for a moment of unvarnished stories, honest questions, and family memories.

Set-up and ready for a perfectly pumpkin porch picnic. (*Photo courtesy of KaLea Lehman*)

These no-rush moments are perfect for passing on family recipe wisdom. We all know there are official measurements, but then there are "mom's normal spoons," "big spoons," "big palms," and "pinch palms." These casual moments set the scene for family storytelling, and they learn to eyeball the key ingredients your *family way.*

Yes, sometimes there were messes – big messes. We eventually learned how to hold back the frustrated scream at the cracked eggs and spilled milk when we learned to be present in the moment and notice their wide eyes and tightened posture. Their oops overtook the inconvenience and softened the abrupt correction. We just started to document the disasters with a quick picture to make light of the mealtime feat. You bet those moments made the refrigerator or scrapbook! We still retell the powder sugar explosion.

Embrace their creations. Before you know it, just like our crews, they will declare they make dinner (or dessert!) better than you. And, that is a good thing!

Little lady bug hard at work mixing up some brownies. *(Photo courtesy of KaLea Lehman)*

By Demand **Spaghetti Bowl**

TIME: 10 MIN (PREP), 45 MIN (COOK)
MAKES: 6 SERVINGS

- -

Ingredients

1 pound ground beef or turkey
3 tablespoons extra virgin olive oil
½ eggplant, diced into ¼ inch squares
4 teaspoons minced garlic
1 small-medium yellow onion
Salt and pepper to taste
1 can of diced, stewed or whole tomatoes
(1) 25 ounce jar of tomato sauce
1 (12 oz) box of spaghetti noodles
1 green bell pepper (optional)
15 slices of pepperoni (optional)

Steps

1. Brown the ground meat in a skillet, drain off excess fat, and set aside.
2. In a large pan, sauté the diced eggplant, garlic, and onion in the olive oil.
3. Season the vegetables with salt and pepper.
4. Stir in the meat and canned tomatoes.
5. Next, add the tomato sauce and allow it to simmer while you boil water for the spaghetti noodles.
6. When the spaghetti noodles are cooked, you can serve separately and top with the sauce or stir the noodles into the sauce to serve.
7. Best topped with Parmesan cheese and fresh basil.

VARIATIONS: If you need a spaghetti shake-up, add 15-20 pepperoni slices (depending on size of pepperoni rounds and preference) or a green bell pepper to the sauce. For a bit of a veggie twist, you can add 2 shredded carrots to the ground beef mixture as it is browning.

"I see my favorite ingredients, and I just start to cook!" (*Photo courtesy of KaLea Lehman*)

SOF STORIES
Peter Piper Picked a Pepper — Anne

My son is the youngest of four, and he was born with an ornery streak. When he was two he would scale my counters with a pan and spaghetti noodles and try to start dinner without me. It was clear I had a chef in training. Amid the deployment rotations, I decided to harness his enthusiasm and set him to work. He would pull up a chair, cut-up the bright veggies, and help mix up the ingredients. It was hilarious because unlike my girls who tended to bake chocolate or sweet items, he was jazzed with a bunch of peppers and greens. He stood on the step stool and declared, "I see my favorite ingredients, and I just start to cook!" Then, when we sat down to eat he proudly proclaimed he cooked better than I did! Now, anything with peppers, spinach, and cream cheese reminds me of my little helper.

"I just can't wait to cook and cut with a knife" *(Photo courtesy of KaLea Lehman)*

Persevere PB and Pick it

TIME: 5 MIN (PREP)
MAKES: 1 SERVING

Ingredients

2 slices of white or wheat bread
2 tablespoons peanut butter
1 tablespoon jelly of choice
⅛ cups sliced fruit (apples or banana)
M&Ms or chocolate chips

Steps

1. Spread peanut butter on one slice of bread.
2. Spread jelly or Nutella on the other slice of bread.
3. Add sliced fruit and chocolate chips if desired.
4. Place the two halves together and serve.

VARIATION: This is a kid's choice sandwich. The idea is a simple peanut butter sandwich and whatever your kiddo gets excited to make and eat. Try swapping the jelly for hazelnut spread.

A family outing in Germany during the Oktoberfest season. *(Photo courtesy of Angie McLaughlin)*

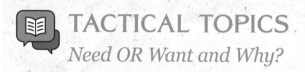 TACTICAL TOPICS
Need OR Want and Why?

Go around the table and have each person name the three items or expressions that you need to see/hear most every day. Share why you need them. Then circle the table one more time to share three items or experiences you want to have and tell why you want them.

Little Bird **Crispy Chicken Fritters**

TIME: 15 MIN (PREP), 10 MIN (COOK)
MAKES: 6 SERVINGS

- -

Ingredients

2 (12.5-ounce) cans white premium chunk chicken breast

1 egg

1 teaspoon Dijon mustard

½ teaspoon salt

¼ teaspoon garlic powder

¼ teaspoon onion powder

¼ teaspoon black pepper

⅛ teaspoon dried thyme

¼ cup plain dried breadcrumbs

Additional breadcrumbs

Vegetable oil

Steps

1. Drain chicken very well by placing pieces in a colander.
2. Roughly chop chicken, about ¼-inch sized pieces. Chopping the chicken also prevents any stray bits from poking out of the crispy coating.
3. Add chicken, egg, Dijon mustard, salt, spices and ¼ cup breadcrumbs to a mixing bowl then stir with a fork until well combined.
4. Pour additional breadcrumbs into a shallow bowl or pie plate (about a cup or so); set aside.
5. Portion chicken mixture into six fritters. Shape each fritter into a tight little hockey puck then coat with additional breadcrumbs.
6. Heat about ¼ inch of oil in a large skillet over medium to medium-high heat. When the oil is hot, pan-fry chicken fritters on each side until golden brown and crispy.

TIP: You can include an egg bath before the final coat of breadcrumbs. These work in an air fryer as well, just be sure to spritz them with a bit of oil first.

VARIATIONS: This can be made with canned salmon, turkey, or tuna. It can also be put together with leftover rotisserie chicken. No breadcrumbs, no problem! You can use crushed Chex cereal, cornflakes, or crackers.

SOF STORIES
Chicken Fritters — Christy

It can be tough to feed both kids and a hungry husband, so when you find an easy dish that pleases all, it becomes a family favorite. My husband was returning from the field, and I was not going to the store that night with my new baby and two young kids. So, I decided to try some pantry magic. I mixed some canned chicken, Chex Mix, and a master-blend of condiments and crossed my fingers. In 10 minutes dinner was done. My children bit into the first one, they loved it! My husband even gave them a thumbs up when he returned.

The first time I made them I used the air fryer. I also pan fried them and found I preferred the taste, but my kids could not tell the difference (neither could my husband). With some experimentation, I learned they froze well. Now, I just pop them in the air fryer for a fast meal especially when I can't stomach another pizza. The kids love these fritters with a light side salad and a lemon vinaigrette. We all wrap up dinner happy.

Joining dad for some extra special push-ups. *(Photo courtesy of Christine Trax)*

Decisive Influence **Mango Spinach Salad**

TIME: 10 MIN (PREP)
MAKES: 2 SERVINGS

Ingredients

1 cup fresh baby spinach
1 cup mango, fresh or frozen (and thawed)
¼ cup red onion, sliced
1 tablespoon olive oil
2 limes, juiced
2 tablespoons honey
Salt and pepper to taste

Steps

1. In a salad bowl, combine spinach, mango, and red onions. Set aside
2. In a jar with a tight-fitting lid, add olive oil, lime juice, honey, salt and pepper. Shake the jar until thoroughly combined.
3. Pour dressing over salad and gently toss it all together.

(Photo courtesy of Lynnsy Snook)

Go around the table and share the worst thing you ever ate. Why was it so bad? Was it just a "strange" texture? Does it have an ingredient you don't like? Would you try it again? Is it "flubbed" enough to be part of a prank? If so, who would you prank and why?

It had eight legs and suction cups all over . . . *(Photo courtesy of Angie McLaughlin)*

Frogman in a Hole

TIME: 5 MIN (PREP), 5 MIN (COOK)
MAKES: 1 SERVINGS

Ingredients

1 teaspoon butter
1 slice bread of your choice
1 egg
Fresh fruit of your choice

Steps

1. Heat a fry pan on medium and spray with butter.
2. With the rim of a water glass or biscuit cutter, cut out the center of a slice of bread.
3. Place bread slice and remaining round in the pan and crack 1 egg in the center of the holed-out bread.
4. Place a lid over the pan and cook for about 2 minutes.
5. As eggs set and whites become cooked, flip bread and egg, also turning bread round.
6. Serve with fresh fruit.

(Photo courtesy of Bridget Orr)

VARIATIONS: Substitute waffles, pancakes, tortillas, or any flat, bread-like food. Make a hole and add an egg. It is that simple!

TACTICAL TOPICS
Sum it up!

Pick three positive words to describe yourself. They could be qualities that make you proud of who you are, or aspects of your personality and character that you feel good about. Examples to get you started: kind, strong, determined, loving, thoughtful, fierce, hilarious, generous, smart, supportive, honest. Stumped at all? Go around the table and have everyone chip in a word. Or, take turns picking three positive words to describe the person next to you.

Battle Buddy **Bar-B-Ketch**

TIME: 5 MIN (PREP)
MAKES: 1 SERVING

Ingredients

½ cup BBQ sauce
¼ cup ketchup

Steps

1. Put BBQ sauce on the plate
2. Add the appropriate amount of ketchup in the middle.
3. Mix as eaten. Enjoy with hot dogs, burgers, or fries.

SOF STORIES
Bar-B-Ketch — Cindy

My son was a picky eater. Textures played a large part in how and what he would eat. Everything was too slimy, or too chunky, too sweet, or too spicy. Our lives revolved around "too." I was tired of the "too." One dinner, we had hot dogs, and he found them too dry plain. Ketchup was too sweet, and the barbecue sauce was too thick and spicy. Fed up, I told him to make something he wanted on the hotdog. He pulled the condiments out of the fridge and started to put a little bit of all of them on the plate, and started tasting. I was floored. Mustard was out, and so was mayo. Too goopy, in his word boggery, for his delicate palate. With those eliminated, we had ketchup and barbecue sauce.

He didn't like them alone, so he mixed them. He loved it. Not too sweet and not too thick and spicy. A perfect combination of the two. My son christened the sauce Bar-B-Ketch. To this day, it graces his (and his siblings) plates with hot dogs, fries, and hamburgers. Now the only "too" is that it's too good!

Say **Cheese Eggs and Ham**

TIME: 5 MIN (PREP), 15 MIN (COOK)
MAKES: 3-4 SERVINGS

Ingredients

1 tablespoon butter
6 eggs, beaten
¼ cup ham, sliced or diced
2-3 slices American cheese
Salt and pepper to taste

Steps

1. Melt butter in a skillet on medium heat.
2. Add in eggs and scramble the eggs in the pan at medium heat.
3. Once the egg white is mostly cooked, push the eggs to one half of the pan and add the ham to the empty side.
4. Allow the ham to get hot, and then stir it into the eggs.
5. Add the diced/sliced cheese to the skillet just before serving.
6. Add salt and pepper to taste.

VARIATION: Use this egg scramble as a blank canvas for your Chopped Cooking Competition!

SOF kids gather for breakfast. *(Photo courtesy of Amanda Hefron)*

WAR GAMES
Chopped Cooking Competition—SOF Pantry Edition

See what is in your pantry and put together an ingredient basket. Who can come up with the most tasty creation?

Kids "Chopped" challenge *(Photo courtesy of Lynnsy Snook)*

- Think of fun themes for your ingredient baskets. Try themes like camping edition, after school snack edition, holiday edition, or even "this is what we have in the pantry so we're gonna figure it out" edition!
- Try silly additions, like a blind taste-test. Take turns wearing a blindfold and see if you can guess whose creation you are eating.
- Give fun award categories for extra laughs—Weirdest Combo, Best/Worst-Tasting, or Funniest Looking.

Littles Love **Lollipops and Hard Candy**

TIME: 15 MIN (PREP), 1 HR AND 15 MINS (COOK)
MAKES: VARIES

- -

Ingredients

1 cup sugar
⅔ cup water
⅓ cup light corn syrup
½ cup butter, cold
Liquid food coloring
Extract flavor of choice: wintergreen,
    cinnamon, butterscotch, lemon
Candy thermometer
Parchment paper
Lollipop or sucker molds, optional
Lollipop sticks, optional

Steps

1. **For hard candy**, prepare a flat baking
   sheet by placing parchment paper on
   it and rubbing a stick of butter on the
   parchment paper.
2. **For lollipops**, place the prepared lollipop
   molds on the prepared sheet with lollipop sticks in place.
3. Combine water, light corn syrup, and
   sugar in a saucepan. Cook over high
   heat until it boils and reaches the hard
   crack stage on the candy thermometer.
4. Add in 1 teaspoon extract and 6 drops of
   color and stir quickly.
5. Pour in molds or on the prepared baking
   sheet.
6. Allow to fully cool. Once cool, the candy
   should be solid and able to crack into
   pieces or enjoy as a lollipop.

A kid's candy dream. (*Photo courtesy of Angie McLaughlin*)

TIP: If the candy does not reach soft crack stage, it will not fully harden once cool.

The Only Easy Day was Yesterday

A Note to the Reader: *Some stories in this section deal with tragedy and loss. Please take care when reading, and know that you are not alone if your own SOF Story features similar chapters.*

AT TIMES, LIFE IN THE SPECIAL OPERATIONS COMMUNITY can feel a bit like the movies and cause you to pause and do a quick reality check. The pictures, stories, and unique family-life moments are remarkable. Living witness to their spectacular skills and professionalism is something to be proud of. You can bet our grandchildren and others in future generations will want to hear first-hand military stories retold. These are the exciting moments that people think of. Those of us who have lived this life know there are also tragic moments of enormous loss, and hard moments that have nothing to do with the uniform.

Their service may make news highlights, but real life in our community is anchored to the often unthought of moments of persevering at home. Over the years, we've each had our own mountain to climb. Each of our cliff-sides were unique – a battle with cancer, a child lost through miscarriage or illness, the unexpected loss of a parent or sibling, a suicide of a loved one, and then for some, the unfathomable knock for a service member who would not be coming home.

A Special Forces family at their Green Beret's interment at Arlington National Cemetery.
(Photo courtesy of Tabitha Farmer)

Some climbs seemed unbearably steep, and we couldn't imagine what it was like to scale the great wall and navigate the boulders before them. These were truly lonely moments where there was no same boat buddy. Even for those of us close who were spotting the climb, there were no words that could help in that moment. All we could do was be near and present, be a willing listener, validating how real and hard their situation was, and maybe help with meals or kid pick-ups. For those of us who prayed, we prayed for their comfort and peace without ceasing.

There were times a flood of every emotion came, and we were there. We let them come and go with a steady hand on their shoulder, a calm demeanor, and a special cup of their favorite coffee. Our hope was they could draw comfort from our calm and know that even in their struggle that they were not alone. Eventually, they would achieve the climb, and we would be there to celebrate their triumph and in time listen to their reflection of the journey.

Remembering a fallen family friend. *(Photo courtesy of Christine Trax)*

Chef Farmer's **Creamy Mustard & Caper Scallops**

TIME: 1 HOUR 10 MIN (PREP), 15 MIN (COOK)
MAKES: 2 SERVINGS

- -

Ingredients

Marinade

Salt and pepper

1 teaspoon Melting Pot Garlic & Wine
  seasoning mix (or garlic powder)

1 cup dry white wine

Scallops & Sauce

½ pound sea scallops (about 7-8 medium
  size scallops)

2 tablespoons olive oil

1 tablespoon butter

5 garlic cloves, minced

1 cup dry white wine

3 tablespoons capers, drained

2-3 tablespoons Dijon mustard
(to your liking)

Steps

1. Rinse the scallops and pat dry. In a mixing bowl, toss scallops with salt, pepper, and Melting Pot Garlic & Wine seasoning mix. Add enough dry white wine to cover the scallops, and marinate for 1 hour in the refrigerator.

2. In a medium nonstick skillet, heat olive oil over medium-high heat. Place the scallops, flat side down, in the pan and cook for about 2 minutes on each side or until they are golden brown. Remove from heat and set aside on a plate.

3. Melt butter over medium heat and sauté garlic for 2-3 minutes, until fragrant.

4. Add the wine, capers, and mustard to the pan. Bring the mixture to a simmer and cook for about 6-7 minutes or until the wine has reduced slightly.

5. Toss the scallops gently in the sauce and serve warm.

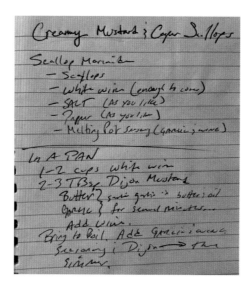

Jon Farmer's last recipe in development before he was killed in action. (*Photo courtesy of Tabitha Farmer*)

SOF STORIES
Chef Farmer — Tabitha

Our kitchen was always the foundation of joy and bliss in our home, especially while Jon and I were cooking together for our four children. Jon would pour me a generous glass of wine, while he had a whiskey. Then, I would watch, and sometimes assist, as my incredibly handsome husband would design the most delicious dinners from whatever he found in our pantry. I called him my "mad scientist" in the kitchen because his meals could never be recreated . . . because the man never wrote anything down. His passion for cooking matched

A Special Forces spouse receives the flag from Command at her husband's interment. *(Photo courtesy of Tabitha Farmer)*

his passion for life, but it wasn't close to his passion for family. The most important ingredient in every meal was a dance.

It was enough that the meal was delicious or that he could clean the dishes as he cooked, but nothing was as important as that moment together. Especially if our wedding song "Can't help falling in love with you" by Elvis would play, he would stop everything and ask for my hand to dance. Our kitchen was small for the mountain of a man that he was to maneuver, but our memories are unmeasurable.

After Jon was killed in action, our kitchen table was turned into a command center. The memories created by his passion for cooking were joined by my closest Special Forces wives and my Casualty Assistance Officer, who I met on the worst day of my life. We were planning Jon's return home, his return to Florida, his funeral, then his final resting place at Arlington, and our "new normal". It's the little things that stab at the heart the most. Food no longer had a taste, and I felt lost. I broke down constantly in the grocery store because I would instinctively look down the aisle to try to see my tall, handsome husband planning the next science experiment in our kitchen. Then, I realize I will never see him again. I never thought I would cook again without him.

Months after Jon was killed, I found a recipe book that had the last meal he ever made. The mad scientist had finally written something down, and was perfecting it up to the date of his last deployment. Our four children all share their Daddy's natural intuition in the kitchen, and I have regained a love for cooking through them. We haven't made his final meal yet, a simple meal with scallops. But when we do, it'll contain the love of four brilliant children and one extremely handsome Angel we know will be proud.

Night Stalkers Don't Quit! Enchiladas

TIME: 15 MIN (PREP), 40 MIN (COOK)
MAKES: 6-8 SERVINGS

- -

Ingredients

4 cups cooked protein choice (pinto/black beans, ground beef, and/or shredded chicken)

1 cup shredded Mexican cheese blend

1 small onion, diced and cooked

1 cup salsa

12 corn tortillas

6 tablespoons extra virgin olive oil

Sauce

2 tablespoons extra virgin olive oil

2 tablespoons flour

8 ounces tomato sauce

1 teaspoon cumin

¼ teaspoon oregano

2 tablespoons chili powder

¼-½ teaspoon salt

Steps

1. To make the sauce, combine all ingredients in a saucepan. Mix well, then add 2 cups of water and stir over medium heat until thickened. Set aside.
2. Preheat the oven to 350°F.
3. To make the filling, combine your protein choice with cheese, diced onion, and salsa in a bowl.
4. Brush each tortilla with olive oil and warm in the microwave for 30 seconds.
5. Spoon filling mixture onto a corn tortilla, roll up, and place in a 9x13 in pan.
6. Fill the pan with filled and rolled tortillas, then cover with sauce.
7. Bake enchiladas for 35 minutes.
8. Add more shredded cheese to the top about 5 minutes before you remove from the oven.
9. This dish is great served with sour cream, corn salsa, and guacamole.

VARIATIONS: Flour tortillas may require extra enchilada sauce. Double the sauce recipe and refrigerate the extra sauce or use it as a dipping sauce.

CUSTOMS AND CAMARADERIE
Tragic Loss of Extortion 17

We Honor in Remembrance. On August 6, 2011 the special operations community lost 38 operators when a CH-47D Chinook (call sign Extortion 17) was shot down by a Taliban rocket propelled grenade. The Army's 160th Special Operations Aviation Regiment (SOAR) and the Navy SEALs lost many of their best when Extortion 17 went down. The helicopter was shot down, after refueling mid-raid, as it was attempting to land in support of an ongoing mission in Juy Zarin, Afghanistan. The operators lost in the attack on Extortion 17 are honored and memorialized by units, foundations, and many other efforts in the special operations community today.[39]

Rear Adm. Sean Pybus, commander of Naval Special Warfare Command, right, and Force Master Chief (SEAL) Stephen Link unveil a memorial dedicated to the men killed in the Extortion 17 crash. *(U.S. Navy photo by Mass Communication Specialist 3rd Class Geneva G. Brier/Released)*

39. Darack, E. (2015, March). *The Final Flight of Extortion 17.* Smithsonian.com. Accessed from https://www.smithsonianmag.com/air-space-magazine/final-flight-extortion-17-180953947/

Master Sergeant **No Ricotta Lasagna**

TIME: 15 MIN (PREP), 50 MIN (COOK)
MAKES: 10 SERVINGS

Ingredients

2 pounds lean ground beef
½ cup white onion, chopped
5 garlic cloves
2 tablespoons Italian seasoning
Salt and pepper to taste
1 (24-ounce) jar tomato and basil marinara
   sauce
3 cups fat free cottage cheese
½ cup Parmesan (and a little extra for
   topping)
1½ cups low fat shredded mozzarella cheese
9 ounces oven ready lasagna noodles

Steps

1. Preheat the oven to 350°F.
2. In a large pan, sauté ground beef over medium-high heat. Drain off excess fat and set aside.
3. Sauté sliced onions and minced garlic. Mix ground beef back in and add seasonings.
4. Add the jar of marinara and stir until heated through.
5. In a mixing bowl, combine cottage cheese, Parmesan, and shredded mozzarella.
6. In a baking dish, add a spoonful of meat sauce, then a layer of oven ready noodles, and finish with a layer of cheese mixture.
7. Repeat until all ingredients are used and end with meat mixture on top. If desired you can sprinkle with additional Parmesan.
8. Cover with foil and bake for 30 minutes. Remove foil and and bake for an additional 10-15 minutes or until bubbly and the top is slightly crispy.

VARIATION: You can swap out the ground beef for shredded chicken or ground turkey. You can also add 1 bag of wilted spinach to the meat mixture if desired.

 SOF STORIES

No Ricotta Lasagna — Emily

I have a good, healthy and hearty lasagna recipe. It soothes the soul on a long day, but my son doesn't always agree. He is one of those kiddos that is picky about textures and tastes, and nothing can kill the comfort of a perfect meal like a hungry kid displeased with the plated option. Everyone loves lasagna, but he says, "it's a texture thing." So, I set out to create a version of lasagna that he would eat. Finally, No-Ricotta Lasagna was the one that fit the bill for us! It is packed with protein and doesn't clash with his texture dilemma. It's a nice win-win for us all.

Personnel Recovery
Spinach and Rice Vegetable Bowl

TIME: 10 MIN (PREP), 45 MIN (COOK)
MAKES: 6 SERVINGS

Ingredients

2 cups uncooked Jasmine rice
3 cups water or chicken broth
1 teaspoon salt
3 tablespoons extra virgin olive oil
1 onion, diced
4 tablespoons minced garlic
1-2 portobello mushrooms, diced
3 cups chopped baby spinach
2 tablespoons butter
Salt and pepper to taste

Steps

1. Cook rice in water or chicken broth and oil in a rice cooker according to manufacturer directions.
2. In a separate pan, sauté the diced onion, garlic, diced mushrooms, and baby spinach in butter.
3. When this sauteed mixture is done, stir in the cooked rice and season with salt and pepper to taste.

TIP: This is a great fast recipe for leftover white rice.

 **TACTICAL TOPICS**
Remember When?

Go around the table and share a special childhood memory. This is a great way for spouses to learn more about each other and for kids to learn about their parents growing up.

A family trip to see the Chihuly Nights exhibit at the Biltmore estate. *(Photo courtesy of KaLea Lehman)*

SOF STORIES
Burying Gianna Rose — Collin and Jennifer

We arrived in Florida for the beginning of our last chapter in the military. We were ready for some family time, some peace and calm after several "all-in" years of squadron command and deputy group command. Shortly after settling into life at AFSOC HQ, we were thrilled to find out that we would be adding another little one to our large family.

By week 7 of our pregnancy, we knew something was wrong. A trip to the doctor confirmed our fears. Our little one didn't survive the first trimester. We had been down this road twice before already, and we knew the weeks ahead would be difficult. We had to take the news head-on, while in a new environment. Our life-long military friends from around the world held us up when we needed them most. Unfortunately, that

Family laying their two children born prematurely to rest. *(Photo courtesy of Jennifer Caldwell)*

miscarriage was followed by another one only a few months later. By the time we were pregnant for a third time in Florida, we felt hesitantly joyful when we made it to the second trimester. But, once more, there was an abnormality and we had to say goodbye to another little one far too soon. Gianna Rose, born June 16, 2022, was 15 weeks old (gestation). Her fingers, her little toes and her face were all so incredibly perfect. While we were sad, we had a profound peace through the process. We were uplifted by our eight amazing military kids . . . and our military friends from around the world. Above all, God was our strength and our peace, and His love for us and our family showed through in incredible ways in the days after Gianna's death.

Pictured you will see our family laying to rest our little ones lost to miscarriage and gained as saints in heaven. We still lean into God's divine comfort each and every day, strengthened by the suffering we've had, and returning our thanks to Him by continuing to trust that His ways are far above our own desires and understanding. "The LORD's love for us is strong; the LORD is faithful forever. Hallelujah!" (Psalm 117:2)

Honor and Heritage **Banana Bread Cookies**

TIME: 5 MIN (PREP), 15 MIN (COOK)
MAKES: 18 SERVINGS

Ingredients

1 ripe banana, mashed
¾ cup applesauce
¼ cup butter, softened
¾ cup all purpose flour
¾ cup oats
¼ teaspoon baking soda
½ cup brown sugar
1 egg
⅛ tsp ground cinnamon

Steps

1. Preheat the oven to 350°F.
2. In a large bowl combine all ingredients. Make sure to mix all ingredients and mash the banana well.
3. Prepare a baking sheet by brushing with oil or melted butter, or line it with parchment paper.
4. Place approximately ½ cup of dough on a baking sheet each about 2 inches apart.
5. Bake for 12-15 minutes depending on cookie size.
6. Serve warm. These cookies make a great addition to a scoop of vanilla ice cream.

 **WAR GAMES**
Popcorn Word of the Day

Go around the table and give a spontaneous one-word description of your day. Pop around the table till the poppin' stops! To further "butter the dish," try naming a category of word for each round, such as feeling, color, noun, food, animal, etc., that is related to how your day went.

Popcorn party during a daddy deployment. *(Photo courtesy of Britt'n Morrison)*

Little Legion S'mores Popcorn Bars

TIME: 5 MIN (PREP)
MAKES: 16 SERVINGS

Ingredients

¼ cup butter, melted
8 ounces mini marshmallows
1 bag popcorn, popped
½ cup crushed graham cracker
¼ cup chocolate chips

Steps

1. Melt butter in a large pot. Quickly add mini marshmallows and stir.
2. Once marshmallows begin to melt, stir in the popcorn.
3. When mixture begins to brown, stir in graham crackers and chocolate chips.
4. Quickly pour into a buttered casserole dish.
5. Once cool, cut or pull apart and serve

VARIATION: If you want it to be very sticky, double the marshmallows and melted butter. Substitute Cheerios, Fruit Loops, or Golden Grahams cereal for popcorn. Try topping with ½ cup of crushed cookies or chopped candy bars.

(Photo courtesy of KaLea Lehman)

SEAL kids watch a Selection event. *(Photo courtesy of Dan and Leslie Luna)*

5. All Together Now

★ ★ ★

YOUR FAMILY GROWS EXPONENTIALLY when you are part of the special operations community. Even with all of our differences in personality, upbringing, faith, and ideas of fun—we are a tribe. The unpredictability and intensity that accompanies life in the special operations community weave a unique culture. Belonging is rarely felt through conventional practices of military custom and tradition. Instead, our service members find it through an admiration of excellence and readiness. Our families sense belonging in familiar faces, smiles, or a hug for clearing life's hurdles.

Belonging—that feeling of comfort and familiarity in a community—comes with time. Each one of us had to learn to recognize the unique ways of the special operations community. We hang out, support, celebrate, and sometimes grieve together at a unit lunch, reunion barbecue, holiday smorgasbord, family jump day, or memorial. It doesn't always come easy or natural. This is especially true at those more formal gatherings and ceremonies. Many times making a dish or blocking-off the time to attend a "mandatory fun event" or the soldier/SEAL/airman lunch seemed like a bridge too far. But showing up to unit events has its sweet spots. Too often, we recognize them only in hindsight—seeing an old friend we didn't expect to see or saying a final goodbye to a great commander, war hero, or teammate.

When we make time for unit events or gatherings, we build relationships that last. We find go-to friends and learn about resources and opportunities we didn't know were out there. We form memories and learn to see where we fit in the traditions and rituals that give the special operations way of life intense meaning. In time, the beach gatherings, receptions, reunions, and campfires we worked into our schedule add up, and the SOF community becomes like family.

Special Forces kids trying out some obstacles during a Reunion week picnic. *(Photo courtesy of KaLea Lehman)*

Unit family day! Even the kids all get to play on team trucks. *(Photo courtesy of KaLea Lehman)*

Big Bunch Lunch

WHOLE UNIT GET-TOGETHERS are somewhat infrequent opportunities because it can be complicated to hone in on a time when a majority of a unit is home. The training work-ups, deployments, and other trips add up so there are very few windows of opportunity in the year to gather. Family time is critical so when a unit function happens, it's worth it to go, enjoy a good meal, let the kids run, and savor moments with unit friends.

These opportunities come for a variety of reasons—a hail and farewell, a reunion, a team or small unit potluck, change of command or responsibility, a holiday party, retirement, or a casual soldier/airman/SEAL lunch hosted by the family support/readiness organization. Whatever the reason there are tables filled with tasty spreads and familiar favorites. Each event takes on a bit of its own personality. One time it is a unit-inspired chili cook-off and another is family led. The common thread is the familiar faces from the unit, the handful of curious junior explorers, and enough food that no one leaves hungry.

A special operations community meal in Germany. *(Photo courtesy of Angie McLaughlin)*

Special Aviator **Green Chile Chicken Stew**

TIME: 15 MIN (PREP), 1 HOUR (COOK)
MAKES: 6 SERVINGS

Ingredients

4 (14.5-ounce) cans Great Northern beans

2 medium onions, chopped

1 tablespoon olive oil

3 (4.5-ounce) cans chopped green chiles, undrained

4 garlic cloves, minced

2 teaspoons ground cumin

2 teaspoons dried oregano

6 cups chicken broth

5 cups chopped chicken meat

3 cups shredded Monterey Jack cheese with jalapeno peppers

½ teaspoon salt

¼ teaspoon pepper

¼ cup chopped fresh cilantro, optional

Steps

1. Drain beans and set aside.
2. Sauté onion in a hot Dutch oven or large pot over medium–high heat until tender.
3. Add green chiles, garlic, cumin and oregano, cook for 2 minutes, stirring constantly.
4. Add beans and broth. Bring to boil, cover, reduce heat and simmer for 45 minutes or until beans are tender, stirring occasionally.
5. Add chicken, 1 cup cheese, salt and pepper. Bring to a boil, reduce heat and simmer, uncovered, 10 minutes, stirring often.
6. Stir in cilantro, if desired.
7. To serve, ladle stew into individual soup bowls. Top each serving with remaining cheese.

VARIATION: You can substitute the canned beans for 1 pound of dry beans, cooked as directed on the package.

(Photo courtesy of Lynnsy Snook)

SOF STORIES
Chili Cook-off Challenge! — Casey

Unit Chili Cook-Off Prizes *(Photo courtesy of Lynnsy Snook)*

We were married before my husband made the move into special operations, and it seemed the women always had to carry the weight of making social events happen. Even potlucks get to be tedious when you seem to be in a constant state of deployments and training, but we had one First Sergeant who flipped this soldier's lunch spouse burden. He loved chilis and he would experiment with peppers and all sorts of flavors. He welcomed every chili ingredient debate you could imagine and his passion for chili seemed to liven the spirits of everyone, making the serious laugh, the tired alert, and the competitive strategize to prove their place.

When he moved from the team to the company, he challenged the whole unit to a chili cook-off. It was amazing to watch all the operators take up the challenge and see who came to joust. Many threw everything they had into the cook-off challenge, and even more came from across the battalion, and in some cases the Group, to spectate, taste, and throw barbs. and reap the delicious rewards. The event was such a hit, it became a bit of a tradition.

Now, every time I see chili I am taken back to that cook-off in the unit classroom. Just like they raised the bar for unconventional warfare, they reset my view on what a unit event could be and become.

Stick to Tradition **Chili with Beans**

TIME: 10 MIN (PREP), 40 MIN (COOK)
MAKES: 6 SERVINGS

Ingredients

1 pound of ground beef

2 cans of pinto beans, drained and rinsed

1 can of red bean or red kidney beans,
   drained and rinsed

1 onion, diced

4 celery stalks, diced

¼ teaspoon garlic salt

¼ teaspoon oregano

1 cube of chicken bouillon

1 can of diced tomatoes

18 ounces of tomato juice or V8 juice

3 tablespoons chili powder

2 tablespoons cumin

2 tablespoons paprika

2 teaspoons salt

Steps

1. Brown the ground beef and drain off the fat.

2. Add all ingredients into a pot and let simmer for 20-30 minutes before serving.

VARIATIONS: Sweet Memory Seconds Chili can be made by combining 1 cup of craisins to your pot of chili leftovers. Let it refrigerate overnight, warm up and enjoy the sweet and spicy combination. It will light up your palate and your memory.

Santa comes to visit SOF style! *(Photo courtesy of Christine Trax.)*

On Point **Pork and White Bean Chili**

TIME: 15 MIN (PREP), 35 MIN (COOK)
MAKES: 4 SERVINGS

Ingredients

2 tablespoons olive oil, divided

1 pound boneless pork loin, cut into 1-inch cubes

2 cups chopped onions

2 tablespoons chili powder

1½ teaspoons ancho chile pepper

1 teaspoon ground cumin

1 teaspoon garlic powder

1 teaspoon Mexican oregano leaves

2 (14.5-ounce) cans cannellini beans, drained and rinsed

1¾ cups chicken stock

1 avocado, peeled, pitted and chopped

2 tablespoons chopped fresh cilantro

2 tablespoons fresh lime juice

Steps

1. Heat 1 tablespoon of the oil in a large skillet on medium-high heat.
2. Add half of the pork and brown on all sides. Remove pork from skillet.
3. Repeat with remaining pork, adding additional 1 tablespoon oil as needed.
4. Stir onions into skillet and cook for 4 minutes or until tender.
5. Add seasonings and cook 1 minute or until fragrant.
6. Add pork, beans, and stock and mix well.
7. Bring to a boil. Reduce heat to low and simmer, uncovered, for 15 to 20 minutes or until pork is tender, stirring occasionally.
8. Mix avocado, cilantro and lime juice in a small bowl. Serve chili topped with avocado mixture.

VARIATION: You can substitute chicken or turkey for the pork.

(Photo courtesy of Andrea Orr)

BUDS **Beef Barbacoa and Taco Bar**

TIME: 10 MIN (PREP), 3-4 HOURS (COOK)
MAKES: 6 SERVINGS

- -

Ingredients

1 (7-ounce) can chipotle peppers in adobo sauce

1 diced onion

3 garlic cloves, minced

¼ cup soy sauce

¼ cup Worcestershire sauce

Juice from 2 limes

2 tablespoons sugar

1 tablespoon finely chopped fresh oregano (or 1 teaspoon dried oregano)

1 tablespoon ground cumin

2 teaspoons paprika

1 teaspoon kosher salt

½ teaspoon pepper

2-3 pounds boneless beef chuck roast, trimmed and cut into 2-inch cubes

Steps

1. Preheat the oven to 325°F.
2. In a Dutch oven stir together chipotle peppers, onion, garlic, soy sauce, Worcestershire sauce, lime juice, sugar, oregano, cumin, paprika, salt and pepper.
3. Stir in beef and toss to coat.
4. Bake in the oven until the meat reaches at least 200°F and easily shreds with a fork (approximately 3-4 hours).
5. Shred meat in the pot or on a cutting board. If you don't want all the chilies, strain juice and discard the solids. Return meat and juices to pan. Serve and enjoy!
6. Store the leftover barbacoa beef with its juices in an airtight container in the refrigerator for up to 5 days. Freeze the beef barbacoa with its juices in an airtight container for up to 3 months.

TIP: Serve with corn or flour tortillas, pico de gallo or salsa, shredded cheese, fresh cilantro, chopped onion, lime wedges, tomatoes, and sour cream.

VARIATION: If you prefer a mild dish, you can use only the adobo sauce or just use adobo sauce and one pepper. DO NOT OMIT, the bulk of the flavor comes from this.

SLOW COOKER OPTION: In a 6-quart slow cooker, stir together chipotle peppers, onion, garlic, soy sauce, Worcestershire sauce, lime juice, sugar, oregano, cumin, paprika, salt and pepper. Stir in beef and toss to coat. Cover and cook until beef is very tender; about 6-8 hours on LOW or 3-4 hours on HIGH. Remove beef and shred with forks. Stir the beef back into the cooking juices. Use a spoon or tongs to serve.

TO REHEAT beef barbacoa: warm the barbacoa in a slow cooker on the "WARM" setting until heated through or place the beef with its juices in a saucepan on the stovetop over low heat. Cover and cook, stirring occasionally, just until the meat is warm.

SOF STORIES
Between Rotation Tacos — Amanda

Years ago, when we were still pretty new to Special Forces, our battalion tried to build in opportunities for families to get together for lunch. It was a low stress way to meet families and the guys my husband worked and deployed with.

One favorite potluck theme was tacos. To make these lunches easy and low stress, a bunch of us would bring slow cookers of main dish options. A spouse that had been around longer shared with me her slow cooker chicken taco recipe. It was so easy and delicious I shared it with our extended family. That recipe is now a family favorite and is often pulled out for easy family celebrations. All thanks to the wisdom from wives more seasoned than I.

A day at the obstacle course, just for the spouses. *(Photo courtesy of KaLea Lehman)*

Quick Strike **Meatball Sub** **& Slow Cooker Spaghetti Sauce**

TIME: 15 MIN (PREP), 6-8 HOURS (COOK)
MAKES: 4-6 SERVINGS

Ingredients

3 large or 4 small zucchini

5 (29-ounce) cans tomato puree

1½ tablespoons rosemary

1½ tablespoons oregano

1½ tablespoons parsley

1 tablespoon minced garlic

1½ tablespoons salt

4-5 tablespoons sugar

2 tablespoons black pepper

Choice of meat: Chief's Meatballs (see page 29) or 3 pounds ground beef, browned and drained

Steps

1. Peel and chop half of the zucchini and add to a blender.
2. Cover with some tomato puree and blend thoroughly. Add mixture to the slow cooker.
3. Chop up remaining zucchini and add to the blender.
4. Add all spices to the blender and cover with more tomato puree. Blend thoroughly and add to the slow cooker.
5. Pour remaining cans of tomato puree into the slow cooker and stir all together.
6. If using ground beef, brown the meat, drain, and place in a covered bowl in the refrigerator for later.
7. Put the sauce on low and allow to cook 6-8 hours, stirring every hour to keep sauce from burning on the bottom.
8. Half an hour to one hour before serving, add your choice of browned ground beef or cooked meatballs to the slow cooker and stir.
9. Serve meatballs and sauce over sub rolls, or serve meat sauce over pasta of your choice.

TIP: This is a fairly large batch of sauce so you can portion out quart size bags for the freezer, which saves time on other dinners.

TACTICAL TOPICS
Remember Me

Who was the first person who greeted you when you got to this unit? How did you meet them? Do you prefer to get to know people at a large gathering or meet them one-on-one?

Special Operations staff goes all out throwing a "shower" for an expecting female service member with just a little help from their own spouses. *(Photo courtesy of KaLea Lehman)*

Little Creek **Party Snack Mix**

TIME: 10 MIN (PREP), 1 HOUR (COOK)
MAKES: 12-15 SERVINGS

Ingredients

2 ⅔ cups Rice Chex
2 ⅔ cups Corn Chex
2 ⅔ cups Wheat Chex
1 cup pretzels (any shape)
1 cup mixed nuts
1 ¼ teaspoons seasoned salt
¼ teaspoon garlic powder
¼ cup butter
5 teaspoons Worcestershire sauce

Steps

1. In a large bowl or stock pot, combine all the Rice Chex, Corn Chex, Wheat Chex, pretzels, and nuts.
2. Mix in the seasoned salt and garlic powder and stir throughout the cereal mix.
3. In a small bowl, melt the butter and stir in the Worcestershire sauce.
4. Drizzle the butter mixture over the cereal while stirring. Make sure to stir well so everything gets coated with seasoning.
5. Bake for 1 hour at 250°F before serving.

VARIATION: If you do not want to use the nuts, they can be left out of the mix or you can add 1 cup extra pretzels or M&Ms.

TACTICAL TOPICS

My Pick.

THE FAMILY DINNER PROJECT.ORG

If you could only eat one food for the rest of your life, what food would you choose?

Air Commando **Cookie Bars**

TIME: 15 MIN (PREP), 30 MIN (COOK)
MAKES: 12-15 SERVINGS

Ingredients

¾ cup butter
2½ cups brown sugar
3 eggs
2¾ cups flour
½ teaspoon salt
2½ teaspoons baking powder
2 cups of choice baking chocolate chips

Steps

1. Preheat the oven to 350°F.
2. Melt the butter in the microwave and with an electric or counter mixer combine it with the brown sugar and eggs.
3. Cream together well, then stir in the flour, salt, and baking soda.
4. Last, stir in baking chocolate chips. This batter will be thick so prep your strong arm or run your counter mixer on low.
5. When the baking chips are mixed in, spoon the cookie batter into a greased 9 x 13-inch baking dish.
6. Bake for 25-30 minutes.
7. When cool, cut into squares to serve. You can drizzle caramel, or melted chocolate over the top for extra fun.

Framlingham Castle from the back of a CV-22 Osprey on a spouse appreciation day flight *(Photo courtesy of Lynnsy Snook)*

VARIATION: You can choose your flavor of baking chips to use: combine dark chocolate and white chips, or try something unique and add butterscotch or mint. Have fun with the flavors you add!

We Spouses Gather Together

THERE ARE TIMES WHEN WE ALL GATHER as units, teams, or families, but there are also events just "to the ladies."[1] But these days, our units also have male and dual military spouses. It doesn't matter where you come from or how long you've been in the community, unit spouse occasions still serve as opportunities for camaraderie, sharing of resources, a momentary break, and a little bit of fun . . . Because, regardless of their gender, military status, or occupation, the special operations experience is a unique journey for any spouse.

Spouses team up on a high ropes course. *(Photo courtesy of KaLea Lehman)*

1. United States Field Artillery Association. (n.d.). *The Military Ball*. The Military Ball - United States Field Artillery Association. Accessed from https://www.fieldartillery.org/the-military-ball

From unit to unit and commander to commander the flavor and title of spouse and family events changes. Sometimes there are "coffees" or mock dining-ins, which are like snazzy get togethers with more wine (or mixed drinks!) than coffee. Then there are welcomes, farewells, luncheons, meetings, play groups, book clubs, and many other meet-ups. Much of the military spouse customs of past lore are gone. Times have changed and the spouse experience changes. Between working couples, late marriages, and a robust deployment and training tempo, fewer spouses find value in many of the old traditions. Occasionally there are glimmers of old customs, but mostly what remains today are universal human truths.

Ladies of the Legion remember (*Photo courtesy of KaLea Lehman*)

Truths like:

- It is nice to feel welcomed and be welcomed.
- Names are sometimes hard to remember.
- This lifestyle is hard, and families manage it differently.
- We all need support and a friend.
- Simple gestures build goodwill and foster community. A thank you, a baby gift, a warm meal, and other actions say "I see you," "thank you," or "we are in this together."
- Smiles are contagious.
- Gossip is never good, and kindness is always king.
- Everyone feels special if leadership families know who they are and make time for them—even in small ways like text messages or a simple thank you.
- It is thoughtful when others notice your time to transfer to a new unit, PCS, or leave service is near.
- Be open to new ideas, settings, and ways to connect with fellow spouses.

We gather because we are in this life together, in both good times and challenging times. We journey a path that few others have to navigate, and collectively we've come up with creative and sometimes surprising tactics to find our way. You don't have to dress up, put on a face, or squeeze into a box to join in. That isn't what these gatherings are about. Our fellow spouses have amazing stories, talents, and goals and our diverse backgrounds and often strong personalities mean we may or may not cook, dress up, craft, or even be familiar with how things have been done in the past. All these characteristics just add to the flavor of the gathering. Resist forcing traditions that don't resonate and cling to the purpose behind them. The real meat of these gatherings come from the friendships ignited, the experiences and resources shared, and connecting to the bigger reason we are all in this boat together.

Green Beret's daughter decorating a home-made gingerbread house at Christmas. *(Photo courtesy of Danielle Foote)*

Gingerbread cookies await a nibble from Santa Claus. *(Photo courtesy of KaLea Lehman)*

Green Beret Gingerbread with Royal Icing

TIME: 1 HOUR (PREP), 1 HOUR (COOK)
MAKES: 20 SERVINGS (SMALL COOKIES)

Ingredients

Gingerbread

½ cup butter, at room temperature
½ cup dark brown sugar
¼ cup light molasses
1 tablespoon cinnamon
1 tablespoon ginger
1½ teaspoons ground cloves
1 teaspoon baking soda
2 cups flour
2 tablespoons water

Royal Icing

4 cups powdered sugar
3 tablespoons meringue powder
12-15 tablespoons water
Candies and sprinkles for decorating

Steps for Gingerbread

1. Preheat the oven to 375°F.
2. In a large mixing bowl, cream the butter, brown sugar, molasses, cinnamon, ginger, cloves and baking soda together until the mixture is smooth.
3. Blend in the flour and water to make a stiff dough.
4. Form into a flattened circle, wrap in plastic wrap, and chill for at least 30 minutes or until firm.
5. Roll out dough to ¼ inch thick between two pieces of parchment paper, and cut into desired shapes with a sharp knife. You can print and trace a template from the internet, or get creative on your own.
6. Bake for 10-15 minutes. Let cool on a flat surface to maintain shape.

Steps for Royal Icing

1. To make the Royal Icing: in a mixing bowl, add powdered sugar and meringue powder and whisk together.
2. Using a counter mixer or a hand mixer, slowly begin to mix the water into the sugar mixture until it is smooth. If the icing is very crumbly, add more water, 1 tablespoon at a time until it creates a thick but smooth consistency.
3. Beat until the icing is shiny, about 6 to 8 minutes with a stand mixer and about 8 to 10 minutes with a hand mixer. The icing should be thick, but not so thick you can't stir it with a spoon.
4. Fill a plastic piping bag or zip-top freezer bag with icing, and snip the corner to pipe.

TIPS: Consider ordering a Gingerbread House cookie cutter online. If you are building a Gingerbread House, attach two sides of the house to each other and your base (cardboard wrapped with foil works well) using a thick line of royal icing. Attach the remaining two sides to the base and the previous sides. Pipe royal icing inside any seams, inside and outside of the house, to fill any voids. Allow it to set at room temperature for at least 1 hour before adding the roof pieces. Add the roof pieces with royal icing and set for at least 3 hours or overnight. Cover and store leftover royal icing at room temperature or in the refrigerator during this time.

ONCE the house is completely set, use remaining royal icing in a piping bag to decorate your house with candies and sprinkles.

WHEN you are not working with your royal icing, place a clean, damp dish towel over the top of the icing so that it doesn't start to harden.

VARIATIONS: If a house is too much of a lift for the moment, make simple cookies from the dough and decorate. If baking fresh gingerbread is just not in the cards this season, simply mix up a batch of royal icing and make mini houses from graham crackers or go with a ready-made kit. Just make some memories, and don't forget to take pictures!

SOF STORIES
My House, Your House, A Gingerbread House Party — Danielle

Early on when my husband was a new Captain, I was skeptical of military customs and anything organized. We were young and our interactions with the "Big Army" had left a bitter taste in my mouth. We were both excited about the different, low key and mission focused environment life in special operations promised. I was leery when I was invited to the house of the Family Readiness Group leader to decorate gingerbread houses—a family tradition she grew up with as a military kid.

As I walked in my skepticism melted quickly as I met everyone and laid my eyes on a table full of giant, homemade gingerbread houses and pounds of homemade icing. In that house, there was no pretense, no haughtiness, just caring spouses equipped with their favorite candies to deck their house with. That was the first gingerbread house I ever made. It left an imprint on me that grows a bit stronger with time.

Set-up and ready for a memorable spouse social gathering. Everyone has their very own gingerbread house for the holidays. (*Photo courtesy of Danielle Foote*)

A decade later, I am still in awe of the energy and kindness that the leader mustered to bake all those houses. Now, every year I decorate gingerbread with my kids and tell them about the first time I decorated a gingerbread house.

Key Spouse Tea Sandwich Spread

TIME: VARIES
MAKES: 12 SERVINGS

Cucumber Sandwiches Ingredients

8 ounces whipped cream cheese
⅛ teaspoon onion powder
¼ teaspoon garlic powder
1 teaspoon green onions or chives
2 teaspoons fresh dill, chopped
1 teaspoon lemon zest (optional)
1 teaspoon lemon juice
1 loaf of white bread
1 long English cucumber

Steps

1. In a mixing bowl, combine the cream cheese, onion powder, garlic powder, green onions/chives, chopped dill, lemon zest, and lemon juice.
2. Evenly spread the cream cheese mixture across all bread slices.
3. Cut the cucumber in ¼ inch slices and place neatly in overlapping rows on the cream cheese mixture.
4. Place another piece of bread with the cream cheese spread on top of the cucumber layer, making a sandwich.
5. Cut each sandwich to match the occasion. For more special occasions, remove the crust and consider using a cookie press to cut into desired shapes.

Tuna Sandwiches Ingredients

1 (12-ounce) can chunk light tuna, drained
2 teaspoons red or yellow onion, diced (optional)
2 tablespoons sweet relish
½ cup mayonnaise
1 loaf of white or soft wheat bread
1 long English cucumber or 6 pieces of romaine lettuce

Steps

1. In a mixing bowl, combine the drained tuna, onion, relish, and mayonnaise.
2. Evenly spread the tuna salad mixture across both soft bread slices.
3. Cut the cucumber in ¼ inch slices and place neatly on the tuna salad mixture. Alternatively, place the lettuce on the tuna instead.
4. Top with a piece of bread with more tuna salad spread. You can cut in squares or triangles, with or without the crust. Place on a plate and serve chilled.

Tea sandwiches and treats for a unit spouse event. *(Photo courtesy of Lynnsy Snook)*

TACTICAL TOPICS

Ice Breaker

What are some things you've experienced that help you nix the nerves or feel like you belong? Was it a fun themed event, a buddy, or maybe a gift that you received?

Spouse ornament exchange party during the holiday season *(Photo courtesy of Lynnsy Snook)*

Maggie Raye **Red Wine Sangria**

TIME: 15 MIN (PREP)
MAKES: 8 SERVINGS

Ingredients

½ cup simple syrup
2 bottles red table wine
1 cup brandy
½ cup Triple Sec
1 cup orange juice
1 cup pomegranate juice
Orange slices
Apple slices
Blackberries

Steps

1. To make simple syrup, combine equal parts sugar and water in a saucepan. Heat until sugar dissolves. Cool before using

2. Mix all ingredients together and let stand in a tightly sealed container or pitcher for at least 24 hours in the fridge before serving.

(Photo courtesy of Bridget Orr)

CUSTOMS AND CAMARADERIE
Legend of Maggie Raye

Historic Highlight. Martha "Maggie" Raye was an actress who spent a lot of time entertaining troops in World War II, the Korean War, and Vietnam. In addition to entertaining, she was often found nursing the wounded. For her efforts to support the troops, she was given a Green Beret and earned the title of "Lieutenant Colonel" from President Johnson.[2] Colonel Maggie also received the Presidential Medal of Freedom and was granted a special exception to be buried in the Ft. Bragg military cemetery. Today her legendary support lives on in the U.S. Army Special Forces Command's Colonel Maggie Raye Volunteer Award, which recognizes spouses or civilians who contribute significantly to the quality of life of soldiers and families in the Special Forces Regiment.[3]

Girls shoot, too. *(Photo courtesy of KaLea Lehman)*

2. Eckert , R. A. (n.d.). *Remembering Martha Raye WW II, Korea, Vietnam*. American Legion. Accessed from https://www.legion.org/yourwords/personal-experiences/252896/remembering-martha-raye-ww-ii-korea-vietnam

3. Aguirre, V. (n.d.). *1st Special Forces Command celebrates Col. Maggie Raye Volunteer Award recipients* . www.army.mil. Accessed from https://www.army.mil/article/177189/1st_special_forces_command_celebrates_col_maggie_raye_volunteer_award_recipients

Master of Influence **Bruschetta Chicken**

TIME: 10 MIN (PREP), 40 MIN (COOK)
MAKES: 8-12 SERVINGS

Ingredients

3-4 chicken breasts
Salt and pepper

Bruschetta

4-6 slices of sourdough bread, cut in half
2 tablespoons melted butter
⅛ teaspoon of garlic salt

Tomato Topping

4-5 small tomatoes, chopped or sliced
   cherry tomatoes
1 garlic clove, minced
2 tablespoons olive oil
2 tablespoons balsamic vinegar
⅛ teaspoon sea salt
Handful basil, chopped

(Photo courtesy of KaLea Lehman)

Steps

1. Preheat the oven to 375°F.
2. Sprinkle some salt and pepper over the top of the chicken, cover and bake for about 35 to 40 minutes until juices run clear.
3. Meanwhile, combine tomatoes, garlic, olive oil, balsamic vinegar, sea salt and basil in a bowl, and refrigerate until chicken is ready.
4. Combine melted butter and garlic salt and brush on both sides of the sourdough bread.
5. Bake sourdough slices for approximately 10 minutes or until golden brown, flipping halfway. Be attentive not to burn.
6. When chicken breasts are cooked, slice and place on top of the sourdough toast.
7. Spoon tomato mixture over top of the chicken and serve.

VARIATION: Grill the chicken breasts instead of baking.

243

TACTICAL TOPICS
Symbols Tell a Story – I belong here

Simple gift given to spouses at 5th Special Forces Group. *(Photo courtesy of KaLea Lehman)*

Night Stalker broach for spouses. *(Photo courtesy of Andrea Dadisman)*

SEAL trident gift for the home. *(Photo courtesy of Andrea Geraldi)*

Have you ever received a simple gift from a unit that made you feel connected to the mission and people? What was it? How did you receive it? When do you feel comfortable wearing or using it?

Steel Magnolia **Sweet Quinoa and Feta**

TIME: 15 MIN (PREP), 20 MIN (COOK)
MAKES: 6 SERVINGS

Ingredients

1½ cups chicken broth
¼ teaspoon salt
1 cup quinoa, rinsed
½ cup diced white onion
½ cup sliced almonds or pine nuts, optional
1 cup feta cheese crumbles
1 cup craisins

Steps

1. Combine the chicken broth, salt, and quinoa.
2. Let boil for 3-5 minutes then turn heat down to cook until the quinoa spirals show. Set aside to cool.
3. Once cooked quinoa is cool, toss in remaining ingredients and serve cold.
4. May be served over salad greens or baby spinach.

TACTICAL TOPICS
Name . . . What's your name, again?

How do you keep tabs on all the new names of people you encounter at community events? Have you found a hack? Or, are you simply thankful that sometimes people still wear name tags?

Spartan Spouse **Curry Chicken Salad**

TIME: 15 MIN (PREP)
MAKES: 6 SERVINGS

Ingredients

1½ cup mayonnaise
3 teaspoons medium yellow curry powder
1 tablespoon soy sauce
4 cups cooked chicken, diced
1 pound seedless grapes, halved
16 ounce can pineapple chunks
1¼ cup sliced almonds

Steps

1. Combine mayonnaise, curry, and soy sauce in a small bowl.
2. Mix remaining ingredients in a larger bowl, then fold the dressing combination into the chicken mixture.
3. Refrigerate until ready to serve.

TACTICAL TOPICS
My People

How do you know when you can trust a person?

Ladies night. A Mock Dining In. *(Photo courtesy of KaLea Lehman)*

Shield Maiden **Strawberry Pizza**

TIME: 15 MIN (PREP), 15 MIN (COOK)
MAKES: 6 SERVINGS

Ingredients

Crust

2 cups flour
4 tablespoons sugar
1 cup butter melted
1 cup of chopped pecans

Strawberry Topping

8 ounces cream cheese
1 container Cool Whip
1 cup powdered sugar
1 package fresh strawberries, diced
1 cup pretzel (optional)

Steps

1. To make the crust, mix ingredients together and press into a baking dish or pizza pan.
2. Bake at 350°F for 15 minutes. Set aside to cool.
3. To make strawberry topping, cream the Cool Whip, cream cheese, and powdered sugar in a mixing bowl.
4. Spread over a cooled crust.
5. Top with diced strawberries.
6. To add a savory flair, you can sprinkle crumbled pretzels on the top with strawberries.
7. Cut and serve.

 ## TACTICAL TOPICS
Sage Advice

What is one part of special operations life that surprised you—good or bad? What could you say or do to help prepare new spouses and families for this lifestyle?

Tea Time! Thoughtfully designed gift for a senior spouse who loved tea. *(Photo courtesy of Megan Arnold)*

A Moment of Silence

- -

THE SOUND OF THE THREE VOLLEY SALUTE leaves an imprint on every sinew in your body. You can see it in the eyes of each special operations service member and family who has attended the funerals, family and unit memorials, luncheons, team shots for the fallen, or a Gold Star ceremony or reception. These are the rare occasions where sometimes a moment of silence is the only appropriate action. The professionalism and awareness of the ultimate cost of war is never far from those who serve in our units. We have fields marked with monuments and trees that memorialize the cost of the mission and the significance of the person who is no longer at our side.

Every team, unit, family, and individual handle grief in their own way. This kind of loss stops you in your tracks and brings you to your knees, and each must find their own way to tussle with the pain and make sense of their loss, the mission, and this lifestyle. Our community rallies around the families of our fallen, and the preparation of food is a simple way to offer support and compassion. Those in a new Gold Star's inner circle accompany them, share memories, and respond to the needs few others can see and understand. Those of us left to stand witness in our community, grieve and prepare simple food to facilitate the memorial and the conversations that must happen to make meaning of such a life-changing moment.

A deliberate moment to remember and memorialize a fallen brother. (*Photo courtesy of Ruben Arriaga*)

Few Americans are aware of the cost of war. Our community is very aware, but even still we each grow into understanding the weight of family and unit memorials that honor those who do not come home. We will not take for granted the lives lost on the battlefield or back home in training or through other tragedies. We are a community, a strong tribe, and we are family. Of all of our traditions, our units stand united in respect and remembrance for those who gave it all and the family they left behind. Their sacrifice is a reminder of the risk we all live with. Honoring their lives reinforces the values that drive the ethos of our special operations units that remain in defense for our nation and the oppressed.

Remembrance **Rum Balls**

TIME: 20 MIN (PREP)
MAKES: 15 SERVINGS

Ingredients

2 cups crushed vanilla wafers or graham crackers

½ cup powdered sugar

3 tablespoons cocoa powder

1 cup chopped pecans or walnuts

¼ cup pitted dates, soaked in warm water and drained

3 tablespoons rum (spiced, coconut, or classic)

Topping of your choice: grated coconut, powdered sugar, granulated sugar, sprinkles, cookie crumbs

Steps

1. Place cookie crumbs, powdered sugar, cocoa powder, nuts, and soaked dates into the food processor.
2. Pulse for 1 minute to combine.
3. Turn on the food processor and drizzle in rum until the mixture forms a dough.
4. Scoop into bite sized balls and roll in desired toppings.
5. Store in muffin cup liners in the refrigerator or freeze for up to 6 months.

(Opposite) (Photo courtesy of Lynnsy Snook)

SOF STORIES
Every Gold Star Deserves Some Rum — Katie

Annual Gold Star Memorial ceremony at 5th Special Forces Group (*Photo courtesy of KaLea Lehman*)

Each year our unit hosts a Gold Star Memorial Ceremony followed by a reception for the families of the fallen. The first few years there, I didn't really understand this ceremony was a unit event for everyone to attend. It seemed like it was an almost sacred event not meant for a common crowd.

The Gold Star Memorial was a moment to honor those who gave the ultimate sacrifice, support their families, to learn their service member's story, and to better grasp the significance of the work our units do. I understood this better as a fellow spouse shared her tradition of providing rum balls for the reception. As she told me about her annual Gold Star reception contribution, I thought, why rum balls? Then she explained that the family of anyone honored under these circumstances deserved a little rum to get through the day. Then I understood that it got to the heart of what the day was about . . . Memorial events are bitter-sweet. They are days for great memories and storytelling, but there is a biting pain that comes with reminders of the loved one who didn't make it home.

Hero **Ham & Brie Sliders**

TIME: 15 MIN (PREP), 25 MIN (COOK)
MAKES: 20-24 SERVINGS

Ingredients

24 Hawaiian sweet rolls
¾ pound black forest deli ham, sliced
¾ pound munster or brie cheese
½ cup melted butter
1 tablespoon Dijon mustard
2 teaspoons dried, minced onion
2 teaspoons Worcestershire sauce
¼ teaspoons salt

Steps

1. Preheat the oven to 350°F.
2. Remove the Hawaiian sweet rolls from the package without tearing them apart. Carefully slice the entire loaf of rolls in half with a long serrated knife. Place the bottom half in a large baking sheet or pan.
3. Layer ham and cheese slices to cover the whole sheet of rolls. Place the remaining half of the loaf of rolls on top.
4. In a separate bowl, melt butter and mix in the Dijon mustard, minced onion, Worcestershire sauce, and salt.
5. Pour evenly over the top of the pan of rolls.
6. Cover the pan with aluminum foil and bake for 25 minutes. Cut the sandwiches apart and place on a serving platter. Best served warm.

CUSTOMS AND CAMARADERIE
Operation Red Wings and the "Memorial Day Murph"

Remembering the fallen by completing a Memorial Day Murph. *(Photo courtesy of Ruben Arriaga)*

We Honor in Remembrance. In June 2005, nearly four years after 9/11 and the Afghanistan invasion, four Navy SEALs were on a reconnaissance mission high in the mountains. When their position was compromised, a firefight erupted and all four SEALs were injured. Lt. Michael P. Murphy took exceptional risks to call for extraction. Answering the call, eight Navy SEALs and eight Army Night Stalkers responded in a Chinook faster than the armed attack helicopters could travel. The Chinook was shot down and all 16 onboard were killed. The four SEALs continued to battle the Taliban and ultimately only one survived.[4] The CrossFit "hero workout of the day" known as a "Murph" honors the courageous and selfless acts of Lt. Murphy during Operation Red Wings. It is among the most challenging physical workouts, but also known to many outside the military.[5]

4. LT Michael P. Murphy Navy SEAL Museum. (n.d.). *Operation Red Wings*. MurphySealMuseum. Accessed from from https://murphsealmuseum.org/operation-red-wings/

5. Smith, S. (2021, September 29). *What Are You Doing This Memorial Day? Try the Murph*. Military.com. Accessed from https://www.military.com/military-fitness/workouts/what-are-you-doing-this-memorial-day-try-the-murph

Three-Volley Salute **Lemon Dill Potato Salad**

TIME: 15 MIN (PREP), 20 MIN (COOK)
MAKES: 4 SERVINGS

- -

Ingredients

5-6 medium red potatoes

¼ cup olive oil

Juice of 1 lemon

2 tablespoons Dijon mustard

1½ tablespoons red wine vinegar

2 garlic cloves, finely minced

3 tablespoons flat leaf parsley, chopped

¼ teaspoon thyme

3-4 tablespoons fresh dill, chopped and divided

Salt & pepper to taste

½ small red onion, finely chopped

Steps

1. Bring a large pot of salted water to a boil.
2. Scrub potatoes and cut into ¼ inch slices.
3. Cook potatoes for about 15-20 minutes until fork tender.
4. Meanwhile, combine olive oil, lemon juice, Dijon mustard, red wine vinegar, garlic, parsley, thyme, 3 tablespoons dill weed, salt, and pepper in a medium mixing bowl.
5. Whisk a minute or two until thoroughly combined.
6. Drain potatoes well and place in a large serving bowl, along with chopped red onion.
7. Pour vinaigrette over potatoes and onion and gently combine.
8. Garnish with remaining chopped dill.
9. Serve immediately or store covered in the fridge for up to five days.

(Photo courtesy of Christine Trax)

TACTICAL TOPICS
Always Remember

Who do you know who didn't make it home? What did that person mean to you? How is their family doing now? Is there something special you do to honor that person?

Navy SEAL and his dad reunite after a deployment to Afghanistan. He suffered fatal injuries in a training jump just a few weeks later. *(Photo courtesy of Dan and Leslie Luna)*

THE WARRIOR'S TABLE

Until Valhalla **Stuffed Mushrooms**

TIME: 15 MIN (PREP), 35 MIN (COOK)
MAKES: 12-15 SERVINGS

Ingredients

1 quart or about 18 medium baby bella
mushrooms
1 small yellow onion, diced
8 ounces sweet or spicy Italian sausage
2 teaspoons minced garlic
½ teaspoon onion powder
6 ounces cream cheese
⅓ cup Parmesan cheese
⅓ cup shredded mozzarella cheese
2 tablespoon butter
1 tablespoon thyme, chopped (optional)

Steps

1. Preheat the oven to 375°F.
2. Remove the stem from the center of
each mushroom.
3. Set the mushroom caps aside and dice
the stems.
4. Remove sausage casings if using
sausage links. In a medium frying pan,
brown and crumble the sausage.
5. Drain all grease from the sausage pan,
then add in the diced onion, mushroom
stems, garlic, onion powder, and all
cheeses. Mix until it is well combined.
6. Melt the butter and brush it on to the
mushroom caps.
7. Fill each cap with the sausage mixture
and place on a baking sheet. Repeat
until all caps are filled.
8. Bake in the oven for 10-15 minutes.
9. Garnish with fresh thyme if desired.

(Photo courtesy of Bridgett Orr)

CUSTOMS AND CAMARADERIE
When the Missing Man is a Woman

We Honor in Remembrance. Most people think of a man when they think of a special operator, but sometimes the operator is in fact a woman. Throughout history women served in war, especially on the unconventional side. Senior Chief Petty Officer Shannon Kent was a US Navy Cryptologist, spouse of a former Green Beret, mother of two young boys, cancer survivor, and much more. The legend of Shannon Kent began long before her death because she was the epitome of what it meant to live a life marked by selflessness, purpose, excellence, and honor. The Kent's two sons are a testament of this as both are named to honor fallen SOF—one name is a tribute to Navy SEAL Blake Martson and the other in tribute to Green Beret Brett Walden. Shannon spoke nearly 11 languages including 5 dialects of Arabic, English, Spanish, French, Portuguese, Latin and others. Among Shannon's many military medals and awards, she was recognized as the DOD Linguist of the year in 2010 and the DIA HUMINT collector of the year in 2012. Shannon completed 4 combat deployments to Iraq and Afghanistan prior to her final deployment to Syria, primarily attached to SOF Teams as a Signals & Human Intelligence/Interpreter. (Personal details shared with MSOFC courtesy of Kent's sister, Mariah Smith. 2023.) Senior Chief Petty Officer Kent was killed by a suicide bomber in Manbij, Syria on January 16, 2019 along side Special Forces Chief Warrant Officer 2 Jonathan Farmer, former Navy SEAL Scott Wirtz, and Ghadir Taher, an American interpreter. Her dedication and achievements directly contributed to the kill or capture of over 300 high value targets and enemy insurgents.[6]

Senior Chief Petty Officer Shannon Kent deployed and in front of statue of Rojava in Syria and re-enlisting into continued service. (*Photo courtesy of Mariah Smith*)

6. Skovlund, M. (2022, April 18). *The Legend of Chief Shannon Kent*. Coffee or Die. Retrieved October 13, 2022, from https://www.coffeeordie.com/shannon-kent

Gold Star Lemon Gingersnaps

TIME: 20 MIN (PREP), 10 MIN (COOK)
MAKES: 6 SERVINGS

Ingredients

2 cups brown sugar
1 cup shortening or margarine
2 eggs
2 teaspoons lemon extract
¼ teaspoon butter flavoring
2 teaspoons baking soda
2 teaspoons cream of tartar
2 teaspoons ground ginger
1 teaspoon salt
3 cups flour
Granulated sugar for rolling

Steps

1. Cream sugar and shortening. Beat in eggs and extracts.
2. Add baking soda, cream of tartar, ginger, and salt, and mix well.
3. Mix in flour, 1 cup at a time.
4. Chill dough several hours or overnight.
5. Preheat oven to 375°F
6. Form into small balls and roll in a bowl of granulated sugar.
7. Place on an ungreased baking sheet. Do not flatten.
8. Bake for 7-9 minutes.

CUSTOMS AND CAMARADERIE
Symbols Tell a Story

Did You Know? Unit patches, branch insignia, and many other military symbols depict a part of a story of duty and service. The blue star and gold star are two symbols for the military family. Each tells a piece of the military family story. Beginning in World War I in 1917, the blue star banner became the symbol of a family with a deployed service member.[7] If the deployed service member died in service, the blue star on the banner is replaced by a gold star. These symbols recognize the sacrifice and honor that accompany service. In special operations units, Gold Star families hold a special place of honor. Each unit, team, and individual operator have varying traditions that remember the fallen. Some take a shot of whiskey, visit a memorial tree or grave site, or attend a special ceremony. Regardless of the practice, each loss is felt and remembered.[8]

---

7. The American Legion. (n.d.). *Blue Star Banner*. American Legion. Accessed from https://www.legion.org/troops/bluestar
8. U.S. Army. (n.d.). *Gold Star Survivors*. www.army.mil. Accessed from https://www.army.mil/goldstar/

Team memories are defining life moments that should always be remembered and never forgotten. *(Photo courtesy of Herb Thompson)*

Good American **Apple Crisp**

TIME: 15 MIN (PREP), 35 MIN (COOK)
MAKES: 6 SERVINGS

- -

Ingredients

Crumb Topping

½ cup all-purpose flour
½ cup rolled oats
⅓ cup brown sugar
½ teaspoon baking powder
¼ teaspoon ground cinnamon
⅓ cup unsalted butter, cut into small pieces
Dash of salt

Apple Filling

3-4 large Granny Smith apples
1 tablespoon lemon juice
2 tablespoons all-purpose flour
¼ cup brown sugar
½ teaspoon ground cinnamon
Dash of salt

Steps

1. Preheat the oven to 375°F.

2. Combine the crumb topping ingredients in a medium size bowl and mix with a fork or pastry blender until it resembles small crumbs. Refrigerate while you prepare the apple filling.

3. Peel and cut apples into bite sized pieces. Toss with lemon juice.

4. In a small bowl, combine flour with brown sugar, cinnamon, and salt.

5. Pour mixture over apples and toss to coat.

6. Pour apple mixture into an 8x8-inch baking dish and spread into an even layer.

7. Sprinkle crumb topping evenly over the apples.

8. Bake for 30-35 minutes or until golden brown and top is set.

9. Remove from the oven and allow to cool for at least 10 minutes before serving.

TIP: Serve with vanilla ice cream if desired.

VARIATION: You can make the apple filling ahead of time but add an extra splash of lemon juice to keep the apples from turning brown. Store in an air-tight container in the fridge for up to one day.

MAKE the crumble topping and store separately in the fridge.

TO FREEZE, prepare and bake the apple crisp as directed. Cool completely, then cover with a double layer of aluminum foil. Freeze for up to 3 months. Thaw overnight in the refrigerator, then warm in a 350°F oven for 20-25 minutes or until heated through.

YOU can also swap out the flour in the crumb topping for oat flour, spelt, or another whole grain for extra fiber.

Raise Your Glass **Pineapple Rum Punch**

TIME: 10 MIN (PREP)
MAKES: 10-12 SERVINGS

Ingredients

3 cups ginger ale or Sprite
3 cups pineapple juice
1 cup vanilla or coconut rum
1 cup fresh pineapple, diced
1 cup diced mango (optional)
¼ cup maraschino cherries (optional)

Steps

1. In a large pitcher, combine all liquid ingredients.
2. Dice the pineapple and other fruit, mix, and serve in a large punch bowl with a ladle for scooping.

VARIATION: If you need a kid-friendly version, simply substitute the rum for an extra cup of ginger ale or Sprite. You can also add/substitute the mango for strawberries or blueberries.

The best family friends travel the distance to celebrate milestone moments. *(Photo courtesy of Bridget Orr)*

Fancy, Formal, and Filling

MOST PEOPLE THINK ABOUT MILITARY BALLS when they hear about fancy military life moments, but we should expand our thinking on these "formal" opportunities. While most units host frequent balls, cocktail attire affairs, or other special events, those experiences are typically infrequent in the special operations community. Yes, they happen; but more often than not, they happen amid a deployment, a work trip, or some other practical barrier that pops up.

When a group of special operations guys dress up, something is about to go down. *(Photo courtesy of KaLea Lehman)*

Like us, you may miss the ball for years in a row. We rarely saw those oh-so-handsome dress uniforms or savored the treats on formal menus. But, it was okay. There is no need to hang your heart on a rare opportunity to go to a glitzy event. Whenever your glamorous opportunity comes, seize it! Unit Balls make for poignant memories and funny stories to retell. They put "meat on the bones" of quality time. Yet, if you find yourself waiting on the moments you expected to happen when you married into the special operations community, instead choose to overcome the hurdles and seize the moment to create memories with those close to you. Make the effort to attend "the far away" friend's wedding. Book a sitter and enjoy a special spa day. Hop on a flight or make the drive. Embrace a beach weekend get-away. Go on vacation. Explore the bucket-list adventure with friends or family, or say yes to an end of tour extravagant rendezvous. These experiences will be memories you can't replicate, but you can relive through pictures and the stories captured in each memory.

A Navy SEAL and his spouse at a formal unit event. *(Photo courtesy of Dan and Leslie Luna)*

A special operations family logs some together time in the run-up to a unit formal. *(Photo courtesy of Jennifer Caldwell)*

Mess Dress **Beef Wellington**

TIME: 30 MIN (PREP), 2 HOURS (COOK)
MAKES: 6-8 SERVINGS

- -

Ingredients

Mushroom Duxelles

1 pound fresh mushrooms
¼ cup butter
½ cup finely chopped shallot
1 garlic clove, minced
¼ cup snipped parsley
Salt and pepper to taste
½ cup dry sherry

Beef Wellington

2½ pounds center cut beef tenderloin
2 tablespoons soft butter
Salt and pepper
1 egg
1 tablespoon water
½ of a 17.3 ounce package Puff Pastry
    Sheets (1 sheet), thawed

Steps

1. Finely chop the mushrooms in a food processor.
2. Melt the butter in a nonstick skillet. Add the mushrooms, shallot, garlic, parsley, and a pinch of salt and pepper.
3. Cook the mushroom mixture on medium to medium-high until the liquid released by the mushrooms evaporates and the mushrooms appear dry and begin to brown.
4. Add the dry sherry and cook, stirring often, until the sherry evaporates and the mushrooms are cooked until dry.
5. Preheat the oven to 425°F.
6. Tie kitchen twine at several points around the tenderloin to retain shape and create an even piece of meat.

Spread butter over the top and sides of the meat. Season with salt and pepper.

7. Place the beef into a roasting pan and roast for 20 minutes or until an instant-read thermometer inserted into the beef reads 120°F.
8. Allow the meat to cool for at least 30 minutes. Remove the twine and pat dry with paper towels.
9. Reheat the oven to 425°F.
10. Beat the egg and water in a small bowl with a fork.
11. Prepare the work surface with a sprinkle of flour. Unfold the puff pastry sheet on the work surface. Roll the pastry sheet into a rectangle large enough to enclose the beef completely. Extend the pastry 3" on each side of the longest side of the beef.
12. Spread the mushroom duxelles onto the pastry sheet to within 1 inch of the edge. Place the beef in the center of the pastry. Fold the pastry over the beef and press to seal.
13. Place the beef seam-side down onto a baking sheet making sure all seams are sealed. Brush the pastry with the egg mixture.
14. Bake for 25 minutes or until the pastry is golden brown and an instant-read thermometer inserted into the beef reads 140°F.
15. Let rest for 10 minutes, and use a sharp knife to carefully cut the beef wellington into 1-inch slices for serving.

TIP: You can make the duxelles ahead of time and store or freeze for easy assembly of the beef wellington. You can decorate the beef wellington by using the extra pastry dough and small cookie cutter designs, such as holly leaves. Decorate the beef wellington with the cut outs after it is brushed with the egg mixture. Brush additional egg mixture on the decorations.

SOF STORIES
To Each Their Own — Angela

In almost 20 years, I can count how many balls we've attended (including semi formals) on one hand. Most military units have socials and formals frequently. Reflecting on these special occasions I have a bucket of memories and the only guiding theme is "to each their own." Our very first ball, our Team Sergeant insisted on going in a stretch Hummer, which wasn't our style, but it was hard to say no to his over-the-top excitement. That ball was on a river boat, and I froze the whole evening. I remember a real historical figure from the movie "Charlie Wilson's War" addressing us, and all I remember is how much more entertaining the movie was!

The next few events we attended I was super pregnant and re-wore the same bump-friendly gown. I remember admiring the pack of spouses who went together and danced the night away refusing to miss out because of a poorly-timed deployment. Those ladies knew every line dance there was, and more power to them for refusing to miss out due to a deployment rotation.

Then there was the formal where a Son Tay Raider spoke (the Son Tay Raiders conducted a mission to rescue American POWs held at a Vietnamese Prisoner of War Camp in 1970). My only memory is of my husband and his first sergeant waiting in line to shake his hand and get a picture. They were like two kids in a candy store, but instead of candy they wanted to witness living history. I could hardly get him on the dance floor, but he still talks about how cool it was to meet that raider.

Our last ball was equally unique because it was the end of an era for my husband and I, and a night to remember for others. We were the old ones nearing the end of our time on active duty service, and we were aware this would likely be our last gala. We felt awkward, but admired the teams gathering on the dance floor, living up the night, holding back nothing. We looked on, laughed, and embraced the team's spirit as they danced with their spouses and ran around the ballroom with their team guidon (the flag that signified their Special Forces team). They made the most of every moment.

Dress Blues **Ginger Carrot Soup**

TIME: 5 MIN (PREP), 20 MIN (COOK)
MAKES: 3-4 SERVINGS

- -

Ingredients

2 tablespoons coconut oil
2 garlic cloves, minced
½ yellow onion, finely diced
2-3 cups chopped carrots
2 cups vegetable broth
1 (14-ounce) can coconut milk
3 tablespoons fresh ginger, finely minced
salt and pepper, to taste

Steps

1. Place a saucepan over medium heat, add in coconut oil, garlic, and onions. Cook until onions are translucent.
2. Add carrots, broth, coconut milk, ginger, and a dash of salt and pepper. Cook until carrots are soft, about 12-15 minutes.
3. Use an immersion blender, food processor, or blender to mix until soup is smooth and creamy.
4. Top with a protein and some cilantro to kick it up.

CUSTOMS AND CAMARADERIE
Son Tay Raiders

Historic Highlight. The story of the Son Tay Raiders is legendary in the special operations community, especially among Special Forces and Air Force Special Operations. The raid was an extremely high risk mission to free prisoners of war (POWs) held by the North Vietnamese at the Son Tay POW camp. There were no casualties yet no rescued prisoners, as they had already been moved to other locations. Even still, the planning, expertise, and courage exemplified by the raiders still inspire special operators today. In many ways they demonstrated the value and capabilities of joint special operations missions and set the bar for future generations of elite warfighters.[9]

The moment of a lifetime. A conversation with a Son Tay Raider. *(Photo courtesy of KaLea Lehman)*

9. Isby, D. C. (2021, November 23). *The Son Tay Raid*. Defense Media Network. Accessed from https://www.defensemedianetwork.com/stories/son-tay-raid-50-years-november-21-1970-special-operations-vietnam-war/

Service Dress **Smoked Salmon and Cucumber**

TIME: 15 MIN (PREP)
MAKES: 6 SERVINGS

Ingredients

½ loaf bread
8 ounces whipped cream cheese
1 teaspoon minced garlic
2 tablespoons fresh dill, chopped
1 English cucumber
½ pound smoked salmon
1 thinly sliced lemon (optional)

Steps

1. Toast the bread and cut each slice into 4 triangles.
2. In a separate bowl, combine the cream cheese, garlic, and dill.
3. Spoon about 1 teaspoon of cream cheese mixture over a toast triangle and top with a thin slice of cucumber.
4. Spoon ½ teaspoon of cream cheese mixture and top with a small piece of smoked salmon.
5. Garnish with a lemon slice, if desired.

(Photo courtesy of Bridget Orr)

CUSTOMS AND CAMARADERIE
Rarely-Worn Uniform Explainer

Did You Know? Special operators operate at full speed chasing the mission, adventure, or goals. So, the opportunity to fully dress up is rarely called for. When that rare occasion arrives you'll find them tediously preparing their dress uniform. Just like their conventional brothers and sisters in their service branch when formal times happen, special operations service members dress to the nines.[10] Can you match who wears what uniform?

1. Navy
2. Army
3. Marine Corps
4. Air Force

A. Evening Dress Uniform (hint: This uniform features a red or scarlet cummerbund)

B. Mess Dress Uniform (hint: This uniform is not worn with a name tag or hat/cover)

C. Blue Mess Dress Uniform (hint: This uniform honors George Washington and the troops who served under him)

D. Dinner Dress Uniform (hint: This uniform can be worn a variety of ways featuring both blue or white uniform pieces)

Answer Key: 1:D, 2:C, 3:A, 4:B

10. VeteranLife. (2022, February 4). *U.S. Military Dress Uniforms: What Each Branch Wears To Look Their Best*. VeteranLife. Accessed from https://veteranlife.com/lifestyle/military-dress-uniforms/

Rare Moment Sweet or Savory Whipped Cheese

TIME: 10 MIN (PREP), 10 MIN (COOK)
MAKES: 4 SERVINGS

Whipped Ricotta with Balsamic Glazed Berries

2 cups whole fat ricotta cheese

2 tablespoons sugar

1 cup balsamic vinegar

2 tablespoons honey

4 cup berries (blackberries, strawberries, raspberries)

2 tablespoons chopped mint

2 tablespoons thinly sliced basil

Steps

1. In a food processor, whip together ricotta and sugar for 1 minute.
2. In a small saucepan, heat balsamic vinegar and honey over medium-low heat until vinegar reduces in half and let cool.
3. In a small bowl, mix together berries, cooled balsamic reduction and fresh herbs.
4. Serve berries over whipped ricotta.
5. Garnish with mint and basil.

Whipped Goat Cheese with Rosemary Bacon and Dates

6 slices bacon

12 dates

1 tablespoon chopped rosemary

8 ounces cream cheese or chevre

2 tablespoons extra virgin olive oil

½ teaspoon paprika

1 garlic clove, minced

½ teaspoon sea salt

2-4 tablespoons honey

Steps

1. Preheat the oven to 400°F.
2. Place bacon, dates, and rosemary on a foiled lined baking sheet.
3. Bake for 15-20 minutes or until bacon is cooked.
4. Meanwhile, in a food processor, whip together cream cheese, olive oil, paprika, garlic, and salt for 1-2 minutes.
5. Spoon cheese into a serving bowl.
6. Chop bacon and dates over whipped cheese.
7. Drizzle with honey and serve.

 TACTICAL TOPICS

Dinner Daydream

If you could do any special thing you wanted with no limitations of money or location, what would it be? Who would be with you? Would you go to Paris and dine in the Eiffel Tower at night? Would you enjoy a brunch at the White House, walk a red carpet event, or simply choose a quiet dinner for two?

(Photo courtesy of KaLea Lehman)

Missing Man **Manchego, Prosciutto, and Olive Salad**

TIME: 15 MIN (PREP)
MAKES: 6 SERVINGS

Ingredients

1 yellow bell pepper

6 ounces Manchego cheese, sliced

1 (8-ounce) jar spanish black olives or kalamata olives

2 teaspoons minced garlic

¼ pound prosciutto or 5 pieces of cooked maple bacon, chopped

2 teaspoons white wine vinegar

3 tablespoons olive oil

1 teaspoon fresh rosemary

1 tablespoon chopped cilantro

Pita chips

Steps

1. Dice the bell pepper or slice into 1 inch strips.
2. Combine cheese, olives, minced garlic, and prosciutto or bacon in a salad bowl.
3. Combine the vinegar, olive oil, rosemary, and cilantro in a small bowl then pour the dressing over the salad ingredients.
4. Chill until ready to serve.
5. Serve with plain or seasoned pita chips.

SOF STORIES
A Little Black Dress Occasion — Kati

One year during our unit's reunion week my husband and I were invited to an evening social hosted by the local Special Forces Association. I didn't know what to expect, but I was grateful it wasn't a fancy ball that came with hours of prep or a giant babysitter tab. It turned out to be a simple evening that was perfect for a comfortable little black dress. It was a thoughtfully catered night with friends we served with for a decade.

The speakers told stories highlighting the heart of the community we were blessed to be part of. But for some reason, the image in my head that stands out most from that night was a small table in the front of the hall set aside for those who never made it home. The evening was not a night about prisoners of war or the fallen. It was a legacy event for the unit. Yet amid the delicious dishes and sweet moments with friends, that table was a very real reminder to stand straight and keep your friends and family close. Sweet moments like this event were to be appreciated and savored. Our community was hard, but there is no doubt we live each day grounded in our values worth fighting for.

FID **Flourless Chocolate Cake**

TIME: 20 MIN (PREP), 50 MIN (COOK)
MAKES: 16 SERVINGS

- -

Ingredients

½ cup water

¼ teaspoon salt

¾ cup granulated sugar

18 ounces bittersweet chocolate

1 cup unsalted butter

6 eggs

Steps

1. Preheat the oven to 300°F.
2. Grease one 10 inch round cake pan and set aside.
3. In a small saucepan over medium heat combine the water, salt, and sugar. Stir until completely dissolved and set aside.
4. Either in the top half of a double boiler or in a microwave oven, melt the bittersweet chocolate. Pour the chocolate into the bowl of an electric mixer.
5. Cut the butter into pieces and beat the butter into the chocolate, 1 piece at a time.
6. Beat in the hot sugar-water.
7. Slowly beat in the eggs, one at a time.
8. Pour the batter into the prepared pan.
9. Put the cake pan in the larger pan and fill the pan with boiling water halfway up the sides of the cake pan.
10. Bake cake in the water bath for 45 minutes. The center will still look wet.
11. Chill cake overnight in the pan.
12. To unmold, dip the bottom of the cake pan in hot water for 10 seconds and invert onto a serving plate.

CUSTOMS AND CAMARADERIE
The Missing Man Table

Did You Know? Military traditions and practices are steeped in significance. They give meaning to the day-to-day sacrifices that accompany service. Everywhere you look, whether it is a uniform or around a unit, there are symbols that tell a story embodied by excellence, honor, duty, and sacrifice. Formal balls, mock dining-ins, and other celebratory occasions are no different. You will find a small, round table waiting in a prominent spot, and designated for the guest of honor – the service member who never came home. The Prisoner of War/Missing in Action table is dressed in white, typically set for one with an upside-down glass, and hosts a Bible, solitary candle and vase wrapped in yellow ribbon holding a red rose. Finally, a plate rests with a slice of lemon and a small pile of salt.[11] These symbols represent:

- Round table: Our enduring concern
- White table cloth: Pure motive in service
- Bible or religious text: Faith in their return
- Red Rose: Service member's life and that of their family
- Upside down glass: Inability to toast
- Lemon slice: Bitter fate of those captured or missing
- Pile of salt: Tears of the missing and their families
- Empty chair: Their absence[12]

The presence of this table means that regardless of the cause for celebration and play, those attending never venture far from the duty, sacrifice, and seriousness of their service.

11. U.S. Department of Defense. (2021, September 15). *The POW/MIA or Missing Man Table*. Accessed from https://www.defense.gov/external-content/story/Article/2776327/the-powmia-or-missing-man-table/

12. Virginia War Memorial Foundation. (n.d.). *The Missing Man Table*. Virginia War Memorial. Accessed from https://vawarmemorial.org/the-missing-man-table/

Father and sons return from a duck hunt.
(Photo courtesy of Cher and Jay Powers)

6. Kill it and Grill it

★ ★ ★

MANY IN OUR SPECIAL OPERATIONS COMMUNITY hunt for food—and for adventure. Deer, bear, or ram hunt, gator catch, or deep sea fishing . . . Name any wild game and they've stalked it. Following snake-eating exploits in SERE school or experiencing Syrian-served mystery meat, the opportunity to chase an American boar is just plain exciting. Even those who grew up in the city or a less outdoorsy family possess a similar drive to explore, push limits, and do what few others can physically or mentally do. They are gone before the sun rises or out until it sets, preparing for the next mission, buying new gear, or training-up the next generation to succeed at all costs. It is simply built into their spirit.

Hunting becomes a family quality-time tradition for some. (*Photo courtesy of John and Angie McLaughlin*)

An ODA at dinner. (*Photo courtesy of KaLea Lehman*)

For those of us at home, we join the adventure when possible and soak up quality time even if it demands we rough it. We are along for the ride, wild as it may be, unless the need arises to make the case for a vacation (which is sometimes necessary). We don't take the catch or the story for granted. Instead we anticipate the opportunity to savor the juicy venison burger with friends or reminisce with our family over classic American meatloaf. It can be a little wild (like that darn ram meat that needed extra sage) but it is part of our story. We do our best to prepare for each season.

Tip of the Spear

- -

SPECIAL OPERATORS ARE FIRST TO GO TO WAR and last to return home. SOF are the unknown, often quiet boots on the ground. In small teams or flying solo, they train partner forces, set the conditions for success, and serve as "eyes on the ground." They can be found slipping in and out of danger without being noticed or soaring in the skies above. Sometimes they sweep into places that house terror for a quick hit. They meet the needs of the nation when and where duty calls. Our units stand ready, and we keep the homefront humming along, however that looks, in each of our homes.

Sweet Moments. A surprise return home. *(Photo courtesy of John and Angie McLaughlin)*

We see the new gear roll in, listen to their stories and frustrations, see them off again, anticipate their return, and repeat it over and over. Being in the special operations community means embracing the adventure by focusing on the "hunt," goal, or priority of the moment. To make it through a season—any season—you have to recognize and focus on the skills they hone for the hunt, their appetite for adventure, and the pride they have in executing the mission or hunting expedition with excellence. Sometimes the hunt can get exhausting. We felt like we were always waiting for the catch. In those moments, we had to get creative to cook up a decent dish. We called on our friends for company and tips and together we pulled together the right seasonings to salvage the game and the moment.

To withstand the risk and uncertainty of it all, our families have to maintain a pantry stocked with a few staple ingredients (awareness of the need for self-less, military service) and distinctive seasonings (an appreciation for the unique, hard, and high demands of our units). If these key ingredients ran low, we had to step in, with boldness and honesty, and revisit the ground rules of our warrior's table (see page 18). There we found the energy for the next season of our adventure together.

(Opposite) Afghan table spread *(Photo courtesy of Hilary Peters)*

Bagging a wild turkey
(Photo courtesy of John and Angie McLaughlin)

Gray Eagles' Bacon-Wrapped Wild Turkey

TIME: 2 HOURS (PREP), 20 MIN (COOK)
MAKES: 6 SERVINGS

Ingredients

¼ cup olive oil

2 tablespoons white vinegar

2 tablespoons Worcestershire sauce

½ teaspoon ground pepper

1 teaspoon garlic powder

1 teaspoon salt

1 tablespoons brown sugar

1½ pounds wild turkey, cut into 1½ inch cubes

1 pound bacon

2 fresh jalapeño peppers, cut into slices lengthwise

Steps

1. Prepare the marinade by mixing olive oil, white vinegar, Worcestershire sauce, pepper, garlic powder, salt, and brown sugar in a medium bowl.

2. Toss in the turkey cubes to coat, and marinate for at least 2 hours.

3. Cut each piece of bacon in half. Place one slice of jalapeño and one cube of turkey in the center of the bacon slice. Tightly roll bacon over turkey and hold in place with a toothpick.

4. Heat grill to medium heat, around 300-350°F.

5. Place rolls on sides and cook slowly, turning every few minutes.

6. Be sure to keep a spray bottle handy because you will be chasing flare-ups from the bacon grease the entire time.

7. Once the bacon is fully cooked, your meat should also be fully cooked.

8. Let stand for 5 minutes before serving. If you are making these for a gathering, they can sit in a warm oven until ready to serve.

VARIATION: You can also cook these on a pan on the stovetop.

SWAP out fresh jalapeño peppers for canned or jarred jalapeño peppers.

SOF STORIES
Wild Turkey — Claire

I'll never forget the time my husband went on a work trip, hunting turkey. I had never prepared wild turkey before, and I just stood in the kitchen staring down two of the largest turkey breasts I have ever seen. Unsure of what I was doing I cleaned the meat and pulled out some stray feathers. Then, I suddenly felt a very small, hard object. I worked at it, and out slid buck shot! Forty-five minutes later I had a small bowl of buck shot and some mighty fine, wild turkey breasts. That was a first I didn't expect, like so many we've experienced in this unit, but at least this one left a tasty mark!

Dam Neck Next-Level Kebabs

TIME: 6-8 HOURS (PREP), 30 MIN (COOK)

MAKES: 6 SERVINGS

- -

Ingredients

Steak Kebab Ingredients

½ cup vegetable oil

¼ cup soy sauce

3 tablespoons brown sugar

1 tablespoon vinegar

½ teaspoon ginger

1 teaspoon minced garlic

1½ pounds beef sirloin steak

Vegetable Ingredients

3 portobello mushrooms

1 red onion

1 yellow onion

3 bell peppers (any color)

1 zucchini

Citrus Glazed Chicken and Shrimp Kebab Ingredients

¼ cup BBQ sauce of choice

2 tablespoons soy sauce

2 tablespoons brown sugar

2 tablespoons lemon or pineapple juice

1 pound boneless chicken breast or thighs, cut in 1 inch cubes

½ pound uncooked medium shrimp, peeled and deveined

Steps

1. Combine the oil, soy sauce, brown sugar, vinegar, ginger, and garlic to use as a marinade.
2. Dice the steak into approximately 1 inch cubes, and place in a plastic bag or glass dish to refrigerate in the marinade.
3. Steak will have the most flavor if it sits in marinade for 6-8 hours, but this can be shortened if you are short on time.
4. When ready to assemble skewers, soak wood skewers in water for 15-20 minutes.
5. Chop vegetables into 1 inch pieces. Set aside until skewer assembly.
6. Next, prepare the sauce for the chicken and shrimp kebabs. Mix the BBQ and soy sauce, brown sugar, and juice. Set aside.
7. Skewer the marinated steak, alternating with vegetables. Repeat with chicken and shrimp.
8. Glaze the chicken and shrimp with the sauce prepared in step 6.
9. Grill steak kabobs over medium heat for 12-15 minutes or until the meat is cooked to preference. Rotate skewers every 4-5 minutes.
10. Chicken should be grilled over medium heat for about 7 -8 minutes. Make sure to rotate skewers every 4-5 minutes.
11. Grill shrimp kebabs for 2-3 minutes on each side until the color is pink and shrimp is opaque.

(Photo courtesy of Wendy Jo Peterson)

 **WAR GAMES**
Bear Hunt

Going on a bear hunt, going to pack a . . . Go around the table and take turns naming something you would need to go on bear hunt. Then, share what makes that part of your essential gear, but don't let your pack get too heavy!

Red Horse **Chicken Cacciatore**

TIME: 15 MIN (PREP), 30 MIN (COOK)
MAKES: 4 SERVINGS

Ingredients

Cooking spray
1 pound chicken thighs
1 teaspoon dried oregano
½ teaspoon dried basil
¼ teaspoon crushed red pepper
2 cups sliced mushrooms
¾ cup bell pepper
1½ cups tomato-basil pasta sauce
¼ cup red wine
Salt to taste
¼ teaspoon black pepper
½ cup Parmesan cheese

Steps

1. Heat a large non-stick skillet over medium-high heat. Coat pan with cooking spray.
2. Sprinkle chicken thighs evenly with oregano, basil, and red pepper. Sauté 2 minutes or until lightly browned.
3. Add mushrooms and bell pepper to the pan and sauté for 5 minutes.
4. Stir in pasta sauce and wine. Bring to a simmer. Cover, reduce heat, and simmer for 20 minutes.
5. Stir in salt and black pepper. Sprinkle with cheese.

VARIATION: You can swap out the wine for broth if desired. If you prefer boneless chicken, reduce simmering time by about half to avoid rubbery chicken, but be sure it's cooked through.

(Photo courtesy of Wendy Jo Peterson)

CUSTOMS AND CAMARADERIE
Raids that Made Waves

Did You Know? The special operations community performs many missions, but of all the difficult, special missions they conduct, the most well-known are those tied to direct action. Can you match which units led the way in these kill and capture missions and raids?

1. 2011: Abbottabad Raid and Osama Bin Laden
2. 2003: Ad Dawr Raid and Saddam Hussein
3. 2019: Syrian Raid and Abu Bakr al-Baghdadi
4. 1945: Raid on Cabanatuan Prison to free POWs

A. Operation Red Dawn led by Special Operations Task Force 121 (1st Special Forces Operational Detachment—Delta and supported by many other special operations elements)
B. Led by 1st Special Forces Operational Detachment—Delta
C. Operation Neptune Spear led by Navy SEALs, supported by 160th SOAR and other special operations
D. Led by Army Rangers and supported by Philippine guerrillas

Answer: 1:C, 2:A, 3:B, 4:D [13] [14] [15] [16] [17]

Rangers deployed. *(Photo courtesy Paul Lushenko)*

13. Osborn, K., & Lin, H. (2022, April 6). *The operation that took out Osama bin Laden*. Military.com. Accessed from https://www.military.com/history/osama-bin-laden-operation-neptune-spear
14. Sof, E. (2022, April 4). *Task Force 121: The Capture of Saddam Hussein*. Accessed from https://special-ops.org/task-force-121-saddam-hussein-capture/
15. USAICoE Command History Office. (2013, December 6). *Operation RED DAWN nets Saddam Hussein*. www.army.mil. Accessed from https://www.army.mil/article/116559/operation_red_dawn_nets_saddam_hussein
16. Sisk, R. (2019, October 27). *ISIS Leader Baghdadi Killed In Daring Special Ops Nighttime Raid In Syria*. Military.com. Accessed from https://www.military.com/daily-news/2019/10/27/isis-leader-baghdadi-killed-daring-special-ops-nighttime-raid-syria.html
17. Krivdo, M. E. (2018, November 2). *Rescue at Cabanatuan*. U.S. Army Special Operations History. Accessed from https://arsof-history.org/articles/v14n2_cabanatuan_page_1.html

JSOC Venison Chili

TIME: 30 MIN (PREP), 3 HOURS (COOK)
MAKES: 6 SERVINGS

- -

Ingredients

12-16 dried chiles—any combination of
  ancho, guajillo, pasilla, or mulato chiles
1 cup black coffee
½ pound chopped bacon
2-3 pounds venison, ground or diced
1 large yellow or white onion, diced
6-8 garlic cloves, chopped
2 tablespoons sweet or smoked paprika
2 tablespoons cumin
1 tablespoon ground coriander
1 tablespoon chipotle powder (optional)
Salt to taste
3 tablespoons tomato paste
3 tablespoons molasses (optional)
1 quart beef broth
2 (14.5-ounce) cans pinto or black beans
Cilantro, shredded cheese, and pickled
  onions to garnish

Steps

1. Remove the stems and seeds of chiles
   and tear them into pieces. Cover with
   boiling water and let stand for 30
   minutes.
2. Grind to a purée with the consistency of
   gravy, adding the coffee and about 1 cup
   of the soaking water.

3. Meanwhile, fry the bacon over medium
   heat in a Dutch oven or other large,
   lidded, oven-proof pot. Once the bacon
   is crispy, remove it and set aside.
4. Add the venison and brown over high
   heat, stirring occasionally. Salt it as it
   cooks.
5. Once all the meat is ready, add the
   onion to the pot and cook for 5 minutes,
   stirring often. Add the garlic, stir and
   cook for 1 minute.
6. Add the paprika, cumin, coriander,
   chipotle powder and salt one at a time,
   stirring to combine each time. Add chile
   purée and tomato paste and stir to
   combine well.
7. Add the molasses and enough beef
   broth to cover everything. Stir to combine all this well, bring to a bare simmer
   and cook gently for 3 hours or so,
   stirring occasionally.
8. Put the lid halfway over the pot as it
   cooks. You want it to eventually cook
   down and be thick.
9. Add beans and bacon for the last 20
   minutes of cooking.
10. Serve the chili with rice or cornbread
    and top with cilantro, cheese, and some
    pickled onions.

TIP: If you need to leave the house, put the chili in a 325°F oven, covered. I strongly advise
you to stick to the types of chiles I list: anchos, guajillos, pasilla, New Mexican, etc. This
prevents you from blowing everyone's heads off with heat. You can always make it hotter
later.

VARIATION: Literally any meat works here, and if you want to go vegetarian, use chopped
mushrooms.

No gift more cool for a little boy than this rack from a Green Beret who loves to hunt. *(Photo courtesy of KaLea Lehman)*

TACTICAL TOPICS
Practical Support

What is one action you take to support your family that you are most proud of? What is one thing you do for your family that is mundane? How did you first take on this chore?

Chow Time Campfire **Conikai**

TIME: 15 MIN (PREP), 45 MIN (COOK)
MAKES: 4-6 SERVINGS

- -

Ingredients

6 large Idaho or russet potatoes, sliced thinly

2 medium yellow onions, sliced

12 ounces beef or turkey kielbasa or smoked sausage, sliced

1 head of cabbage, sliced

¼ cup butter

1 teaspoon salt

Pepper to taste

½ cup of shredded cheddar cheese (optional)

½ cup of shredded mozzarella cheese (optional)

Steps

1. Lay out 30" x 12" rectangles of heavy duty aluminum foil and rub with butter.

2. Layer the cabbage, potatoes, and onions in the center of the foil.

3. Sprinkle it with salt and pepper and place small pieces of butter on the vegetables.

4. Add the sausage slices to the top of the vegetables, then fold the sides up to close the foil. The foil should be folded up so it is crimped tightly and the food is fully enclosed. Extra foil may be needed to fully enclose the ingredients.

5. Place on grill, and over medium heat for 40 minutes.

6. Open the foil packets and add cheese to the top of the foils for 5 minutes if cheese is desired.

7. Serve and enjoy!

VARIATION: Sliced steak can be used as a sausage substitute.

Away but chilling by the fire *(Photo courtesy of KaLea Lehman)*

Fish it and Dish it

LIKE OUTDOOR SPORTS, THE SPECIAL OPERATIONS FAMILY goes through seasons. Some seasons mount a great challenge and sometimes the catch seems elusive. Learning the ropes of the wild outdoors demands real skills, unique knowledge, a heap of personal discipline, and some direct action. The challenge is developing the skills you will need ahead, in preparation for consequential moments. This challenge mounts with time, experience, and responsibility, regardless of whether you are the special operations family member or the service member.

Nice catch on a day at the lake. (*Photo courtesy of John and Angie McLaughlin*)

Sports like deep sea fishing, fly fishing, and spearfishing require strength, patience and balance. Special operations families also must hone these skills. We ride along in the boat and breach the waves if only to capture the moment of the trophy catch. Sometimes we have to make tough calls, and we need thick skin to wait out an unplanned adventure. And in other times, waiting out the storm or rough water is the wrong answer. When rough waters grow too familiar, boldness is just as necessary as patience. This is the real challenge of this lifestyle. A false front of strength and patience only weakens the family and risks losing the catch of a lifetime.

A SEAL kid fly fishing. (*Photo courtesy of Andrea Geraldi*)

This is especially true for the families of special operations leaders of any level. What keeps a team, a unit, and our whole force strong begins with our relationships at home. This isn't a job that floats out of service members' thoughts when they walk through the door. At some point, their work will come home in their head or on the phone. Short fuses and mealtime tension happen, especially between trips home and away. There may be a secret gorilla weighing on their back (or yours), and family can help set the conditions for it to depart. There may be a funny story that can engage the senses and spur rewarding family interactions.

A flash flood in the desert, a blizzard in the mountains, goat brains or bugs—we all have a story that can be told or jobs we can dish out. Encourage little hands to take on mealtime responsibilities, like lighting a candle or setting the table. It helps channel excitement and energy when everyone has a role in making meal-time work.[18]

Embrace the journey, thrive with authenticity, and develop a respect for the mission of our special operations community. Over time, we learned this recipe and we were proud to serve the dishes that few others could catch.

Kids on a National Seashore where Great Whites frequent. *(Photo courtesy of KaLea Lehman)*

18. The Family Dinner Project. 2019. Eat, Laugh, Talk: The Family Dinner Playbook. Familius LLC.

Command Commitment Crab Cakes

TIME: 45 MIN (PREP), 15 MIN (COOK)
MAKES: 6 SERVINGS

- -

Ingredients

1 large egg

¼ cup mayonnaise

2 teaspoons Dijon mustard

2 teaspoons Worcestershire sauce

1 teaspoon Old Bay seasoning (or more for a bigger kick)

1 teaspoon fresh lemon juice, plus more for serving

⅛ teaspoon salt

1 pound fresh lump crab meat

⅔ cup Saltine cracker crumbs (about 14 crackers)

Steps

1. Whisk the egg, mayonnaise, parsley, Dijon mustard, Worcestershire sauce, Old Bay, lemon juice, and salt together in a large bowl.
2. Place the crab meat on top, followed by the cracker crumbs.
3. With a rubber spatula or large spoon (or even your hands!), very gently and carefully fold together. You don't want to break up that crab meat.
4. Cover tightly and refrigerate for at least 30 minutes and up to 1 day.
5. Preheat the oven to 450°F.
6. Generously grease a rimmed baking sheet with nonstick spray or line with a silicone baking mat.
7. Using a ½ cup measuring cup, portion the crab cake mixture into 6 mounds on the baking sheet. Don't flatten them.
8. Use your hands or a spoon to compact each individual mound so there aren't any lumps sticking out or falling apart.
9. Bake for 12-14 minutes or until lightly browned around the edges and on top.
10. Drizzle each with fresh lemon juice and serve warm.
11. Cover leftover crab cakes tightly and refrigerate for up to 5 days or freeze for up to 3 months.

VARIATION: The Commissary and Costco sometimes sell Philips brand crabmeat in a can, if you can't get fresh locally. You can also try Dungeness Crab!

(Photo courtesy of Andrea Geraldi)

SOF STORIES
Command Commitments — Allison

It seemed we were always being pushed to attend various Team functions. Family time was rare so added events can get exhausting. I'd ask, "Whose house?" "Do I even know them?" "Why are we obligated to go, again?" I tried to get out of so many events, only to be guilted into joining my husband. Truthfully, I really enjoyed seeing everyone from the Team, and when we got home, I always told my husband that I was glad I went. And every time, he gave me that familiar look of "I know!"

When we moved to Virginia Beach I quickly learned not to hesitate on joining any function, as they were usually held at Chick's Oyster Bar. I loved the feeling of being on the bay and hearing the seagulls around me. I also loved how the music was jamming, the keg was flowing and people were chatting away, having a great time. These were the years right after 9/11 and the Iraq War broke out and our lives were flipped upside down. But we always knew we could count on a good time at Chick's, and even more importantly, a great crab cake.

Red Rose **Salmon and Broccoli** with Chile-Caper Vinaigrette

TIME: 15 MIN (PREP), 30 MIN (COOK)
MAKES: 4 SERVINGS

Ingredients

1 head of broccoli, cut into florets
4 tablespoons olive oil, divided
Salt and pepper
4 (6-ounce) skinless salmon filets
1 red Fresno chile or jalapeño, thinly sliced into rings, seeds removed if desired
2 tablespoons unseasoned rice vinegar
2 tablespoons drained capers

Steps

1. Preheat the oven to 400°F.
2. Toss broccoli florets and 2 tablespoons oil on a large rimmed baking sheet. Season with salt and pepper.
3. Roast, tossing occasionally, until browned and crisp-tender, 12–15 minutes.
4. Remove the baking sheet from the oven and rub salmon with 1 tablespoon oil and season with salt and pepper.
5. Push broccoli to edges of baking sheet and place salmon in the center. Roast until salmon is opaque throughout, 10–15 minutes.
6. Meanwhile, combine chile, vinegar, and a pinch of salt in a small bowl and let sit until chiles are slightly softened, about 10 minutes.
7. Mix in capers and remaining 1 tablespoon oil. Season with salt and pepper.
8. Serve salmon and broccoli drizzled with chile vinaigrette.

Authentically smoked salmon lights up the imagination and tummy of the whole family.
(Photo courtesy of Angie McLaughlin)

SOF STORIES

The Brilliance of a Candle — Kevin

I grew-up having dinner with my family. We clung tight to this tradition in our home, but it hasn't always been easy. When I left active duty my kids were young, and dinner was chaos. It would be enough movement and noise that conversation felt impossible. My temper would flash, and I just couldn't take it. I needed a calmer table to join my family.

The holiday season came and there were candles on the table, and the kids all clamored to light them. My wife let them light the candles, and our two kids sat still just fascinated

A simple family Thanksgiving dinner with candle-light and littles. *(Photo courtesy of KaLea Lehman)*

by the flame. That holiday meal was like an "ah-ha" moment for us. We started lighting candles for each family dinner. The kids had to take turns lighting the candles and then blowing them out. It quickly became a dinner responsibility they were proud to earn. Dinner became less chaotic, and we slowly started having great family conversations. I never would've guessed such a small thing would make such a huge difference in our evening routine and family life.

Legion of **Baked Baby Scallops**

TIME: 5 MIN (PREP), 20 MIN (COOK)
MAKES: 6 SERVINGS

Ingredients

2 cups frozen baby scallops, thawed
4 tablespoons butter, melted
½ cup seasoned bread crumbs or Panko
1 teaspoon onion powder
1 teaspoon garlic powder
3 garlic cloves, minced
¼ cup of Parmesan cheese
½ teaspoon parsley (optional)
Red pepper (optional)

Steps

1. Preheat the oven to 400°F.
2. Stir all ingredients together in a bowl. Place in a glass cooking dish.
3. Bake for 20 minutes and serve.

TACTICAL TOPICS
My Waves

What is your favorite water sport? Why do you enjoy it so much? If you could do this sport anywhere in the world, where would that be?

Family fishing outing on the Gulf.
(Photo courtesy of Jennifer Caldwell)

SOCOM **Shrimp & Grits**

TIME: 5 MIN (PREP), 50 MIN (COOK)
MAKES: 6-8 SERVINGS

Ingredients

1 cup uncooked grits
1 teaspoon salt
6 tablespoons butter, divided
4 teaspoon minced garlic, divided
1 pound medium or large shrimp, shelled
   and deveined
1 cup cheddar cheese

Steps

1. In a saucepan, boil 4 cups of water. Add grits, salt, and 2 tablespoons butter and stir regularly.

2. Allow the grits to simmer for about 30-40 minutes until it thickens. Stir grits occasionally while they simmer.

3. Meanwhile, ensure shrimp are thawed and remove the tails.

4. Add the remainder of the butter and 2 teaspoons of garlic to a medium frying pan.

5. Once the butter is melted, add the shrimp to sauté.

6. Return to grits and add in 2 teaspoons garlic and cheddar cheese and stir.

7. Serve shrimp over a plate of fresh grits.

VARIATION: The shrimp can also be prepared over medium heat on a grill. Just combine ingredients on a grill pan and cook for 8-10 minutes on the open grill.

 # CUSTOMS AND CAMARADERIE
To Don a Dagger

Did You Know? Knives have many purposes, both in battle and in day-to-day life. In special operations, certain blades have deep ties to military history. Recognizing the utility and historical meaning, some units give an operator a dagger upon their selection to special operations. For Special Forces it is often a Yarborough Knife, inspired by the "father of modern Special Forces," Lt. Gen. William P. Yarborough.[19] For Navy SEALs and often Marine Raiders, the KA-BAR knife is the favored gift.[20]

19. *The Yarborough Knife: Symbol of a legacy*. Professional soldiers. (2010, March 28). Acessed from https://www.professionalsoldiers.com/forums/showthread.php?t=28311
20. KA-BAR. (n.d.). *About*. Kabar. Accessed from https://www.kabar.com/customer/aboutUs.jsp;

Cunning, Speed, Surprise **Salmon Chowder**

TIME: 15 MIN (PREP), 30 MINS (COOK)
MAKES: 8 SERVINGS

- -

Ingredients

½ cup butter, melted
½ cup flour
3 cups chicken broth
3 tablespoons butter
2 stalks celery, diced
1 onion, chopped
1 teaspoon minced garlic
5 potatoes, diced
3 carrots, diced
1 teaspoon salt
1 teaspoon pepper
1 teaspoon dried dill weed
2 (16-ounce) cans salmon, drained
1 (15-ounce) can corn, drained, or 1 ½ cup
    frozen corn
1 (12-ounce) can evaporated milk or 1 ½
    cups heavy cream
1 cup shredded cheddar cheese (optional)

Steps

1. In a medium pan, sauté the onion, celery, and garlic in 3 tablespoons of butter.
2. In a large stew pot, stir ½ cup melted butter and flour until they form a thick slurry. Make sure to keep stirring or it will burn.
3. Slowly whisk in the 3 cups of chicken broth.
4. Add the sauté mixture to the large pot of broth. Stir in potatoes, carrots, salt, pepper, and dill. Bring to a boil, reduce heat, and let simmer for 20 minutes.
5. Drain the canned salmon and make sure to check for bones.
6. Stir in salmon, corn, evaporated milk, and cheese, and cook until the chowder is hot throughout, stirring occasionally.
7. Garnish with more dill and serve with warm bread.

VARIATIONS: To make with fresh baked salmon or leftover salmon, just substitute with approximately 1 pound of baked salmon. Drizzle fresh salmon filets with olive oil and salt. Set the oven to 400°F and bake for about 12-15 minutes. Chop the salmon up and toss in the chowder.

TO make **clam chowder**, substitute the 2 large cans of salmon with 4 well drained, (6.5 ounce) cans of clams. Omit and do not include the cheddar cheese or dried dill for this chowder variation.

(Photo courtesy of KaLea Lehman)

Phantom Knights & Wild Game

SOME MISSIONS SHARE THE SPIRIT of a wild hunt. Occasionally, there are seasons where the special operations lifestyle or a mission, or job—"the wild game"—spurs concern. Some trips and deployment rotations stretch your imagination. The texts, messages, emails or calls seem too hairy. They challenge your nerves and unsettle your stomach. There were times when the "game" they were after, or in, was intense for us all. We've all gone through these moments and seasons.

It takes a unique palate to appreciate the rare spirit demanded by this SOF lifestyle. Just as a recipe goes one step and one ingredient at a time, these missions flow one call, one breath, one to-do list task or accomplishment at a time. Embrace the wild, roll with it (to some degree), and learn to tell the story according to the character of your family, the warrior, and our military units. This is the way of a special operations family.

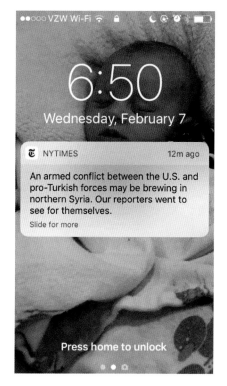

Real life in the news. (*Photo courtesy of KaLea Lehman*)

Sniper on target. (*Photo courtesy of KaLea Lehman*)

Wild Bill Donovan **Ram Balls**

TIME: 10 MIN (PREP), 40 MIN (COOK)
MAKES: 4-6 SERVINGS

Ingredients

1 pound ground wild ram

2 eggs

1 teaspoon vegetable or chicken bouillon
  paste

1 small yellow onion, diced

¾ cup rolled oats

1 cup crushed Ritz crackers

1 tablespoon salt

¾ cup ketchup or canned tomato sauce

⅛ teaspoon pepper

¾ teaspoon sage

BBQ sauce

Steps

1. Combine all ingredients except BBQ sauce in a large mixing bowl. Can be mixed by hand, but a stand mixer is very efficient. Combine and mix until all ingredients are smoothly incorporated.

2. Form meatballs by rolling the mixture into 1-1½ inch balls.

3. Place on a baking sheet and bake at 350°F for 25-30 minutes.

4. Remove from the baking sheet and coat in your favorite BBQ sauce, bake 5-8 mins longer and serve.

TIP: Great served with any potato or vegetable medley and bread.

VARIATION: You can substitute beef for ram meat and reduce sage to ½ teaspoon. For a meatloaf: Pat meat mixture into a 8x11-inch baking dish or a meatloaf pan and bake for 1 hour at 350°F. When done, top with sauce.

Ram Hunt (Photo courtesy of John and Angie McLaughlin)

SOF STORIES
Wild Ram because Why Not? — Meg

One winter, propane prices were sky high. I was trying hard to cut corners on groceries about the time a friend was trying to make freezer space. Her husband had just returned from post deployment, bucket-list hunts and they were maxed out on venison, turkey, and . . . wild ram. So I took some off her hands thinking ram meat would be similar to beef. The ram turned out to be a bit "wild." It needed a lot more sage and a bit less salt than ground beef.

In the end, I had to get creative to cook with the ram meat. That year gas, propane, and baby formula took every penny of our paycheck. The more I tried to use up the meat, it occurred to me how much it was like our life. Ram meat seemed to be a metaphor for our family during team time. No resiliency training quite captures the patience and heart needed to just keep going. I never was particular and I was fairly adaptable (in general or in the kitchen). But some nights there wasn't enough sage in my soul to keep at it without a total fit. I had kitchen skills, but our taste buds needed a more tender and savory treat.

Even my husband called for a vacation from the ram. We were all glad to run out of that meat and welcome summer that year.

TACTICAL TOPICS
Ready or Not

Go around the table and share a story about one time you were not ready for a challenge or something you were about to do. Or, think of a time when you were prepared but others were not. Why were you prepared or not? Did the experience change how you do things now?

PJ Rodeo **Slow Roasted Pulled Mojo Pork**

TIME: 10 MIN (PREP), 10 HOURS (COOK)
MAKES: 6-8 SERVINGS

Ingredients

2 teaspoons cumin
½ teaspoon peppercorns
4 garlic cloves, pressed or minced
1 teaspoon thyme or oregano
Zest of 1 orange
⅓ cup freshly squeezed orange juice
Zest of 1 lime
¼ cup fresh lime juice
⅓ cup dry sherry or dry white wine
Pork roast loin, bone in
1-2 cups chicken broth

Steps

1. Mix all ingredients, except for pork and broth, in a bowl.
2. Brown pork on all sides until golden brown.
3. Place pork roast in a slow cooker and top with marinade. Add enough broth to keep pork from drying out.
4. Set the slow cooker to low for 10 hours.
5. When ready pork will be very tender, remove from slow cooker and remove bones. Shred or chunk pork to serve.

VARIATION: To roast in the oven, use as marinade and leave for 24 hours. If using a grill, add oil to marinade.

(Photo courtesy of Wendy Jo Peterson)

RASP **Ribs**

TIME: 5 MIN (PREP), 35 MIN (COOK)
MAKES: 6-8 SERVINGS

- -

Ingredients

3 tablespoons brown sugar

3 teaspoons sea salt

2 teaspoons garlic powder

2 teaspoons smoked paprika

1 teaspoon ground black pepper

4 pounds baby back pork ribs

1 cup water

1 cup apple cider vinegar

BBQ sauce

(Photo courtesy of Wendy Jo Peterson)

Steps

1. Add the the brown sugar, sea salt, garlic powder, smoked paprika and pepper to a small bowl, and stir to combine

2. Remove membrane from back of ribs, rub seasoning mix over ribs, and cut into slabs to fit the size of your pressure cooker or multi-cooker.

3. Add water and apple cider vinegar to a pressure cooker or multi-cooker, and place the trivet on the bottom of the pot.

4. Place seasoned ribs on the trivet, cover, move the valve to sealing position, and set to pressure cook for 20 minutes.

5. Allow to naturally release for 10 minutes, then move the valve to quick release until the pin drops.

6. Open lid, remove ribs to a foil lined baking sheet, and brush barbecue sauce over ribs.

7. Place ribs in the oven, and broil for 5 minutes or until ribs bubble and edges look crisp.

8. Remove ribs from the oven, cut, and enjoy!

VARIATION: Try apple juice instead of apple cider vinegar.

Black Dagger **Mushroom Burger**

TIME: 15 MIN (PREP), 15 MIN (COOK)
MAKES: 6-8 SERVINGS

Ingredients

½ pound fresh mushrooms of choice, sliced

1 yellow onion, sliced

2 teaspoons minced garlic

1⅛ teaspoon salt, divided

1 tablespoon balsamic vinegar

2 tablespoons extra virgin olive oil

2 pounds lean ground beef

2 teaspoons Worcestershire sauce

2 eggs, beaten

1 teaspoon onion powder

¼ cup ketchup

Steps

1. Mix beef, Worcestershire sauce, eggs, 1 teaspoon salt, onion powder, and ketchup together in a bowl.

2. Shape mixture into 6-8 hamburger patties. Recommend ¾ in thick patties.

3. In a large saucepan, sauté the mushrooms, onions, and garlic until the onion is translucent.

4. Add in the ⅛ teaspoon salt, balsamic, and olive oil and sauté for 2 more minutes. Set aside but keep warm until burgers are ready to serve.

5. Grill burger patties over medium heat for 6 minutes on each side or until cooked to liking.

6. Serve on a bun of choice with mushroom and onion topping, plus steak sauce, or other condiments of choice.

VARIATION: The mushroom topping will have the most flavor if you mix the mushrooms to include a combination such as baby bella, portobello, and shitake. However, baby bella mushrooms will be adequate. Add 1 cup chopped baby spinach to the mushroom and onion mixture if desired.

 TACTICAL TOPICS
No-Go Crow

Think of a time where your plan, your approach, or your thinking just didn't pan out. When push came to shove, you had to admit you were wrong and had to "eat the crow." Take turns telling about the moment you "ate crow." What did you learn from that experience? Looking back, is it still a bitter event or did you learn something from the experience?

(Photo courtesy of Wendy Jo Peterson)

Combat Talon **Huli Huli Chicken**

TIME: 8 HOURS (PREP), 15 MIN (COOK)
MAKES: 8-10 SERVINGS

Ingredients

½ cup brown sugar
½ cup ketchup
⅓ cup soy sauce
⅓ cup pineapple juice
2 tablespoon sriracha
1 teaspoon garlic powder
½ teaspoon ground ginger
8-12 boneless, skinless chicken thighs
Sliced green onions (optional)

Steps

1. Stir together brown sugar, ketchup, soy sauce, pineapple juice, sriracha garlic powder, and ginger in a medium bowl.
2. Place ½ cup of mixture in a bowl to reserve to baste the chicken with.
3. Place remaining marinade in a large plastic zip top bag. Add chicken. Seal bag and refrigerate for 8 hours.
4. Remove chicken from marinade. Grill chicken over medium heat for 6 to 8 minutes per side.
5. Baste several times during the last 5 minutes with reserved marinade.
6. Garnish with chopped green onions if desired.

SOF STORIES
A Take-out Ritual — Karina

I'm not sure how it started, it kinda evolved into our family tradition. My husband takes on the family dinner by "ordering" out. He proclaims he "is cooking tonight!" And now, my step-son and I know that means he needs the favorite restaurant name and our dinner wish list. It gets delivered or he goes with his son to pick it up and we all set the table together. It's a fun and totally stress-free meal.

This is now a family tradition we enjoy—a way not to quit on dinner and quality time spent together. We all eat what we love, our son sees us happy and less stressed because there's no required prep or much to clean up. This became our tradition the day before he stepped off and the day after he returned from a deployment or long training event. It was golden because it took one stressor off the ever changing timeline.

Flying a kite in Okinawa (Photo courtesy of Steven Miller)

7. Treasured Times

★ ★ ★

IN OUR COMMUNITY, THE MISSION IS paramount. This intense fixation on the mission is the spirit that both grounds and drives the morale of our units, but it can also overshadow individual and family milestone moments that should be acknowledged and treasured. Treasured times occur amid simple routines and rituals with the people with love most. They serve as Healthy Checkpoints that are essential for well-being.

Special operations family rides their horses out West. *(Photo courtesy of Matt and Elin Pitts)*

These moments can mark a once-in-a-lifetime occurrence, a break from the grind with friends, or key experiences that thread together your family story. They appear in a season of change and fade as time moves along. Then there are rituals that help form us into the individuals we are. Our rituals are unique and they mark our faith, our roots, our family, our age, and our unique self. Collectively, these moments help us make sense of who we are, gain familiarity with where we came from, and chart our trajectory as we move forward.

An Air Force special operations couple dancing at their wedding. *(Photo courtesy of Jennifer Byrne)*

Reflecting on decades of these moments, we found ourselves shaking off our saltiness. Some occasions, like special times spent with friends, were easy to value, unpack, and storytell. They naturally come to mind and roll from memory to the tongue. One story ignites the memory of a time we are proud we didn't quit or cut sling-load. Instead, we kept the figurative and physical lights on at home. These moments with friends are treasured because they are defined by our vulnerability and the people who rallied to respond with real friendship and support. These times were just for us.

But, we also had to talk through and unknot moments more closely tied to our intangible, individual and family needs and routines. We struggled to make sense of the heavy lift that seemed to accompany common and predictable but still important moments – you know, the birthdays, the promotions, the anniversaries, and holiday or family traditions – the rituals that we seemed to take for granted without ever realizing it. These fundamentals seemed easy to dismiss because they involved the people closest to us, who "should" understand and know we love them and forgive us for missing, overlooking, or underplaying notable routines or big life moments. We found ourselves wanting to let them slide in exchange for a deep breath, although we felt deep in our gut these moments mattered.

At first celebrations seemed like a herculean lift, but in a fairly quick time, they became a type of tradition, too. The rare and fancy foods we brought to the table were simple ways to point out gifts – of talent, skill, accomplishment, or simply of being. The punch, cake, or recipe discovered while on a mission helped us recognize the moment, and it replaced the pressure of words. Many times, our table said it all. Recognizing opportunities that will become treasured family moments took awareness and work. So don't be fooled into thinking these are frivolous moments that don't hold a candle to the mission. Truth be told, it was these instances of quality time rooted at home that fuel the heart and soul of our community and keep our warrior's spirit alive and ready for the next ridgeline.

The rituals we wove into our lives formed family traditions and times for celebration that helped remind us that we were part of something bigger. Traditions gave meaning when there were no adequate words. They were magical moments composed of expressions, sounds, and sights that instilled their meaning through our senses. No further explanation was needed because our joyful participation spoke for us. Food played a key part in each of these rituals. In so many ways, food was the guardrail for our routines. It was our special skill that helped us scale key moments. It helped us express what we believed in, and what we hoped our children believed in, too. Other times, it became the stage for celebration.

We all need support from people in our lives to feel and know we are valued and we belong. These Healthy Checkpoints helped us authentically build community and care for each other. They enabled us to cultivate a sense of meaning and support. Without these experiences, we would have found ourselves, our family, and eventually our legacy on a destructive road.

So when the opportunity to celebrate arises, embrace the moment and enjoy! Take off the mom hat, let the demands of the day slide, and let your guard down with your spouse, closest friends, or family. Embrace real conversation. Be in the company of your people. Acknowledge the weight they carry and the mountains they've climbed – they being everyone and not just the warrior of the house. Reflect on your journey together and celebrate! Give yourself permission to be interested and invested, and adventure, connect, and unwind with those close to you. These treasured times ignite our senses, rejuvenate our souls, and give us the support and energy we need for this long walk of life.

A spread for the unit deployed. (Photo shared with MSOFC)

Just for Us

IN OUR COMMUNITY, we spend a disproportionate amount of time "holding down the fort." Our service members spend a good majority of nearly every year of service away, on call, or separated from the demands at home. What often sustains our heart, mind, and motivation on the homefront is the time we carve out for moments just for us.

Girls night out to see Garth and Tricia in concert in 2017. *(Photo courtesy of KaLea Lehman)*

Enjoying Ladies Day at the races in Newmarket, United Kingdom. *(Photo courtesy of Lynnsy Snook)*

Call it a survival tactic, Mom-Escape Games, or something simple like Fire Pit Friday, we all needed and savored intentional time spent with friends. The more we adjusted to the constant home and away routine flip-flop, we actually found ourselves looking forward to our away routine where a "staple" event was a gathering with a small group of trusted friends. They were simple, candid times of friendship. We felt supported and found belonging, confidence, and affirmation as we vented frustrations. We shared tips, hobbies, goals, and bucket lists, confessed embarrassing moments, and sought honest advice. Each meet-up we sprinkled with splurges of some of our favorite things—a favorite recipe, wine, bubbly, chocolate, or a cheese spread. We all pitched in to make the moment happen, and together we embraced and indulged in a bit of life.

Over the years our meet ups changed flavor, just like every deployment or away routine. Sometimes we pulled together to paint a house and help each other with a to-do list and other times a new, fun, and frivolous theme emerged. The constant ingredient in these moments just for us was the support we felt from close friends who were dependable and judgment-free. Together we made the impossible happen. Together we found humor in what sometimes felt like mere survival. And together we found confidence and strength flying solo.

(Photo courtesy of Bridget Orr)

Live Fire **Champagne Float**

TIME: 5 MIN (PREP)
MAKES: 6 SERVINGS

Ingredients

1 quart sorbet of your choice
1 bottle of favorite champagne

Steps

1. Scoop one scoop of sorbet into a nice wine glass.
2. Top with roughly ½ cup of champagne and serve.

SOF STORIES
Finding a Sweet Spot and Deployment Fun — Wendy

During a really tough deployment season, a spouse started a trend of Sunday Cosmos with Sex and the City. We would rotate homes of those willing to host the nightly cocktails, sometimes we'd dress up for the episode, and each of us would chip in with appetizers. This fancy fluff was exactly what we needed to laugh, find joy in a tough season, and it set our week on a happier path. Find a favorite show and see what can work for your crew.

During another deployment, we organized monthly dinner parties with a theme. The host spouse would decide on the theme and recipes, and then she'd email out recipes to each spouse to contribute. We would celebrate each theme and learn something new. We tried so many fabulous recipes, some of which I continue to include today. Some of my favorites were the Chinese New Year and Holiday Family Classics. What would your theme be?

Tier 1 **Caprese Bites**

TIME: 15 MIN (PREP)
MAKES: 25 SERVINGS

- -

Ingredients

1 cup balsamic vinegar
12 ounces cherry tomatoes
12 ounces mozzarella balls
Basil leaves
6 inch skewers

Steps

1. Gently heat balsamic vinegar in a non-reactive saucepan, preferably one with a thick bottom, until it starts to simmer. Lower the heat to keep the vinegar simmering, and patiently allow the vinegar to reduce into a syrupy glaze. It will continue to thicken slightly as it cools.

2. Arrange cherry tomatoes, mozzarella balls and basil leaves as desired in a pattern on skewers.

3. Place all skewers on a platter and drizzle with balsamic reduction.

4. Serve while fresh.

TACTICAL TOPICS
Support through the Senses

Pick an item for each of the five senses: think of things that bring you comfort, or funny things that make you laugh. Have fun with it!

- Sight: Name something you can see that makes you smile. It may be a picture of something or someone that puts a smile on your face or maybe it is a silly sight of another kind.

- Touch: Name something that feels good to hold, like a fuzzy sweater or a smooth rock from your favorite river.

- Hearing: Think of a sound that soothes you. It may be a song you love or the sound of the beach or something connected to some other memory.

- Smell: Name your favorite scent. What smell ignites your imagination, revs up your hunger, or calms your soul? Is it lavender, the smell of a rich dark chocolate, or another scent altogether?

- Taste: Speaking of chocolate . . . It's time to add your favorite flavor to the spread!

(Photo courtesy of Lynnsy Snook)

Faithfully Waiting White Bean, Asparagus, and Mushroom Cassoulet

TIME: 15 MIN (PREP), 40 MIN (COOK)
MAKES: 4 SERVINGS

Ingredients

1 pound asparagus, sliced to 2 inch pieces

2 tablespoons extra-virgin olive oil, divided

10 ounces chanterelle or oyster mushrooms, sliced

⅓ cup finely chopped shallots

6 garlic cloves, minced

¼ cup dry white wine

1½ cups vegetable broth

½ teaspoon dried marjoram or dried oregano

2 (15-ounce) cans cannellini beans, rinsed and drained

¼ teaspoon freshly ground black pepper

2 ounces French bread, cut into 1 inch cubes

1 tablespoon butter, cut into small pieces

½ cup grated Parmigiano-Reggiano cheese

Steps

1. Bring 5 cups of water to a boil in a large stainless-steel skillet, and add asparagus to the pan.

2. Cover and cook for 2 minutes. Rinse asparagus with cold water. Drain well and set aside.

3. Return the pan to medium-high heat. Add 1 tablespoon of oil, swirling to coat.

4. Add mushrooms, shallots, and garlic and sauté for 8 minutes or until mushrooms are tender.

5. Add wine and cook for 3 minutes or until liquid evaporates.

6. Stir in broth, marjoram or oregano, and beans. Bring to a simmer.

7. Reduce heat to medium and cook for 12 minutes or until thick and the beans are very tender. Stir in black pepper.

8. Preheat broiler.

9. Place French bread and butter in a food processor, and pulse until coarse crumbs form.

10. Add the remaining 1 tablespoon oil and cheese to coarse breadcrumbs and pulse until combined.

11. Stir asparagus into bean mixture.

12. Sprinkle coarse breadcrumb mixture evenly over bean mixture. Broil 3 minutes or until crumbs are golden brown.

Rough Terrain **Toffee Crackle**

TIME: 10 MIN (PREP), 35 MIN (COOK)
MAKES: 6-8 SERVINGS

Ingredients

40 saltine crackers
1 cup unsalted butter
1 cup brown sugar
2 cups semisweet chocolate chips

Steps

1. Preheat to 350°F.
2. Line baking sheet with foil and spray with cooking spray. Spread out the saltines next to one another (5 crackers by 8 crackers).
3. Stir butter and sugar in a saucepan over medium-high heat until boiling.
4. Reduce heat and simmer uncovered, about 5-10 minutes, until thickened and sugar is dissolved.
5. Pour over crackers to coat evenly.
6. Bake for 8-10 minutes or until the toffee is bubbly.
7. Turn off the oven and remove the pan. Let it sit for 3-5 min.
8. Sprinkle on chocolate chips and let soften until you can spread out in an even layer. Place the baking sheet back in the oven to help melt chocolate chips if needed.
9. Let this cool and put it in the fridge to harden.
10. Break into pieces and enjoy!

VARIATION: Sprinkle nuts, dried fruit, etc. on to the chocolate while still soft.

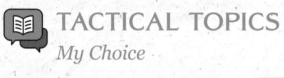

TACTICAL TOPICS
My Choice

THE FAMILY DINNER PROJECT.ORG

If you woke up tomorrow and could do one thing you can't do right now, what would it be?

Visiting the beaches of Normandy, France.
(Photo courtesy of Lynnsy Snook)

Dive Team Delicious Cheesecake

TIME: 10 MIN (PREP), 60 MIN (COOK)
MAKES: 6 SERVINGS

- -

Ingredients

Cheesecake Graham Cracker Crust

1 cup crushed graham crackers
3 teaspoons sugar
½ teaspoon cinnamon
¼ cup melted butter

Cheesecake Filling

(3) 8 ounce packages of cream cheese
¾ cup sugar
3 eggs
¾ teaspoon vanilla extract

Steps

1. Combine all the graham cracker crust ingredients in a mixing bowl. Press the graham cracker mixture into a pan and bake at 350°F for 10 minutes.
2. To make the filling, beat the cream cheese and sugar together using a blender. Add in the eggs and vanilla, and blend until smooth.
3. Pour mixture over the crust and bake for 55-60 minutes at 350°F.
4. Cool, slice, and add toppings of your choice, if desired.

VARIATION: Chocolate chip cookie dough also makes a great crust for this recipe. You can craft your own cookie dough or buy a roll of refrigerated dough. Press evenly into the pan and bake until just dry in the center.

(Opposite) (Photo courtesy of Bridget Orr)

Finding Routine and Recognizing Tradition

LIVING IN A COMMUNITY THAT THRIVES on uncertainty, it seems almost out of touch to talk about creating routine or tradition. Like you, we once scoffed at these words. How do you value Healthy Checkpoints that seem to contradict your lifestyle and at times feel impossible? Those of us who have been in it for a while know that frustration. Our exhaustion ceased many efforts to establish family routine or practice any ritual.

Growing up, things like family dinner just seemed practical, but we didn't realize how formative that ritual was to our family relationships and legacy. In our own homes, we gave up on them, for a bit, as we tried to navigate the unique hurdles that came with life in SOF. Frankly for us, it was a gut-check when we learned these Healthy Checkpoints played a crucial role to our family and our own health and well-being.

A Navy special operations family celebrating Christmas during a deployment. Dad joined virtually. *(Photo courtesy of Dan and Leslie Luna)*

We had slowly learned to dismiss healthy family checkpoints (family dinner, intentional celebrations, claiming tradition, holding to a vacation) to cope with stress in our lives. We convinced ourselves that skipping them didn't matter to cope with the constantly changing calendar. Family dinner just made stress obvious. Whether we were at our table or out to eat it was undeniable that there was chaos and tension in our house. Picky eaters, food allergy friction, loud toddlers, burnt sides, or side tracked cooking—there were plenty of triggers for tension. We didn't know how to control it so family dinner often got nixed and avoided. We didn't think of these challenges as stress. They were simply our life at that moment, and it became the way we lived. The high stress *was* our "normal" and surviving the day became a point of pride.

We are pulled in so many directions today, even blocking off the time for a family meal is really hard. How do you establish a basic routine or any tradition when you can't even plan an hour ahead? We had to get creative to reclaim Healthy Checkpoints even though we weren't always sure where or how to start. Unpacking these SOF family needs helped us recognize when we started to feel stressed. We realized a routine, like family mealtime, was actually a boundary we needed to set. While of course food nourished our bodies, we began to recognize these Healthy Checkpoints strengthened our heart and nourished our soul.

Dad's birthday is a great reason for dessert! *(Photo courtesy of Samantha Gomolka)*

These rituals were our lifeline in some of the most challenging seasons. Family traditions – like the way we celebrate St. Patty's Day or Thanksgiving – sprinkled mundane moments with bits of fun and wisdom passed down through generations of family. They gave us a place in history and helped us write our own story one experience at a time. Some rituals became our family traditions in special seasons – like berry picking in the spring. We told our friends and kids of how grandma used to sweeten her garden berries and bake her party potatoes. Then, some of us practiced spiritual rituals that kept us grounded. If the sky seemed to be falling or the mundane was starting to wear on our soul, our spirit found energy and hope in sacred tradition.

Amid the Iraq War, a Special Forces officer partakes in a Catholic mass in 2011 with the Chaldean Catholic community. *(Photo courtesy of KaLea Lehman)*

These rituals helped us realize that we were never alone. The Healthy Checkpoints we thought were impossible were the healthy baby steps that we needed. Routines like mealtime became an opportunity to intentionally focus on the basics and protect our family life. This realization made us feel truly seasoned. It was a total flip on life as we were living it before—just surviving.

Tradition leaves a Legacy **Oven-Roasted Turkey**

TIME: 15 MIN (PREP), 12 HRS - 48 HRS (MARINATE)
MAKES: 15-20 SERVINGS

Ingredients

15 - 20 pound, thawed turkey

For Brine:

4 stalks celery, diced
1 ½ gallons water
1 ½ cup kosher salt
½ cup brown sugar
4 (4-inch) sprigs fresh rosemary
2 tablespoons savory

For Roasting:

1 cup reserved turkey brine
1 cup apple cider
2 cups chicken stock
2 onions, sliced
1 bulb garlic
4 carrots, peeled and sliced into chunks
1 apple, cored and quartered
Fresh herbs for garnish

Steps:

1. Place all brine ingredients in a large stew pot and heat on high until it boils. Allow brine to cool.
2. Place the thawed turkey in a plastic bag or large pot, add in all the brine, and allow to marinate in the refrigerator for 12-48 hours. Make sure to clear enough space in the refrigerator for the turkey and marinade. Shelves may need to be adjusted.
3. On roasting day, combine apple cider, brine, and chicken stock in a large pitcher or container.
4. Place the turkey, breast-up, in a large roasting pan with the liquid mixture.
5. Let sit at room temperature for 1 hour.
6. Meanwhile, slice the top off of the bulb of garlic to expose the cloves, and pull apart into chunks.
7. Place the celery from the brine in the pan around the turkey, along with the onions, garlic, carrots, apple, and herbs.
8. Heat oven to 450°F and roast the turkey for 30 minutes.
9. Reduce oven temperature to 350°F and roast for 3 ½ hours more, making sure to baste the turkey every 30 minutes with the pan liquid.
10. Once cooked to an internal temperature of 180°F, transfer the turkey to a serving dish and let it rest at room temperature for 30 more minutes.
11. Cut and serve with the roasted vegetables, apples, and herbs. Ladle the pan drippings over the meat to keep it moist.

A perfect turkey freshly brined and ready to roast! *(Photo courtesy of Tabitha Farmer)*

SOF STORIES
Turkey Wings, Please – Denise

I worked for a small school for many years. Every year we had a traditional turkey dinner for the students and invited all the parents and staff. One year during the dinner preparation, my friend threw out all the turkey wings thinking they weren't worth the work. When I heard this, I was mad the rest of the day. The turkey dinner was a school tradition, but savoring the dark, juicy meat on the wings was a personal tradition for me.

As a kid, I always got to eat the meat on the wings. It was something I looked forward to and it was a tradition that brought me comfort. I never threw out the wings. When my friend

Perfectly crisp, turkey wings.
(Photo courtesy of KaLea Lehman)

learned why I was upset, she made sure to note that the wings mattered to me. Every school or personal turkey dinner since, my friend took extra care to ensure that the wings were not only cooked but specifically saved for me. I am retired now, and this is still a tradition between us and also one I passed down to my daughters. They love the wings, too, and all of our daughters love this story.

Two great friends celebrating at a school party. *(Photo courtesy of Andrea Orr)*

Osprey **Apple Spinach Salad** with Making Memories **Maple Cider Vinaigrette**

TIME: 20 MIN (PREP), 15 MIN (COOK)
MAKES: 6 SERVINGS

Ingredients

Sugared Curried Pecans

1 (6-ounce) package of pecan halves
2 tablespoons butter, melted
3 tablespoons sugar
¼ teaspoon ground ginger
⅛ teaspoon curry powder
⅛ teaspoon kosher salt
⅛ teaspoon ground red or black pepper

Maple Cider Vinaigrette

⅓ cup apple cider vinegar
2 tablespoons pure maple syrup
1 tablespoon Dijon mustard
¼ teaspoon kosher salt
¼ teaspoon pepper
⅔ cup olive oil

Salad

10 ounce package fresh baby spinach
1 apple, thinly sliced
1 small red onion, thinly sliced
4 ounce package crumbled goat cheese

Steps

1. To prepare pecans, preheat the oven to 350°F.
2. Toss pecans in butter.
3. Stir together sugar, ginger, curry, salt, and pepper in a separate bowl.
4. Add pecans, tossing to coat.
5. Spread in a single layer on an aluminum foil lined pan.
6. Bake for 10-13 minutes or until lightly browned and toasted.
7. Cool in a pan or on a wire rack for 20 minutes.
8. To prepare the vinaigrette, whisk together vinegar, maple syrup, mustard, salt and pepper, gradually whisk in oil until well blended.
9. Mix the salad ingredients in a bowl.
10. Drizzle with desired amount of dressing and sprinkle with pecans.

SOF STORIES
Fresh Greens — Lauren

When the teams are deployed they eat all kinds of things. One thing I noticed they do not eat is "green." Most of the countries my husband ventured to did not have an abundance of fresh vegetables, and if they did, they usually have some contaminant that makes them regret trying to eat fresh. My husband's main request when he comes home is green food—lots of salads and fresh vegetables. It's an easy thing to fix and the easiest way to welcome him home for family dinner.

Raider Ready **Lasagna Dip**

TIME: 30 MIN (PREP), 30 MIN (COOK)
MAKES: 12 SERVINGS

Ingredients

1½ pounds ground beef

1 pound hot Italian sausage

2 garlic cloves, minced

2 (28-ounce) jars marinara sauce

3 cups low-fat cottage cheese

2 eggs, beaten

½ cup Parmesan cheese, grated (not shredded)

2 tablespoons dried parsley

1 teaspoon salt

1 pound sliced mozzarella cheese

Steps

1. In a large skillet or saucepan, combine ground beef, sausage, and garlic. Brown over medium-high heat, then drain half the fat (or none at all).
2. Add sauce and simmer while you are working on the other steps.
3. In a medium bowl, mix cottage cheese, beaten eggs, grated Parmesan, parsley, and salt. Stir together well and set aside.
4. To assemble: Spoon half the cottage cheese mixture in a baking pan. Spread evenly. Cover cottage cheese with a layer of mozzarella cheese. Spoon a little less than half the meat/sauce mixture over the top. Repeat, ending with meat/sauce mixture. Sprinkle the top generously with extra Parmesan.
5. Bake in a 350°F oven for 20 to 30 minutes, until the dip is hot and bubbling.
6. Serve with toasted bread while bubbly and warm.

TIP: This recipe freezes particularly well after assembly and before baking. If frozen, thaw overnight before baking as directed.

VARIATION: To make this a true lasagna, arrange 4 oven ready lasagna noodles in the bottom of a baking pan, overlapping if necessary. Spoon half the cottage cheese mixture over the noodles. Spread evenly. Cover cottage cheese with a layer of mozzarella cheese. Spoon a little less than half the meat/sauce mixture over the top. Repeat, ending with meat/sauce mixture. Sprinkle the top generously with extra Parmesan.

(Opposite) (Photo courtesy of Lynnsy Snook)

SOF STORIES
Success by Compassionate Standards — Heather

When we were stationed at Air University at Maxwell AFB, we had regular opportunities to connect with familiar faces as students moved through the schoolhouse. One particular time, my husband invited a half dozen of his friends from college, who were in town TDY. With juggling three young kids, I decided my homemade lasagna would be enough to feed these former college football players and give me time to finish tidying up while it baked.

In my attempt to simplify food prep, I made two lasagnas, at the same time, assembly line style, along the counter. Finally, after layering all of the ingredients and getting the lasagnas into the oven to bake, I turned around to clean up my work area to see the cooked noodles still sitting in the colander in the sink. Yes, I had assembled multiple layers of cheese, meat, and homemade sauce with no noodles. There was no recovery, there was no saving the ruined food. In a panic, I called my husband and asked him to swing into the grocery store—"the one with the good bread"—and pick up two loaves of fancy, herbed bread on his way home. That night, as we gathered around the table, I served a large salad, freshly warmed bread, and two big casserole dishes of sauce, cheese, and meat. We affectionately called it "lasagna dip," and moved on with entertaining our guests. We intentionally enjoyed fellowship with friends. Now we have a running family joke about including noodles in the lasagna.

TACTICAL TOPICS
Sense of Home
Hospitality

When you return home or visit someone, what one drink, dish, smell, or feeling makes you instantly feel welcome?

A Navy SEAL dad hugs his son on his return home. *(Photo courtesy of Dan Luna)*

Sweet Escape **Brussels Sprouts with Cranberries and Pecans**

TIME: 10 MIN (PREP), 30 MIN (COOK)
MAKES: 4-6 SERVINGS

Ingredients

12-15 ounces Brussels sprouts
3 tablespoons extra virgin olive oil
¼ teaspoon salt
1 cup pecans
½ cup craisins

Steps

1. Cut off the tough end and quarter the Brussels sprouts.
2. Heat 3 tablespoons of olive oil in a large frying pan over medium-high heat.
3. Add Brussels sprouts to the pan and sprinkle with salt.
4. Sauté for approximately 15 minutes or until the edges brown.
5. Add pecans and craisins to pan and sauté 2-3 more minutes then serve.

(Photo courtesy of KaLea Lehman)

SOF STORIES
Surprise Thanksgiving Potluck — Maria

Thinking way back to our first deployment that fell over my favorite holiday, I laugh remembering the thoughtfulness of my friends and neighbors. My family was a world away, and we didn't yet have kids. Yet, my friends knew Thanksgiving was my favorite holiday, and they were not going to let me feel alone. Somebody brought the turkey and gravy, while the others took care of the side dishes and desserts.

Somehow I ended up solo hosting three couples who barely knew one another, and I didn't even prepare a single dish! How did I end up hosting without making anything for these friends who didn't know the other? I look back and laugh about that memorable Thanksgiving, and the people that went out of their way to make me feel special during a hard time. Now I have been through what feels like a billion missed holidays due to deploy-

An ODA turkey fry. *(Photo courtesy of Britt'n Morrison)*

ments. I still look back at that time and make sure I show others the same care that my neighbors showed me when I was first learning to navigate this way of life. It meant the world to me in that moment and still today.

A Scent to Remember **Wassail**

TIME: 5 MIN (PREP), 40 MIN - 8 HRS (SIMMER)

MAKES: 12 SERVINGS

Ingredients

2 quarts apple cider
½ cup lemon juice
4 cinnamon sticks
⅛ teaspoon ground nutmeg
2 cups orange juice
12 whole cloves
⅛ teaspoon ground ginger

Steps

1. Combine apple cider, orange juice, and lemon juice in a slow cooker.
2. Add in cloves, ginger, and nutmeg to season.
3. Allow the mixture to simmer before serving. It can simmer all day.
4. Serve hot, sip and relax with good company.

 WAR GAMES
The Face of My Day

Special Forces family on pre-PCS vacation has some fun over a picnic lunch. *(Photo courtesy of Steve Miller)*

What is your "face" of the day? If your day isn't going well, what are some steps you can take to turn it around?

Look up a "feelings chart" or create one together! Think of words and corresponding colors or faces. Look to the internet for examples, and then make it uniquely yours. Depending on your kid-dos ages, you can keep it simple or go into more detail and depth. Once created, display the chart in a viewable spot and use it for family check-ins or a conversation starter at meal or snack time.

Learning how to identify and express feelings is a first step to learning how to regulate emotions. We are more equipped to build lasting friendships and succeed when we can recognize and regulate our emotions.

Raise Your Glass **Raspberry Champagne Cocktail**

TIME: 5 MIN (PREP)
MAKES: 1 SERVING

Ingredients

2 teaspoons Chambord black raspberry liqueur

3 fresh raspberries

Prosecco sparkling wine

Steps

1. Spoon Chambord raspberry liqueur into a flute, then drop in a few raspberries.

2. Hold a spoon inside the glass over the top of the liqueur and slowly pour in the Prosecco, pulling the spoon up as you go to create the two-tone effect.

(Photo courtesy of Bridget Orr)

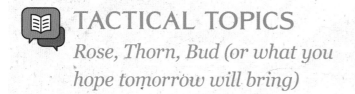 **TACTICAL TOPICS**

Rose, Thorn, Bud (or what you hope tomorrow will bring)

Take turns sharing about your day. What was your favorite part of the day? What was your least favorite? Was there anything funny or silly that happened?

A Need for Celebration

THESE LIFE EVENTS DON'T COME OUT of nowhere. They are formative rituals that help us understand and accept ourselves and gain confidence in who we are, where we have been, and where we may go. Celebrations make you pause and reflect on meaningful moments. Recognizing key dates and accomplishments validates our efforts, interests, friendships, family bonds, and sense of self. These rituals are opportunities to nourish the heart, mind, and soul of the people we love most, but making the party possible can sometimes feel heavy and overwhelming.

Happy Birthday downrange, SOF style. *(Photo courtesy of Britt'n Morrison)*

Celebration itself isn't complicated, but it can feel complicated when there is a key person missing in body or spirit. Their absence makes the effort to celebrate anything seem exhausting, over-the-top, or simply not a priority concern when confronted with the triple challenge of constant change, unpredictability, and a weak support system. Like the myth of stress inoculation, ceasing celebration is a pitfall. We all need to feel special and know we belong, and celebrations, even modest ones, commemorate key moments, give testament to our value, and serve as practical healthy family Healthy Checkpoints.

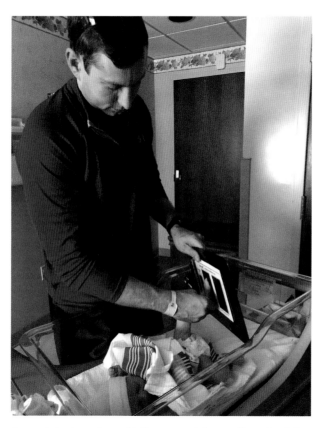

A new baby born in an Air Force special operations family!
(Photo courtesy of Jennifer Byrne)

Celebrations can be simple. Don't overthink it. Think of them as a strategic yet tactical pause. The truth is, milestone moments become the binding that holds the pages of our family story together. If you find yourself lacking a celebratory spirit, you are certainly not alone, but hang in there and reclaim the happy ritual. Cling tight to a habit of deliberate celebration because this family ritual gives dignity to the journey. It will likely catch you off guard. Many times, like us, you won't realize you needed the pat on the back until the moment you receive it. You will find it touching and uncomfortable, but you will also feel the deep joy that is unleashed when you are surrounded by people who believe you are extraordinary. These moments celebrating tough challenges, milestones, or just us – me – you, give us comfort and security that comes with family support and real community.

Proud dad and daughter at her flight school graduation.
(Photo courtesy of Jim Lynch)

(Photo courtesy of Lynnsy Snook)

Significant Accomplishment **Flank Steak** in Celebration **Chimichurri Sauce**

TIME: 2 HRS 10 MIN (PREP), 20 MIN (COOK)
MAKES: 6 SERVINGS

Ingredients

2 pounds flank steak

Marinade Ingredients

⅓ cup extra virgin olive oil
2 garlic cloves, minced
2 tablespoons red wine vinegar
⅓ cup soy sauce
¼ cup honey
½ teaspoon freshly ground black pepper

Chimichurri Sauce

3 garlic cloves
1 large shallot
1 heaping cup cilantro
1 jalapeño pepper (optional)
¼ cup extra virgin olive oil
1 tablespoon red wine vinegar
½ teaspoon salt
½ teaspoon crushed red pepper flakes

Steps

1. To marinate the steak, combine the marinade ingredients in a large zip top bag.
2. Place the steak in the bag and make sure the meat is completely coated with the marinade. Chill and marinate for at least 2 hours and up to overnight.
3. To prepare chimichurri sauce, finely chop garlic, shallot, cilantro, jalapeño pepper (remove seeds and membrane if you want it milder) and place in a small bowl. Add olive oil, red wine vinegar, salt, and crushed red pepper. Mix, cover, and refrigerate until ready to use on steak.
4. Prepare the grill for high, direct heat with one part of the grill for lower, indirect heat. The grill is hot enough when you hold your hand about an inch over the hot side, and you can only hold it there for about a second.
5. Remove the steak from the marinade and gently shake off the excess marinade from the steak. Sprinkle generously on all sides with coarse salt and freshly ground pepper to form a savory crust on the steak.
6. Place steak on the hot side of the grill. Grill for a minute or two on each side to get a good sear. Then move the steak to the cooler side of the grill, cover and cook a few minutes more until done to your liking. Use a meat thermometer to determine when meat is ready. Pull the steak off the grill at 120-125°F for rare, 130-140°F for medium rare, and 145°F for medium.
7. Rest the steak for 10 minutes on a cutting board, then cut across the grain of the meat at a steep diagonal so that the slices are wide. Top with chimichurri sauce.

SOF STORIES
Team Picnic — Christine

In 2017, my husband became a Team Sergeant. It was a triumphant moment for our family because we approached his job in Special Forces as a team. We endured a lot, and the opportunity for him to lead a team was a long-sought goal and honor. We landed on a team of amazing men with solid families, fiancées, and girlfriends and the next deployment was coming. We wanted the team to know each other and feel supported, so we hosted a picnic at our place where everyone could relax and let their guard down.

I pulled together all the foods that my family and I find comfort in. Food that is not fussy, just flavorful and says "Glad to be a part of this." I grilled flank steak dressed in chimichurri sauce, slow roasted pulled mojo pork (see page 303), and apricot and chipotle glazed chicken thighs, then served a corn and avocado salsa (see page 84), rolls, and a simple green salad to accompany it. The team brought their favorite sides and desserts, and we all enjoyed homemade Sangria (see page 241) as we milled around the kitchen, hung out outside, played with our kids and dogs, and devoured everything. By the end of the night, we were no longer strangers or just acquaintances. The team was now a tribe preparing for what would become a for-midable deployment.

Redeployment **Roasted Fennel with Tomatoes and Olives**

TIME: 15 MIN (PREP), 40 MIN (COOK)
MAKES: 6 SERVINGS

Ingredients

3 large fennel bulbs
2 tablespoons olive oil
1½ cups cherry tomatoes
½ cup small black olives

Steps

1. Heat oven to 375°F.
2. Halve and quarter the fennel through the root, then trim off the hard core.
3. Slice the fennel and toss in a roasting pan with the olive oil, salt, and pepper.
4. Roast for 20-25 mins, until starting to soften.
5. Add tomatoes and olives and stir well. Return to the oven for 10-15 mins until the fennel is tender, with just a bit of crunch.

VARIATION: Add boiled potatoes when you add the tomatoes and olives.

SOF STORIES
The Warrior-Chef Returns — Erin

Like all unit families, we all walk our own way—just a bit. I don't cook. It's not my thing, but I still appreciate a good family dinner. My spouse does the cooking and the grocery shopping. When he's gone, I make it work. I take forever in a grocery store and manage to return with only half my list. But he can case a grocery store, return with every item, and whip up an all-star meal. Occasionally, I join him in the kitchen or at the grill, and that is basically a date night for us. When he's away, I send him new recipes to try on his return, and we make plans for cookouts with our friends. He masters the meal, and I stick to the drinks.

He loves it. I love it. Our friends love it. We all love it! It's just our way and his hot meal skills are sexier than any special skill that ever came with a badge or tab.

Party Perfect **Confetti Corn and Frito Salad**

TIME: 20 MIN (PREP)
MAKES: 6 SERVINGS

Ingredients

Salad

6 green onions
1 bell pepper (any color)
1 pint grape or cherry tomatoes
2 (15-ounce) cans whole kernel corn
2 cups cheddar cheese, thickly shredded
1 bag Frito chips

Zesty Dressing

½ cup mayonnaise

½ cup sour cream
1 teaspoon chili powder

½ teaspoon cumin
¼ teaspoon garlic powder
1 teaspoon lime zest

Steps

1. Dice the green onions and bell pepper.
2. Halve or quarter the tomatoes, and drain the canned corn of all liquid.
3. Stir all salad ingredients together in a salad bowl.
4. Mix all the dressing ingredients together well and chill until ready to mix into the salad.
5. Just before serving, stir in the dressing.

TACTICAL TOPICS
Special and You Know It

THE FAMILY DINNER PROJECT.ORG

How do you show someone that they are special to you?

Giant hugs for dad returning home!
(Photo courtesy of Samantha Gomolka)

Party Perfect Confetti Corn and Frito Salad *(Photo courtesy of KaLea Lehman)*

Make it a Party! **Pink Champagne Cake Pops**

TIME: 1 HOUR (PREP), 35 MIN (COOK)
MAKES: 60 CAKE POPS

Ingredients

Buttercream

¼ cup unsalted butter, softened at room
    temperature
1¼ cups powdered sugar
2 tablespoons champagne
¼ teaspoon vanilla extract
1 drop red food coloring

Cake

3 cups all-purpose flour
3 teaspoons baking powder
½ teaspoon salt
1 cup unsalted butter, softened at room
    temperature
2 cups granulated sugar
1 teaspoon vanilla extract
6 large egg whites at room temperature
4 drops red food coloring
2 cups champagne

Pink Champagne Cake Pops

60 (6-inch) lollipop sticks
32 ounces white chocolate or white
    chocolate melts, roughly chopped
½ - 1 cup diamond sugar (optional but
    recommended)

To Prepare the Cake

1. Preheat the oven to 350°F.
2. Grease and flour a 9x13-inch cake pan
   or baking dish and set aside.
3. In a medium bowl, whisk together dry
   ingredients: flour, baking powder and
   salt. Set aside.
4. In the large bowl of an electric mixer,
   beat butter and sugar until light and
   fluffy.
5. Reduce speed to medium and add egg
   whites, one at a time. Then add vanilla.

6. Mix in food coloring. Stop the mixer
   and scrape the sides of the bowl with a
   spatula.
7. With a mixer on low speed, add dry
   ingredients and champagne in three alternating additions, starting and ending
   with dry ingredients.
8. Pour into the prepared cake pan and
   bake for 25-35 minutes or until a knife
   comes out clean from the center.

To Make the Cake Pops

1. Line a baking sheet with wax paper and
   set aside.
2. Next prepare the buttercream. Beat
   butter for several minutes until light and
   fluffy. Add sugar, champagne, vanilla,
   and food coloring and beat for several
   minutes until light and creamy.
3. Break cake into pieces and place in a
   large bowl; crumble cake into small
   crumbs with fingers. Add buttercream to
   the cake and mix with a spoon until all
   cake crumbs are coated.
4. Use a small cookie dough scoop or large
   spoon to scoop balls of dough onto wax
   paper. Use clean hands to roll the cake
   scoops into balls.
5. Cover with another sheet of wax paper
   and place in the freezer for at least two
   hours.
6. Prepare another baking sheet with wax
   paper for finished pops. Alternatively,
   have a large piece of styrofoam available
   for drying cake pops.
7. Put white chocolate in a heat-safe bowl
   and place it over a pot of simmering
   water, stirringly constantly until melted.
8. Remove cake balls from the freezer and
   dip the top of each lollipop stick about
   ¼ of an inch into the white chocolate

and immediately press into the cake ball two thirds of the way through.

9. Dip each cake pop, one at a time, into white chocolate. Lightly tap off excess chocolate and place cake pop on wax paper or stick into styrofoam. Decorate with diamond sugar immediately before chocolate hardens.

10. Repeat until all cake pops are dipped and decorated. Allow to cool and for chocolate to harden before serving.

Every kid loves a good cake pop. *(Photo courtesy of KaLea Lehman)*

Celebrating a birthday with High Altitude Ice Cream Pie (chocolate cookie version). *(Photo courtesy of KaLea Lehman)*

Birthday Blitz **Ice Cream Pie with Shredded Chocolate**

TIME: 5 MIN (PREP), 5-8 HOURS (CHILL)
MAKES: 6-8 SERVINGS

Ingredients

1½ quart of favorite ice cream
1 Oreo or graham cracker crust pie shell
1 white chocolate almond bark
1 dark chocolate candy bar
Sprinkles (optional)

Steps

1. Set out the ice cream on the counter until it softens.
2. Once soft, spoon ice cream into pie crust.
3. With a grater or knife, carefully shred the desired amount of chocolate and sprinkles onto the cake.
4. Cover and return to the freeze for 5-8 hours to firm up.

VARIATION: Chocolate can be replaced with Reese's, Oreo cookies, or chocolate candy bar pieces.

 TACTICAL TOPICS
Past, Present, Future Party!

Go around the table and take turns sharing: What moment or milestone are you most proud of? What celebration (birthday or a religious, school, hobby-related milestone or achievement) is approaching? What do you want to do to celebrate the special occasion? What are some celebrations you are looking forward to in the future?

Celebrating with sparkling cider and a feast. (*Photo courtesy of Lynnsy Snook*)

Green eggs and ham for the win! *(Photo courtesy of Jess Doty)*

8. Breakfast Anytime

★ ★ ★

EGGS FOR DINNER is almost a special operations deployment understanding. We've all had a night where we needed dinner ready in minutes or
we couldn't take another "food fight." "Brinner" (breakfast for dinner) is a fast
backup and the ultimate crowd-pleaser. You can flex a breakfast recipe so it is
fast and protein-packed, veggied-up, loaded with antioxidants and probiotics,
carbo-loaded, or you can make it into a sweet treat. Ask a 5-year-old what's for
dinner and you are certain to get something with cheese or syrup! For those of
us without kids, it is a fast and healthy option to fall back on when you are flying
solo and don't feel like making a big meal.

Brinner is flexible and it helps us be easy on ourselves. We embraced the power
of an incredible, edible egg and the joy that accompanied an extra side of bacon,
syrup, and butter. A good meal doesn't need to be a heavy lift, and breakfast
for dinner is a great way to meet nutritional needs yet save the cooking time to
put toward something that fills your spirit—like a call to catch up with friends or
family, a movie treat, extra reading time, a bubble bath, or maybe journaling or
an art project.

Breakfast Blitz

EVERY NOW AND AGAIN THERE IS AN EASY DAY, often a Saturday, where the calendar is wide open. You have no place to be and no tasks to catch up on. It's a blank canvas. It feels like you are missing something, but it is really an opportunity to take a deep breath and treat yourself with a slow day at home, a bucket list adventure, or a moment to get ahead. A free calendar day means the world is your playground, and you can seize the day! Take advantage of the moment, invest in yourself, and make it a winning weekend for the whole family.

Go a step further than cereal or fast morning fix, and make the morning special. If you have kids, this is a great way to score some quality time and add a fun twist to the normal morning hustle. Breakfast dishes are easy to jazz up. They are fast and almost foolproof recipes to start your cozy weekend off with a little extra chocolate, cheese, or whipped cream!

Special Forces Team spouses enjoy brunch while their guys are away. *(Photo courtesy of Britt'n Morrison)*

Adaptive Strike **Pancakes**

TIME: 10 MIN (PREP), 20 MIN (COOK)
MAKES: 6 SERVINGS

Ingredients

2 cups all-purpose flour
½ cup granulated sugar
¾ tablespoon baking powder
¾ teaspoon baking soda
¾ teaspoon salt
2 large eggs
2 ¼ cups milk
6 tablespoons melted butter, cooled
1 teaspoon vanilla extract

Steps

1. Combine all dry ingredients In a large bowl.
2. In a separate bowl or large liquid measuring cup, whisk together the milk, eggs, butter, and vanilla.

3. Slowly pour the milk mixture into the flour mixture while stirring. Whisk until smooth. Let rest for 10 to 15 minutes.
4. While the batter rests, heat your griddle or large nonstick pan over medium heat.
5. Once hot, coat the pan or griddle with butter or nonstick spray as necessary.
6. Pour about ¼ cup of batter onto the hot griddle for each pancake, leaving a little space between pancakes.
7. When you see large bubbles begin to form and pop on the surface after 2 to 3 minutes, flip and cook until done.

VARIATIONS: Pick a new and exciting flavor and add one of the following ingredients: ¼ teaspoon cinnamon, ¼ teaspoon pumpkin spice, ¼ cup chocolate chips, or ¼ cup canned drained blueberries.

(Photo courtesy of KaLea Lehman)

Tactical **French Toast**

TIME: 10 MIN (PREP), 15 MIN (COOK)
MAKES: 6 SERVINGS

- -

Ingredients

5 eggs
¼ cup milk
1 teaspoon vanilla
3 tablespoon sugar
1 teaspoon cinnamon
2 tablespoons butter, softened
6 slices of whatever bread is on hand
1 teaspoon vanilla extract (optional)

Steps

1. Preheat the oven to 375°F.
2. Grease a 9x13-inch cake pan or baking dish with the softened butter.
3. In a small bowl combine the sugar and cinnamon.
4. Sprinkle ½ of the sugar mixture on the buttered dish.
5. Place 6 slices of bread in the buttered pan and sprinkle the remaining sugar mixture over the top.
6. In a medium bowl, whisk together milk, eggs, and extract.
7. Pour the egg mixture over the bread slices. Make sure the egg mixture is evenly absorbed by tilting the pan and using a fork to poke the bread if needed.
8. Place in the oven and bake for approximately 15 minutes or until the toast is cooked through.

TIP: Cook time can vary based on thickness and density of bread. If you use a bread like Texas Toast, double the recipe and add 10 minutes to bake time. This recipe is great to cut into French Toast strips and freeze for a later date.

VARIATION: You can swap out the sugar for brown sugar, honey, or maple syrup.

- -

CUSTOMS AND CAMARADERIE
The Root of the Ranger Motto

Historic Highlight. The famed Army Ranger Regiment earned its "Rangers lead the way" motto on June 6, 1944 while storming the beaches of Normandy in World War II. US troops were pinned down on the beach and General Norman Cota turned to Max Schnider, a young Lieutenant in 5 BN of the 75th Ranger Regiment, and asked what unit he belonged to. Immediately following his response, General Cota yelled, "If you're Rangers, lead the way!" They responded and led the charge to retake the beach.[21]

- -

21. MacDougall, M. (2022, July 13). *The Real Story Behind the Slogan "Rangers Lead the Way."* VeteranLife. Accessed from https://veteranlife.com/military-history/rangers-lead-the-way-motto/

Irregular Warfare **Waffles**

TIME: 10 MIN (PREP), 20 MIN (COOK)
MAKES: 6 SERVINGS

Ingredients

2 cups all-purpose flour

½ cup granulated sugar

¾ tablespoon baking powder

¾ teaspoon baking soda

¾ teaspoon salt

2 cups milk

2 large eggs

4 tablespoons melted butter, cooled

1 teaspoon vanilla extract

Steps

1. Preheat your waffle iron. Coat waffle iron with butter, oil, or nonstick spray as needed.
2. Combine all dry ingredients In a large bowl.
3. In a separate bowl or large liquid measuring cup, whisk together the milk, eggs, butter, and vanilla.
4. Slowly pour the milk mixture into the flour mixture while stirring.
5. Whisk until smooth — no need for the batter to rest as with the pancakes.
6. Cook waffles according to the manufacturer's instructions for the waffle iron, using more butter, oil, or nonstick spray as needed.

VARIATIONS: Pick a new and exciting flavor and add one of the following ingredients: ¼ teaspoon cinnamon, ¼ teaspoon pumpkin spice, or ¼ cup chocolate chips.

(Photo courtesy of Wendy Jo Peterson)

SOF STORIES
Feed Corn — Jess

After spending three weeks in the field at a school and coming home so late it was early, I came downstairs and saw my husband passed out on the couch. First thought was "gross," and my second thought was, "I had better hit the grocery store." I snuck out of the house to stock up on big breakfast items; bacon, eggs, bread, tomatoes, all the fixings for a well-deserved and filling meal. I came home and unloaded and started to cook. My husband had since left and was in the shower upstairs. I walked up to say "hi" and noticed a yellow seed on the floor, and then another, and another. I followed the corn trail to a pile of clothes on the floor. When my husband came down, I presented him with a breakfast plate . . . full of feed corn. A giant smile came to his face and he exclaimed, "I guess I have a hole in my pocket!" Thanks to his couch nap, every time the couch was moved a trail of feed corn came out. It was like that for years until we finally retired the couch.

It made for great conversations and to this day it makes me smile. It is my favorite slow, Saturday morning story to reminisce and laugh about.

(Photo courtesy of Heather Campbell)

Drop Zone **Brunch Board**

TIME: 20 MIN (PREP)
MAKES: VARIES

Ingredients

Waffles or pancakes (or use frozen if short on time)

Breakfast sausage or bacon, cooked

Eggs, scrambled, hard boiled, or sunny side up

Fresh fruit of your choice (bananas, strawberries, raspberries, blackberries, blueberries, orange slices, etc.)

Fruit jam

Nut or seed butter of your choice

Yogurt of your choice

Toppings, such as chocolate chips, sprinkles, or mini marshmallows

Maple syrup

Butter

Steps

1. Mix and match any ingredients from the above list.
2. Arrange all ingredients on a wooden board or serving platter.
3. Dive in to create your ideal brunch plate and enjoy family time. Don't forget the Tactical Topics and War Games!
4. Store any leftovers in an airtight container for up to 3 days.

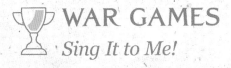

WAR GAMES
Sing It to Me!

Sing a line from your favorite song and see who can guess the musician. Why is it your favorite song? Go around the table and embrace the moment of singing in front of each other.

Guerilla Force **Yogurt Banana Splits**

TIME: 10 MIN (PREP)
MAKES: 4 SERVINGS

Ingredients

4 bananas, peeled and sliced in half lengthwise

2 cups vanilla or plain yogurt

Toppings of your choice: Chocolate chips, marshmallows, chopped nuts, granola, sprinkles, sundae syrups or fresh and dried fruit

Steps

1. Arrange the halved bananas in four individual serving dishes, as you would for a banana split.

2. Place spoonfuls of yogurt down the center of each split.

3. Provide an assortment of toppings and let everyone make their own banana split creations!

TACTICAL TOPICS

About Us

What are three words you would use to describe our family?

Guard Dog Deployment. *(Photo courtesy of Laura Nicholson)*

JTAC **Chorizo Breakfast Bowls**

TIME: 15 MIN (PREP), 1 HOUR (COOK)
MAKES: 6 SERVINGS

Ingredients

Olive oil spray
1 pound baby gold or red potatoes,
  quartered
1 tablespoon olive oil
¾ teaspoon salt
½ teaspoon garlic powder
Fresh black pepper, to taste
8 large eggs
1⅓ cups cooked turkey chorizo
2 tablespoons crumbled Mexican
  cheese, queso blanco, queso fresco
4 ounces avocado, sliced
Cilantro or scallions, for garnish
Cholula hot sauce, for serving

Steps

1. Preheat the oven to 425°F.
2. Spray a 9x12 or large oval casserole dish with cooking spray.
3. Add the potatoes, olive oil, salt, garlic powder, and black pepper and toss.
4. Bake until tender, tossing every 15 minutes, about 45-55 minutes.
5. Meanwhile, heat a large nonstick skillet over medium-low heat, spray with oil and cook the eggs in batches sunny-side up until the whites are just set, about 2-3 minutes for a runny yolk, or longer if a firm yolk is desired.
6. To serve, divide the potatoes in 4 bowls, top each with ⅓ cup chorizo, 2 fried eggs, crumbled cheese, 1 ounce avocado, and garnish with scallions or cilantro.

VARIATIONS: Omit the chorizo if you want to make these bowls vegetarian. Add in black beans for some extra fiber and protein. Omit the cheese for dairy-free. Sub the baby gold or red potatoes for sweet potatoes. Top with pico de gallo.

TACTICAL TOPICS
Know What's Special

What makes a food or a meal special to you? It doesn't have to be upscale. It can be a family favorite that takes extra preparation and perhaps some unique ingredients or maybe it is made by a particular person. What about the meal gives it meaning or makes it special?

Search and Seizure **Southwest Chicken Quiche**

TIME: 10 MIN (PREP), 50 MIN (COOK)
MAKES: 6 SERVINGS

Ingredients

1 (9-inch) unbaked pie shell
1 pound shredded cooked chicken
1 packet taco seasoning
⅓ cup water or chicken broth
1 bell pepper, chopped (red, green, yellow,
   orange — or mix them up)
1 small onion, chopped
1 cup Mexican shredded cheese
3 eggs
1¼ cup light cream or half & half
½ teaspoon salt
Dash of nutmeg
Dash of black pepper & red pepper
Optional: ½ cup diced spinach

Steps

1. Preheat the oven to 400°F.
2. Put pie crust in pie dish, prick with fork, and bake 5 minutes to set crust.
3. Sauté sweet peppers and onion in oil.
4. Add cooked chicken, taco seasoning, and water/broth. Cook until taco seasoning is fairly absorbed.
5. Place meat mixture & cheese in bottom of pie crust in dish.
6. Beat eggs in a bowl. Add cream, salt, nutmeg, black & red peppers, mixing well. Pour mixture over meat & cheese.
7. Reduce heat to 350°F and bake 35 minutes or longer until set.

VARIATION: If you want your quiche to be more spicy, add extra red pepper flakes and dice up some jalapeños to throw in as well

(Photo courtesy of KaLea Lehman)

Carbo-Loaded

WHILE WE MAY GET THE OCCASIONAL, restful weekend, oftentimes the breakfast demands fall on the other end of the scale. There are countless reasons you might need to carbo-load your plate. Maybe you have a big event or race planned, a kid who needs fuel for a big game or competition, or your operator is on a flight crew running night flights only to return starved.

Our crew has some hearty recipes that take less of a toll in prep time. They will fuel your tummy and help your whole family power through. Many of these go-to fill'er-up recipes can be prepped before-hand and not crunch your morning routine. Everyone can feel the love and get on to a winning day.

A special operator takes his spouse and mom up for some high altitude fun. (*Photo courtesy of Dan and Leslie Luna*)

Wolfhounds **Spinach and Potato Frittata**

TIME: 10 MIN (PREP), 25 MIN (COOK)
MAKES: 4 SERVINGS

Ingredients

6 slices bacon, chopped
1 potato, thinly sliced
8 eggs
⅓ cup milk
1 garlic clove, minced
1 cup torn/chopped fresh spinach
½ cup shredded cheddar cheese

Steps

1. Preheat the oven to 350°F.
2. Cook bacon in an oven safe skillet, like a cast iron, over medium heat until cooked. Remove bacon from pan and set aside. Drain all but 1 tablespoon of bacon fat from the pan.
3. Add the potatoes to the pan. Cover and cook for about 10 minutes until tender but firm. Add garlic.
4. In a medium bowl beat together eggs and milk.
5. Spread potatoes evenly in the skillet. Top with garlic, bacon, and spinach. Add egg mixture.
6. Sprinkle with cheddar cheese. Cover and cook on low for 5 minutes.
7. Place the skillet in the oven and cook for 10 minutes covered and then another 10 minutes uncovered, or until eggs are firm.
8. Can be eaten hot or cold.

VARIATION: Use sweet potato, cooked hash browns, or tater tots instead of potato. Omit milk and cheese for dairy free. Make vegetarian by using olive oil instead of bacon fat and remove bacon. You can also change any of the fillings to your liking.

SOF STORIES
Night Flight Brunch — Nikki

For Air Force special ops aircrew, "train like you fight" often means multiple night flights per week to stay proficient on night vision goggles (NVGs or NODS). Not only does this wreak havoc with their internal clock, but it makes nightly family dinner impossible. So on those days my husband wasn't going in until the early afternoon or after he awoke in the late morning from the previous night's flight, I would throw together a brunch of sorts—a frittata made with leftover meat and veggies, or eggs to order if I was feeling up to it. When the kids were little, they enjoyed fruit, yogurt, or cereal alongside us, but now they look forward to those fancy family frittatas.

(Photo courtesy of KaLea Lehman)

Teams **Everything Bagels**

TIME: 15 MIN (PREP), 15 MIN (COOK)
MAKES: 6 SERVING

- -

Ingredients

2 cups almond flour

1 tablespoon baking powder

1 teaspoon garlic powder

1 teaspoon onion powder

1 teaspoon dried Italian seasoning

3 large eggs, divided

3 cups shredded low moisture mozzarella
cheese

5 tablespoons cream cheese

3 tablespoons Everything Bagel Seasoning

Steps

1. Preheat the oven to 425°F. Line a
   rimmed baking sheet with parchment
   paper.
2. In a medium mixing bowl, combine the
   almond flour, baking powder, garlic
   powder, onion powder, and dried Italian
   seasoning.
3. Mix until well combined. Put the mixture
   through a flour sifter to ensure that all
   the baking powder gets mixed in with
   the rest of the ingredients.
4. Crack one of the eggs into a small bowl
   and whisk. This will be the egg wash for
   the top of the bagels.

5. In a large microwave safe mixing bowl,
   combine the mozzarella cheese and
   cream cheese. Microwave for 1 minute
   and 30 seconds.
6. Remove from the microwave and stir
   to combine. Return to the microwave
   for 1 additional minute. Mix until well
   combined.
7. To the melted cheeses, add the remaining 2 eggs and the almond flour mixture.
8. Mix until all ingredients are well incorporated. If the dough gets too stringy and
   unworkable, simply put it back in the
   microwave for 30 seconds to soften and
   continue mixing.
9. Divide the dough into 6 equal portions.
   Roll each portion into a ball.
10. Gently press your finger into the center
    of each dough ball to form a ring.
    Stretch the ring to make a small hole
    in the center and form it into a bagel
    shape.
11. Brush the top of each bagel with the
    egg wash and sprinkle with Everything
    Bagel Seasoning.
12. Bake on the middle rack for 12-14 min-
    utes or until golden brown.

TIP: If you do not have a silicone baking mat or parchment paper, you can also bake these on
foil, in a large donut pan, or on a greased baking sheet.

Never Quit **Quinoa, Broccoli, and Ham Bites**

TIME: 10 MIN (PREP), 40 MIN (COOK)
MAKES: 6 SERVINGS

- -

Ingredients

2 cups quinoa, rinsed

4 cups chicken broth

½ yellow onion

2 cups broccoli

½ cup diced ham

Salt and pepper to taste

⅔ cup shredded cheddar cheese

8 eggs

Steps

1. Preheat the oven to 400°F.
2. Prepare the quinoa as the package states but substitute chicken broth for water.
3. Finely dice the onion, broccoli, and ham.
4. Stir together quinoa, diced ingredients, salt, pepper, cheese, and eggs in a bowl.
5. Pour mixture into a greased, mini cupcake pan and cook for 15 minutes. If you use a regular cupcake pan, you will need to cook them for 25 minutes.
6. The egg bites should have a golden brown color on the top and pop out of the pan when cooled.

Deployed for a JCET where it just kept snowing. *(Photo courtesy of KaLea Lehman)*

SOF STORIES
When the Fall Came to my Table — Agnes

One June morning while sitting at our break-fast table with my teen daughter, my phone alerted me to a notification on LinkedIn. It was a desperate plea for help from a family in Afghanistan. I read it to my daughter and put my phone down. I was just a spouse. I watched my husband train for unconventional war, but I had no business in it. My husband deployed many times, but he never deployed to Afghanistan. How was this war coming to my table?

I ignored the messages for a few weeks but the pleas increased, and now I had friends posting updates on Afghanistan withdrawal efforts. Before I knew it, I was collecting documents and passing on instructions. One moment I was making breakfast for my young kids and the next I was consumed with how to ratline a family with young children out of a country being overtaken by the Taliban. I couldn't even wrap my head around how bizarre the whole scenario was. I couldn't ignore the messages without attempting to help when I knew the network helping.

Orphans in Afghanistan eating dinner. Caring American veterans made sure they had food. *(Photo courtesy of Perry Blackburn)*

Somehow the War in Afghanistan ended as ugly and abruptly as it began. Our Air Force pararescuemen defied the impossible and saved many Afghan allies. Thank goodness I didn't get the plea from the mom stuck standing in the sewage, on the wrong side of the HKIA fence, holding her infant. My friend took that call and so many more. She had the soul of a saint to raise three sweet babies during the day and rescue allies from hell all through the night. She was a veteran who was part of one of the efforts saving lives.

When the last plane left, the pleas for help just multiplied. From my vantage point, I watched active duty service members, veterans, spouses, interagency folks, and caring American civilians work creatively and tirelessly to honor a promise and hold true to their values. For many, it was a war without boundary and a deployment from home. I was without skill to navigate this situation, but I will forever be proud of our community for rallying to save every life they could. They are still putting food on orphanage tables more than a year later because human dignity and lives matter.

NODS Overnight Oats

TIME: 10 MIN (PREP)
MAKES: 1 SERVING

Ingredients

1 cup rolled oats
1-1½ cups liquid of choice (milk, almond milk, coconut milk, etc.)
1 teaspoon sweetener (maple syrup, honey, or brown sugar)
Fruit (optional)
Nuts (optional)

Steps

1. Mix all ingredients together in a sealable container.
2. Store it in the fridge overnight. Enjoy the next day!

(Photo courtesy of Lynnsy Snook)

VARIATION: Frozen or fresh fruit works well. You can add a teaspoon of chia to up the protein. A favorite is maple syrup, raisins, and chopped walnuts with a pinch of cinnamon - tastes like a cinnamon roll!

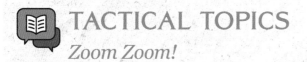 TACTICAL TOPICS
Zoom Zoom!

What gives you energy? It could be a food, an activity, or an idea that gets you going and firing on all cylinders. Maybe you or your crew are "hangry" and need to boost up your blood sugar. What can you do or eat if you feel like you are running on low?

Advanced Skills **Breakfast Pizza**

TIME: 10 MIN (PREP), 45 MIN (COOK)
MAKES: 8 SERVINGS

Ingredients

5 eggs
3 cups frozen shredded hash browns, thawed
½ teaspoon salt
¼ teaspoon pepper
½ pound pork sausage
¼ cup sliced green onions
¼ cup diced red or green pepper
1½ cups grated cheddar cheese

Steps

1. For the crust, beat one egg, then add the hash browns, salt, and pepper. Press very firmly into the bottom and up the sides of a well greased 10 inch tart pan. Bake at 425°F for 20 minutes, or till starting to brown.
2. Meanwhile, brown the sausage in a skillet. Drain and set aside.
3. Beat the remaining eggs and cook in a small amount of oil in the skillet. Set aside.
4. Remove the crust from the oven and sprinkle the scrambled eggs and browned sausage over the top. Add half of the green onions and peppers.
5. Sprinkle the cheese over the top. Return to the oven and bake for 10 more minutes, or until the cheese is melted.
6. Garnish with remaining onions and peppers.

CUSTOMS AND CAMARADERIE
Edson's Raiders

Historic Highlight. The Raiders, the Marine Corps Special Operations Force, has powerful roots in the short-lived, World War II Raider Battalions led by LTC Merritt Edson. Edson's Raiders were the Marine Corps' first special missions force that significantly impacted key campaigns in the Pacific Theater. They were the first to fight in amphibious landings at Guadalcanal, Makin Atoll, Bougainville, and New Georgia. They ran raids and functioned as guerrilla units. The Raider's efforts were legendary in the South Pacific, but they were disbanded following their success.[22] Today, their history continues in the modern Marine Raider units, re-established in 2006 to be "Always Faithful, Always Forward."[23]

22. Navy and Marine Corps WWII Commemorative Committee. (n.d.). *Marine Corps Raiders*. United States Marine Corps University. Accessed from https://www.usmcu.edu/Research/Marine-Corps-History-Division/Brief-Histories/Marines-in-World-War-II/Marine-Corps-Raiders/
23. Marine Forces Special Operations Command. (2020, September 4). *Who we are*. Marine Raider Recruiting. Accessed from https://www.marsoc.com/who-we-are/

Fast and Friendly **Vegetarian Quiche**

TIME: 10 MIN (PREP), 1 HR (COOK)
MAKES: 16-20 SERVINGS

Ingredients

4 tablespoons olive oil

1 onion, diced

1 (8-ounce) package bella mushrooms or 3 sliced portabella mushrooms

2 cups fresh baby spinach, chopped

1 cup milk

12 eggs

2 cups sliced cheddar or colby-jack cheese

3 teaspoons minced garlic

2 teaspoons salt

2 frozen pie crusts, thawed

Pepper to taste

Steps

1. Preheat oven to 375°F.
2. In a large frying pan, sauté the onion, salt, pepper, garlic, and sliced mushrooms for about 8 minutes or until tender.
3. In a separate large bowl, beat the eggs and milk until combined.
4. Stir in the chopped baby spinach, cheese, and sauteed mixture.
5. Press the 2 pie crusts into a large 15x10 inch baking dish. Mold edges with fingers.
6. Pour egg mixture into the crust.
7. Bake at 375°F for 1 hour.

(Photo courtesy of KaLea Lehman)

WAR GAMES
Gratefulness Grab Bag

Give everyone two slips of paper and have them write down two things that they're thankful for (these can be silly or serious!). Place the slips in a bowl, pass it around the table, and have different people read the slips out loud.

Tan Beret **Zucchini Bread**

TIME: 15 MIN (PREP), 1 HR MINS (COOK)
MAKES: 2 LOAVES

Ingredients

3 eggs
1 cup vegetable oil
2 cups sugar
2 cups grated zucchini
3 teaspoons vanilla
3 cups flour
1 teaspoon baking soda
1 teaspoon salt
3 ½ teaspoons cinnamon

Steps

1. Preheat oven to 350°F.
2. Butter or grease 2 loaf pans.
3. Combine all ingredients in a mixing bowl and mix well.
4. Pour half of the batter into each prepared loaf pan.
5. Bake for 1 hour at 350°F.

TIP: Bread is delicious served warm, but it is even better served cold with butter. For a fun addition, add ½ cup of dried fruit.

(Photo courtesy of Wendy Jo Peterson)

A view of Independence Day fireworks from the Pentagon lawn
(Photo courtesy of Lynnsy Snook)

9. Anywhere but
the Table

★ ★ ★

SOME DAYS FEEL LONG. They seem to drag on, and it's easy to feel restless or just plain tired. These days always hit a handful of weeks into a deployment trip or training work-up. The thought of stocking groceries, making time for an uneventful meal, listening to the inevitable complaints, and the task of post dinner clean up just saps us. We need a shake up. We all know this feeling a bit from our universal COVID-19 experience. For some of us, it wasn't the stress or uncertainty that made these days seem "gray." It was the way the feeling seemed to hog tie life, adventure, and connecting with faraway friends and family. That took a toll. We all needed a friend or a simple change of pace to brighten life.

The support of a friend or a reason to let rules slide are refreshing. Our favorite, though least common, reason to flee from the table were opportunities to rendezvous with our service member. We seized the moment, dropped it all, and made dinner happen elsewhere. Spontaneous dinners and mealtime meet ups always got us to bedtime and that cherished glass of wine, beer, or bubbly. Table or not, we were together, everyone was fed, and we made new memories. The burdens of the day always felt lighter. In a way, we were redefining the boundaries of family mealtime by seasoning it with a pinch of adventure.

Mother and daughter take a moment away and explore. *(Photo courtesy of Jennifer Byrne)*

371

Truck Bed Spreads

SOMETIMES THERE IS NO TABLE. Truck bed spreads happen for many reasons. Maybe you PCS'd and camped for weeks, found a weekend to sneak off, or you took advantage of the opportunity to rough it for lunch or dinner next to the range, the drop zone, or who knows where else. One thing is for sure, each meet-up and spread is a memorable moment characterized by your efforts to sneak in just a few brief minutes of quality time.

These meet-ups can be a heavy family lift, but the quality time is worth the family scramble. We either packed it up, purchased it, or stomached what they had to eat. It didn't matter because it was a moment together—breakfast in the bed of the pickup truck near the lake, a fast midtown lunch meet-up, or dinner brought late to their work desk. Meals together can be sparse, so when possible, drop what you are doing and embrace the adventure.

Whatever the reason for the link-up, embrace a simple spread, snap a picture, and enjoy the time together. It's a low key time to take in the sights and sounds around you. If you have kids, it will often bring an opportunity ripe with possibilities for outdoor exploration.

Special Operations kids hanging out *(Photo courtesy of Britt'n Morrison)*

OSS Fast and Furious **Frito Pie**

TIME: 10 MIN (PREP), 20 MIN (COOK)
MAKES: 6 SERVINGS

Ingredients

1 pound lean ground beef

1 (15.5-ounce) can pinto beans

1 (15.5-ounce) can black beans

1 small onion, diced

1 (14.5-ounce) can diced or crushed
  tomatoes

1 packet taco seasoning

1 large bag of Scoops Fritos

1 jar of salsa

1 cup Colby-Jack shredded cheese

1 squeeze bottle of sour cream

Steps

1. Brown the ground beef in a frying pan and drain the excess grease.
2. Drain and rinse the canned pinto and black beans.
3. Add the canned beans, diced onion, and canned tomato to the beef.
4. Stir well, then add the taco seasoning mixture.
5. Once all the mixture is hot, it is ready to serve.
6. This dish can be scooped into individual bags of Fritos and topped with salsa, cheese, and sour cream as desired.

TIP: If you are on the go, put the refrigerated ingredients in a lunch cooler and pack away the taco filling. Once to your ideal spot, the meat can be spooned over individual bags of Fritos and topped with cheese, sour cream, and salsa on the picnic spot!

(Photo courtesy of Lynnsy Snook)

9. ANYWHERE BUT THE TABLE

SOF STORIES

Picnic Here, Picnic There, We've Picnicked Everywhere — Diana

Special ops wives hit the trails then picnic at a park. *(Photo courtesy of KaLea Lehman)*

During our almost 15 years in special operations, we've pretty much mastered the sloppy picnic on the go. Our link-ups evolved with his job, our growing family, and my preferences. We started linking up for quick lunch breaks during his days in Special Forces language school. We were newlywed, and I would pack up a tasty barbecue lunch. By the end of his Q-course we would picnic with our newborn daughter.

These days, my favorite link-up is a tailgate gobbler following family PT (physical training). We meet up on the training grounds, pack our four kids in a double, or sometimes, triple stroller and crank out 3-5 fast miles together on the trail. As we run, my husband takes the kids on an imaginary dinosaur hunt through the woods along the road. Then, we top off our family workout with sandwiches and snacks on his tailgate as the kids attempt pull-ups and adventures into the woodline. When our meet-ups are over, I have a handful of fresh family pictures and my workout logged! Then, we split ways to finish the work day.

Special Tactics **Picnic Sliders**

TIME: 10 MIN (PREP)

MAKES: 8 SERVINGS

Ingredients

1 pack King's Hawaiian rolls

Condiments of choice — Dijon mustard,
  mayonnaise

1 pound sliced deli meat of choice

8 ounces sliced cheese of choice

(Photo courtesy of KaLea Lehman)

Steps

1. Remove the Hawaiian rolls from the package and using a long serrated bread knife, slice into top and bottom sections while still attached together.
2. Spread condiments of choice over bread.
3. Layer meat and cheese as desired on bottom buns.
4. Place top buns on sandwiches, and return the entire stack to the paper tray. Slice along lines to create slider size sandwiches.
5. Return tray to plastic bag and store in fridge for up to 3 days for grab and go, premade sliders. These go are a favorite for picnics, road trips, and beach days.

🏆 WAR GAMES
Nature—Name it

There are new finds and adventures to be found everywhere. Take a moment to stop and look around. Challenge every family member to spot their favorite five picnic items. Why are they your favorite finds? Take a moment to uncover the unique observations of your dinner spot.

Looking for shark teeth on the North Carolina coast. *(Photo courtesy of Lynnsy Snook)*

Reaper Ready **Reuben**

TIME: 10 MIN (PREP), 5 MIN (COOK)
MAKES: 6 SERVINGS

Ingredients

½ teaspoon olive oil
½ pound sliced corned beef or pastrami
2 tablespoons unsalted butter, room temp
6 slices rye bread
6 slices Swiss cheese
½ cup sauerkraut, drained very well
Russian or Thousand Island dressing

Steps

1. In a skillet, over medium heat, add oil. Once hot, add the meat and cook just until heated.
2. Lightly butter one side of each slice of bread. Place the bread butter side down on a plate.
3. Add the toppings to each sandwich by spreading the dressing, topping with the meat, cheese, and sauerkraut.
4. Close bread slices to create a sandwich.
5. In a hot skillet, cook sandwiches over medium heat 4-6 minutes, flipping once.
6. Cook until the cheese melts and the bread is crispy.

VARIATION: Substitute the rye bread with sourdough bread.

TACTICAL TOPICS

Best Moment Looking Back

What was your favorite moment while living the SOF life? If you could relive one day, which would it be?

Boots reflecting fresh out of Afghanistan.
(Photo courtesy of Herb Thompson)

CUSTOMS AND CAMARADERIE
Operation Sauerkraut - A PSYOP

Historic Highlight. Near the end of World War II, German military officers attempted and failed to assassinate Adoplf Hitler. This courageous attempt inspired the Office of Strategic Services (OSS) to launch a psychological operation with a mission to exploit the burgeoning disillusionment of the German military and spur more insider attacks on Nazi leaders of the Third Reich. This effort was codenamed "Operation Sauerkraut."

The female OSS officer, Barbara Lauwers, worked to identify German POWs willing to take bold actions to spur discontent and doubt. These selected prisoners of war were "provided with fake identity papers, cover stories, German uniforms, weapons, survival supplies, and approximately 3,000 propaganda leaflets, then sent back to the front lines." They deployed to disburse the information and spur fear that the Germans were losing the war. Operation Sauerkraut soured the hope of so many Germans that the Allies expanded the operations into other countries where the war was raging.[24]

24. Fratus, M. (2022, September 2). *Killer Vampires, demon dolls, and Sauerkraut: A brief history of american psyops.* Coffee or Die. Accessed from https://www.coffeeordie.com/craziest-american-psyops

ITC **Tortilla Wraps**

TIME: 15 MIN (PREP), 25 MIN (COOK)

MAKES: 6 SERVINGS

- -

Ingredients

¼ cup quinoa, dry

2¼ cups canned low-sodium black beans, drained, rinsed

¼ cup fresh red bell pepper, seeded, diced

¼ cup fresh red onions, peeled, diced

½ cup fresh carrots, peeled, shredded

¼ cup reduced-fat white cheddar cheese, shredded

1 teaspoon chili powder

1¼ teaspoon ground cumin

1¼ teaspoon fresh lime juice

6 whole-wheat tortillas, 6"

1 tablespoon vegetable oil

Steps

1. Preheat the oven to 325°F.
2. Rinse quinoa in a fine mesh strainer until water runs clear, not cloudy.
3. Combine quinoa and ¾ cup water in a small pot. Cover and bring to a boil.
4. Turn heat down to low and simmer until water is completely absorbed, about 10-15 minutes.

5. When done, quinoa will be soft and a white ring will pop out of the kernel. The white ring will appear only when it is fully cooked.
6. Fluff with a fork and set aside. A rice cooker may be used with the same quantity of quinoa and water.
7. Place black beans in a large mixing bowl. Lightly mash beans by squeezing them using gloved hands (at least 50 percent of the beans should appear whole). Be careful not to over-mash beans.
8. To make filling, add to the mashed beans the quinoa, red peppers, red onions, carrots, cheese, chili powder, cumin, and lime juice.
9. For each wrap, place ½ cup of filling on the bottom half of the tortilla and roll in the form of a burrito. The wrap may also be folded in half like a taco.
10. Brush filled wraps lightly with vegetable oil and place on a baking sheet.
11. Bake for 10 minutes. Wraps will be lightly brown. Serve hot.

Long Tab **Fruit Skewers with Marshmallow Dip**

TIME: 15 MIN (PREP)
MAKES: 8 SERVINGS

Ingredients

1 watermelon

1 quart blueberries

1 fresh pineapple

Wooden skewers

4 ounces marshmallow fluff

12 ounces whipped cream cheese (pick your favorite flavor)

Steps

1. Cut the watermelon in ¾ in slices. Use a star-shape cookie cutter to cut stars out of the heart of the watermelon rounds.
2. Then place 7 blueberries on a skewer, 1 piece of pineapple, and top with a star shaped piece of watermelon. Repeat until the fruit is gone.
3. Mix the marshmallow fluff and whipped cream cheese together in a mixing bowl and serve with the skewers.

(Photo courtesy of Lynnsy Snook)

Spontaneous Potluck

DEPLOYMENTS AND WORK TRIPS can be long. Most of the time you find a rhythm and the weeks begin to roll, but one of the best ways to spice up the weeks and speed up time is to fill it with friends. There always seems to be a day when the personal energy bank or your patience just fall flat. The energy and inspiration needed for dinner are long gone, and you are just antsy for a switch-up. So it's time for friends, food, and fun. We are all in this boat together, and there is no reason to complicate it with formality. If there are kids, chaos will certainly happen, but that's part of the fun.

A surprise picnic and visit at school from an old friend. *(Photo courtesy of Andrea Orr)*

The spontaneous potluck is a "come as you are" meal. It may be a thrown together, hodgepodge spread. It doesn't matter. It's about the people, the moment, and the memories. You don't realize it at the moment, but these meals shared together become priceless memories over the years as deployments roll on. They give each trip a little dimension and depth.

An extended weekend visit with old friends. Takeout for the win! *(Photo courtesy of KaLea Lehman)*

For the Cold, Wet, and Tired **Pecan Pie Minis**

TIME: 10 MIN (PREP), 25MIN (COOK)
MAKES: 6 SERVINGS

Ingredients

Crust

1 cup of flour
¼ cup butter, softened
3 ounces cream cheese

Filling

¾ cup brown sugar
1 egg
⅛ teaspoon salt
1 teaspoon vanilla
¾ cup of chopped pecans
1 tablespoon butter, melted

Steps

1. Preheat the oven to 350°F.
2. Mix the crust ingredients together and press into a mini muffin pan.
3. Mix the pecan pie filling ingredients.
4. Pour into the mini crusts carefully. Use caution not to overfill the small crusts.
5. Bake for 20-25 minutes.

(Photo courtesy of KaLea Lehman)

HALO Hearty **Ham and Beans**

TIME: 10 MIN (PREP), 6 HOURS (COOK)
MAKES: 6-8 SERVINGS

Ingredients

1 ham bone or 1 package of ham/pork
  pieces for seasoning
1 yellow onion, diced
4 celery stalks, diced
1 pound dry Great Northern beans
½ teaspoon baking soda
6 cups chicken broth
1-2 ham steaks, diced
Salt and pepper to taste

Steps

1. Add all ingredients except the diced ham to a slow cooker.
2. Cook in a slow cooker for 5 hours on medium.
3. After 5 hours, stir in the diced ham, and cook 30 minutes to 1 hour more at medium heat.
4. Season with salt and pepper and serve.

 TACTICAL TOPICS
Lucky to Have You

What do we each bring to the table? Go around the table and share one quality you bring to the table, and name something that another person contributes to your family.

A Navy SOF kid and an Army SOF kid becoming the best of friends. (*Photo courtesy of KaLea Lehman*)

Eagle, Globe, and Anchor to **Summer Salad**

TIME: 10 MIN (PREP)
MAKES: 6 SERVINGS

Ingredients

2 cups cherry or grape tomatoes, quartered
¼ cup red or white onion, sliced
1 cucumber, sliced
1 cup marinated mozzarella cheese balls, halved
¼ cup balsamic vinaigrette
½ cup croutons, optional

Steps

1. Mix all ingredients and refrigerate 30 minutes before serving.

CUSTOMS AND CAMARADERIE
The Path to Special Operations Command: Iranian Hostage Crisis

Historic Highlight. In November 1979 the U.S. Embassy in Tehran was overrun by Iranian college students who supported the Iranian Revolution. They held 52 Americans hostage for 444 days in what would be known as the Iranian hostage crisis. This crisis drew an outpouring of patriotism and attention from the American public, and President Carter tried to coerce release of the hostages though economic and diplomatic sanctions.

Five months into the crisis, President Carter approved Operation Eagle Claw, a joint special operations mission to rescue the hostages. Eagle Claw brought together special capabilities from 4 service branches – the Army, Navy, Marine Corps, and Air Force – but it ran into a series of mishaps. Ultimately, the mission was aborted, no hostages were rescued, and eight service members were killed when a helicopter crashed into a C-130. The lessons learned from the mission failure revealed many critical gaps in U.S. military capabilities, and it ultimately led to the creation of U.S. Special Operations Command and the extraordinary joint military capabilities we have today.[25]

25. Correll, D. (2022, August 19). *40 years later: How the Iran hostage crisis shaped the future of Special Operations*. Military Times. Accessed from https://www.militarytimes.com/flashpoints/2019/11/04/40-years-later-how-the-iran-hostage-crisis-shaped-the-future-of-special-operations/

Take it Easy **Egg Roll Bowl**

TIME: 10 MIN (PREP), 15 MIN (COOK)
MAKES: 6 SERVINGS

Ingredients

1 pound ground sausage, pork, or turkey
14 ounce bag coleslaw
1 onion, diced
1 tablespoon ground ginger
1 teaspoon minced garlic
2 tablespoons soy sauce

Steps

1. Brown the meat in a large pan.
2. Drain fat and add in the coleslaw, onions, ginger, and garlic, sauteing until softened.
3. Once the onion and cabbage are cooked, stir in the soy sauce.
4. Cook a few more minutes and serve over white rice.

CUSTOMS AND CAMARADERIE
Air Commando Cave Rescue

Historic Highlight. It is most common to think of special operators in war and conflict, but sometimes their special capabilities play an inspiring role in other unconventional ways. A great example of the selfless courage and heroics of special operators happened in 2019 when a youth soccer team became trapped in an underwater cave in Thailand. The world watched as dramatic rescue efforts played out to rescue the young boys. Among those who harnessed their special skills to save the team was Technical Sergeant Kenny O'Brien from the 320th Special Tactics Squadron. TSgt O'Brien helped pull the 13 trapped individuals through 2.5 miles of flooded caves. It was a rare moment for the world to witness the exceptional skills of Air Force special operators.[26]

26. Burke, M. M. (2019, August 9). *One year after Thai Cave Rescue, US airman recalls harrowing effort to save youth soccer team*. Stars and Stripes. Accessed from https://www.stripes.com/theaters/asia_pacific/one-year-after-thai-cave-rescue-us-airman-recalls-harrowing-effort-to-save-youth-soccer-team-1.593762

Let 'em Loose

YOU KNOW THAT FEELING where your body feels like a pressure keg? Maybe it's from excitement, joy, frustration, worry, or boredom. Whatever the reason, we had a need to let loose! Training mission, deployment, unpredictable work days, or it was just vacation and we were out of entertainment ideas. Sometimes it was us and sometimes it was the kids bouncing off the walls. It was time for a quick shake-up!

Making memories exploring a state park with friends. *(Photo courtesy of Britt'n Morrison)*

We have been down this road so many times, and we were never alone. Kids need friends and so do we. There was always a friend ready or at least willing to join us on an adventure. It was the perfect moment to pack up dinner for a picnic, "bag it up" for an evening hike with a buddy, or grab some take out for an easy meet-up.

These quick connections were fast, easy, and exciting. A big playdate or meet-up sometimes felt like a lot so we found a park, a pond, or a trail. The key was to let go, get out, and to be with friends or family, and enjoy the moments of laughter, honest conversation, and break from routine. It was an active, flying solo, twist on the truck bed spread.

Boys will be . . . busy. *(Photo courtesy of KaLea Lehman)*

Dad's Gone Again, **Perfect Roast Chicken**

TIME: 15 MIN (PREP), 1.5 HOURS (COOK)
MAKES: 6-8 SERVINGS

Ingredients

5-6 pound whole chicken
Kosher salt
Freshly ground black pepper
1 large bunch fresh thyme (or teaspoon of dried)
1 lemon, halved
1 garlic bulb, cut in half crosswise
2 tablespoons olive oil or butter, melted
1 onion, thickly sliced

Steps

1. Preheat the oven to 425°F.
2. Remove the chicken giblets. Rinse the chicken inside and out. Remove any excess fat and leftover pinfeathers and pat the outside dry.
3. Place the chicken in a large roasting pan. Liberally salt and pepper the inside of the chicken. Stuff the cavity with the thyme or sprinkle with dried, both halves of the lemon, and all the garlic.
4. Brush the outside of the chicken with the olive oil or butter and sprinkle again with salt and pepper. Tie the legs together with kitchen string and tuck the wing tips under the body of the chicken.
5. Scatter the onion slices around the chicken.
6. Roast the chicken for 1½ hours, or until the juices run clear when you cut between a leg and thigh.

SOF STORIES
Everywhere but the Table — Kate

I tried to keep some "normalcy" when my husband was gone and a roasted chicken always made everyone happy. It provided us with extra chicken for other easy meals and the bones for soup stock. Years ago, I clearly remember my five year old daughter refusing to sit at the table because daddy wasn't home. So she sat under the table . . . or next to the table. I picked my battles and allowed her to fill her belly and her pink IKEA plastic plate on the floor. As a soon-to-be-13-year-old with the same rebellious qualities, I'm happy to report she now sits at the table with a real plate and is a proud vegetarian.

(Opposite) (Photo courtesy of Julianne Ziebell)

Go Time **Grilled Cheese Cut-Ups**

TIME: 5 MIN (PREP), 10 MIN (COOK)
MAKES: 8 SERVINGS

Ingredients

½ cup butter, melted
1 loaf white or wheat bread
¾ pound deli ham, finely shredded or
   pepperoni, sliced
1 pound white American cheese

Steps

1. Brush melted butter on the exterior pieces of bread.
2. Layer bread, American cheese, ham or pepperoni, one more slice of American cheese, then one more piece of bread.
3. Place this on a skillet or a griddle and brown the bread on medium-high heat.
4. Remove from heat, cut into desired shapes, and enjoy.
5. Repeat to make more sandwiches.

TIP: If making a lot of sandwiches, place them on a baking sheet. Bake at 375°F for 8-10 minutes, remove from the oven and serve.

VARIATIONS: To make a pizza version, brush insides of bread with a thin layer of pizza or pasta sauce, and substitute pepperoni or cooked sausage for the ham. Use shredded mozzarella.

JUST Cheese Please: Mix up your cheeses by adding your favorite sliced or shredded cheese - and perhaps a sprinkle of Parmesan.

GETTIN' Fancy: Try brie and fruit jam on sliced sourdough. Pinkies up, ladies and gentlemen!

WAR GAMES
Post Picnic Finds

Challenge everyone to find the oddest, most interesting, or most beautiful discovery. Take 10-30 minutes to explore. Bring back treasures and retell about your discovery stories.

SOF kids show the treasures after a quick state park meet-up. *(Photo courtesy of KaLea Lehman)*

(Photo courtesy of Lynnsy Snook)

Mission Planning **Mexican Pizza**

TIME: 5 MIN (PREP), 25 MIN (COOK)
MAKES: 4 SERVINGS

Ingredients

1 pound ground beef
1 packet taco seasoning
¾ cup water
4 flour tortillas, burrito size
1 tablespoon vegetable oil or spray oil
1 (15-ounce) can refried beans
1 (10-ounce) can enchilada sauce
¼ cup diced tomatoes
1½ cups shredded Colby Jack cheese

Steps

1. Preheat the oven to 400°F.
2. In a large skillet, brown ground beef, breaking up into small pieces. Once cooked, add taco seasoning and water. Bring to a boil, reduce heat and simmer until most of the liquid is absorbed.
3. Place two tortillas on a baking sheet and brush with oil or lightly spray with cooking spray. Bake just until starting to brown, then flip and bake on the other side until crisp.
4. Spread about ¼ cup of beans evenly on each tortilla. Top with taco meat.
5. Drizzle about 2 tablespoons of enchilada sauce evenly over the meat and beans.
6. Sprinkle tomatoes and cheese evenly over the top.
7. Place each pizza on a baking sheet and bake for 8-10 minutes until the cheese is melted and everything is hot.
8. Slice and serve.

TACTICAL TOPICS
Family Fun

THE FAMILY DINNER PROJECT.ORG

What is your favorite thing to do as a family?

A Special Forces family getting away for some weekend fun. *(Photo courtesy of Britt'n Morris)*

Extra Run until the **Bugle Call Snack Mix**

TIME: 10 MIN (PREP)
MAKES: 8 SERVINGS

Ingredients

1 can salted cashews
12 ounces pretzels (any shape)
12 ounces Bugles (corn snack food, may substitute with Fritos)
8-12 ounces Goldfish crackers
1 packet ranch dip seasoning
¾ cup vegetable oil

Steps

1. In a large bowl, combine the cashews, pretzels, Bugles, goldfish crackers, and dry Ranch seasoning. Stir well.
2. Drizzle the mix with vegetable oil and stir until the Ranch sticks to the snack mix. Great for a party snack or to take on the go!

TACTICAL TOPICS.
What is your Unwind?

What is your go to activity to "get away" from the weight of the day? How does this help to relieve stress?

Shaking it up with a day on the river. *(Photo courtesy of KaLea Lehman)*

Homecoming **Hearty Charcuterie Spread**

TIME: 15 MIN (PREP)
MAKES: 4 SERVINGS

Ingredients

2 cups cauliflower florets, cut into bite-size
  pieces
1 cucumber, cut into long wedges
2 carrots, halved and sliced lengthwise into
  2-inch pieces
½ cup dried apricots
½ cup pitted dates
1 cup walnuts
½ cup almonds
½ cup hummus (see recipe on page 113)
½ cup jarred roasted red bell peppers,
  drained

½ pound sliced deli meats (ham, salami, or
  prosciutto)
½ cup marinated artichoke hearts
Kalamata olives
Flatbread or sliced baguette, for serving

Steps

1. On a large serving platter, place each
    item grouped together.
2. Serve family-style and enjoy!

(Photo courtesy of Wendy Jo Peterson)

Counterterrorism **Sweet and Savory Crepes**

TIME: 5 MIN (PREP), 15 MIN (COOK)
MAKES: 6 SERVINGS

Ingredients

¾ cups of flour
½ teaspoon salt
2 eggs
1 tablespoon of melted butter

Steps

1. Mix all ingredients together.

2. Once the mixture is a smooth consistency, pour ½ cup of batter on the griddle.
3. Smooth crepes in circular motion.
4. Cook on each side.
5. Once the crepe is browned, add ham, cheese, salt and pepper for a savory flavor.
6. For a dessert crepe consider: banana slices, strawberries, Nutella, powder sugar, or marshmallows.

SOF STORIES
Channeling Cher — Lynnsy

In the coming of age drama, *Mermaids*, Cher stars as a mom who—among other questionable characteristics—can't cook a full meal. But she can put together a hell of an hors d'oeuvres platter! On those days when I just don't have the energy to follow a recipe or I need to creatively use up leftovers from the fridge, I get out the toothpicks, crank up the 1960s doo wop music, and channel my inner Cher. There is something about a variety of nicely displayed small bites that make any occasion seem just a bit more fun.

Suggested playlist:

- "The Shoop Shoop Song (It's in His Kiss)" by Cher
- "You've Really Got a Hold on Me" by Smokey Robinson and The Miracles
- "Johnny Angel" by Shelley Fabares
- "Just One Look" by Doris Troy
- "Love Is Strange" by Mickey & Sylvia

A memorable family moment at a Navy SEAL's retirement.
(*Photo courtesy of Wendy Jo Peterson*)

10. *The Curtain Closes for Everyone*

★ ★ ★

THERE COMES A TIME WHEN EVERY WARRIOR MUST LEAVE THE STAGE, exit the theater, and give someone else the role. This is common knowledge. Military duties are meant to end for everyone eventually, but it doesn't feel real until that moment of reckoning comes. Especially in special operations where our eyes are always on the mission, this is even true for those of us at home. It is easy to forget, or intentionally ignore, where you are in a military career. It takes extraordinary self-awareness and personal discipline to rise above the challenge of managing life's demands, avoid compartmentalizing life, and actually look ahead to take charge of your journey.

Retirement papers arriving stamping the official end to a career of service in special operations. *(Photo courtesy of Jon Hooten)*

Families are a keystone for what comes after service, and so is staying connected with those who served before, alongside, and after you. SOF is a community, and you are part of the legacy. Keep it strong by living honorably and well regardless of the challenges transition brings. Before the special ops show ends, start writing your next script. It takes time to process the residue[27] from such a notable drama.

The transition from service is hard because it touches every aspect of your life and your family's life. Preparing for the post service mission takes significant time, effort, and awareness—*think 5-7 years before you leave service*. Few mentioned that transition from service actually takes that long. It is the first 1-2 years after service everyone talks about, the practical tasks tied up in finding work, money, relocation, and other similar next steps. The 3-4 years before and after transition are the years that get missed. They lay the foundation for strong new beginnings and carry you through to the next show.

It feels like "the greats" will stay forever, but in reality we all have to take that final bow and move on to another show. The earlier this truth works its way into your family's awareness, the better it is for everyone. Recognizing there is life beyond the unit and the mission is critical to keeping family and friendships strong. It is a necessary truth that keeps us from losing ourselves amid the chaos and coolness. Your family, like ours, will always be part of the special operations community. Legacy matters. When your service ends your role in the community just takes on another part, and the way you live life after service still impacts the SOF legacy.

We could write a whole book on the transition process, but thankfully others already have! Take a peek at our Simple List of Resources on page 443 for a curated list of transition resources recommended by SOF families.

A great, final career moment. A hug from a mentor. *(Photo courtesy of Cher Powers)*

27. Cline, P. B. (2020, April 20). *Residue*. Accessed from https://missioncti.com/wp-content/uploads/2020/06/RESIDUE-V.4-PUBLIC-DISTRIBUTION-4.20.20-1.pdf

A Farewell to Remember— Retirement Party

RETIREMENT FINALLY CAME. All these years it felt like it would never happen. When it did, it didn't feel real for us or our friends. Decades and years of life spent surrounded by America's best. Then—in a flash—it is just part of your family story. It abruptly ends.

Some warriors embrace the opportunity to throw a party, and others prefer minimal fanfare. Any degree of celebration can be uncomfortable, awkward, and take energy. This is especially true if you fall out of the habit of formally recognizing key accomplishments, people, moments, and milestones. The transition from active duty to civilian life is one that should be marked in some way with those close to you. Overcoming the urge to disappear into life post-service is actually a signal of confidence and strength.

Celebrations recognize people and actions that matter. No service member or their family makes it to the end of a career without many people to thank. No one serves alone and the transition out of special operations is no small task. It is if we are temporarily lost at sea, and our family and friends are the dinghy. It is scary as hell, but retirement parties are an opportunity to say thanks, then sit back, share stories, and be in the company of people in your circle. Embrace the time to be with friends and family and the opportunity to chart a new path with equal or greater meaning.

Special Forces soldiers celebrating the retirement of a buddy. *(Photo courtesy of KaLea Lehman)*

Boom **Brats in a Blink**

TIME: 5 MIN (PREP), 25 MIN (COOK)
MAKES: 5 SERVINGS

- -

Ingredients

1 tablespoon light cooking oil

5 Bratwurst links

Salt to taste

Pepper to taste

2 large onions, cut into medium sized
  wedges

1 bottle beer (craft or domestic)

Steps

1. In a large skillet, heat oil over
   medium-high heat until hot.
2. Carefully lay the bratwurst in the skillet
   and sprinkle with salt and pepper.
3. Cook until dark brown, but not burnt.
4. Flip the bratwurst, cover with onion
   wedges, cover with a lid and let cook
   until the other side is also dark brown.
5. Uncover and move the brats around so
   that some of the onions are touching
   the bottom of the skillet.
6. Pour beer over the brats and onions. Set
   the lid back on the pan slightly offset to
   allow some of the steam to escape.
7. As the onions begin to soften, move
   the bratwurst on top of the onions and
   replace the lid, offset.
8. Reduce heat to low and simmer until the
   onions have become caramel colored
   and the beer is mostly evaporated.
9. Serve the bratwurst on a bun topped
   with the onions, and good hot mustard.

TIP: If doubling, only use as much beer as required to cover ¾ of the brats, otherwise you will
be simmering for so long the brats will dry out.

(Photo courtesy of Andrea Geraldi)

SOF STORIES
A Simple Farewell — Andrea

My husband decided to retire while we were on an overseas tour in Germany, which meant he wouldn't be having a traditional retirement ceremony or celebration. He was hesitant about even having one at first, but my friends were not giving him the option to say no. These spouses spoke to their husbands and made this happen, as it's not really about the service member—it's about us, the spouse and the kids being acknowledged for supporting his career. Plus, one doesn't argue with a spec ops wife!

The ceremony itself was intimate and a perfect closure for 22 years spent serving our country. The celebration, though, was the best part with brats and beers, German style! I love how our life in the military taught us so much about many different cultures. It continues to shape our family as we chart this next phase of our lives.

A final sunset looking out and over the next ridge. *(Photo courtesy of KaLea Lehman)*

Boat Team **Beef Brisket**

TIME: 30 MIN (PREP), 8-9 HOUR (COOK)

MAKES: 6 SERVINGS

Ingredients

½ teaspoon garlic powder

1 teaspoon liquid smoke

1 teaspoon soy sauce

¼ teaspoon onion powder

⅛ teaspoon black pepper

2 teaspoons BBQ sauce

1 teaspoon Worchestire sauce

1 tri-tip roast beef brisket

Steps

1. Mix all the seasonings together and coat the brisket.
2. Let marinate 30 minutes to 12 hours.
3. Cook in a slow cooker for 8-9 hours at 250 degrees.
4. Slice across the grain into slabs and drizzle with cooking juices before serving.

WAR GAMES
When I Grow Up

What do you want to be when you "grow up?" This can be for kids or just a funny way to spin what will be done after the active military career is over. Perhaps mom will go back to work or change careers, and Dad wants to stay at home when he "grows up." Go around the table and get some laughs and learn what everyone wants to be, real or imagined!

Dreams fuel little special ops kid's minds. Each has "big boots to fill" in their own unique way. *(Photo courtesy of KaLea Lehman)*

Family Renewal **Roasted Red Pepper and Goat Cheese Alfredo**

TIME: 25 MIN (PREP), 25 MINS (COOK)
MAKES: 4-6 SERVINGS

Ingredients

2 whole roasted red bell peppers, sliced
4 tablespoons olive oil
1 onion, diced
2 teaspoons minced garlic
1 cup half and half
4 ounces garlic and herb goat cheese
⅔ cup grated Parmesan cheese
1 (1-pound) box linguine, spaghetti or penne
  cooked al dente
8 ounces bella mushrooms,sliced
1 cup fresh baby spinach, chopped
Salt and pepper to taste

Steps

1. In a medium frying pan, sauté the onion, garlic, and sliced mushrooms about 8 minutes or until tender.
2. Stir the chopped spinach into the sauté mixture until the spinach is wilted.
3. Keep over low heat and pour the half and half into the saute mixture.
4. Add the goat cheese into the mixture and stir until the cheese melts into the sauce.
5. Slowly stir the grated Parmesan cheese into the mixture.
6. In a food processor or using an immersion blender, puree the cheese mixture with the roasted bell pepper slices.
7. Once the sauce is a smooth alfredo, serve over al dente (cooked but firm) pasta.

VARIATIONS: Add baked chicken, roasted vegetables, or steamed edamame to the alfredo.

CUSTOMS AND CAMARADERIE
Sentiments that Last

Did You know? There are some phrases that become deeply connected to who we are, what our life is about, and what needs to remain as we move forward. These phrases have few words but they reflect our values. The selfless aspect of military service brings out these values and they become interwoven with our experience of military service. These are some of the phrases and mottos deeply felt in special operations units. Each is tied to values and ethos that stick with our warriors and their families long after service. They simply become part of who we are, reflecting qualities we believe are honorable and important.

Take a moment and match the motto or phrase with its proper meaning or associated unit.

1. De Oppresso Liber/DOL to free the oppressed
2. Until Valhalla
3. Rangers Lead the Way (unofficial motto) or Sua Sponte "of one's own accord"
4. Always Faithful, Always Forward
5. Death waits in the Dark (unofficial motto) or Night Stalkers Don't Quit
6. That others may live
7. The only easy day was yesterday

A. Sentiment of respect for the fallen warrior and their enduring spirit
B. Marine Raiders
C. Army Special Forces
D. 160th Special Operations Aviation Regiment (SOAR)
E. Navy SEALs
F. 75th Ranger Regiment
G. Air Force Pararescue

1:C, 2:A, 3:F, 4:B, 5:D, 6:G, 7:E

"Lead the Way." *(Photo courtesy of Paul Lushenko)*

Charlie **Green Bean Salad**

TIME: 5 MIN (PREP), 5 MIN (COOK)
MAKES: 4 SERVINGS

Ingredients

1 (14.5-ounce) can green beans
1 cup cherry tomatoes, halved
1 lemon, zested and juiced
½ medium red onion, thinly sliced
1 teaspoon McCormick's Montreal Steak
  Seasoning (or seasoning mix of your
  choice)
1 tablespoon extra virgin olive oil

Steps

1. Place green beans in a small saucepan and heat over medium heat until
   warmed, about 5 minutes.
2. Meanwhile, in a serving dish add remaining ingredients and toss to mix.
3. Drain cooked green beans and add to
   the fresh ingredients.
4. Stir and serve warm or refrigerate to
   serve cold.

(Photo courtesy of Lynnsy Snook)

TACTICAL TOPICS
Our Traditions

If you could create a new tradition for our family, what would it be? Or how would
you change a family tradition we already have?

Oh So Southern **Sweet Potato Casserole**

TIME: 30 MIN (PREP), 1 HOUR (COOK)
MAKES: 6 SERVINGS

Ingredients

4 sweet potatoes, sliced
1 teaspoon cinnamon
¼ cup butter
½ cup sugar
1 teaspoon vanilla

Topping

½ cup brown sugar

1 teaspoon cinnamon
2 tablespoons butter
½ cup of pecans (optional)

Steps

1. Mix sweet potato mixture and bake at 350°F for 30 minutes.
2. Add topping mixture and bake for 20 more minutes.

SOF STORIES

A Time to Thank our Friends — Jodi and Jim

During my husband's time in service, I recognized the demands that accompanied his calling. I was always involved with the family readiness and support groups. I tried to help wherever there was a need, and I took pride in being able to help where I could.

Our whole marriage, we've done everything together. His retirement party was no exception. We both saw it as our retirement party, and a time to thank and recognize all the people who were

Giving thanks surrounded by a community of friends to celebrate retirement. *(Photo courtesy of Jodi Lynch)*

there to support us all these years. It was our time to celebrate with family and our community. We felt so much pride seeing old friends he served and deployed with.

It was our time to step into retirement. We were ready for the next chapter, especially in that moment celebrating his service and our journey surrounded by people we cherished. We were the people we were because of the people we were both privileged to be with all these years.

Breacher **Peanut Butter Cookies**

TIME: 10 MIN (PREP), 10 MIN (COOK)

MAKES: 24 SERVINGS

Ingredients

1 cup peanut butter, chunky or smooth

1 egg

1 cup granulated sugar

Steps

1. Preheat the oven to 350°F.
2. Mix all ingredients together in a bowl until the dough is smooth.
3. Place dough on a baking sheet in small 1 inch rounds.
4. You can bake designs into the cookie by flattening it with a fork or spoon.
5. Bake for 10 minutes.

CUSTOMS AND CAMARADERIE
The Sound of 21 Guns

Did You Know? Most military traditions are deeply tied to history and civilizations that are no more. Artillery salutes date back to the 14th century. In the United States, artillery salutes by cannon or gunfire have been adapted over-time for a demonstration of honor. We have two salutes with 21 fires. The 21-gun salute also known as the "national salute" is 21 separate fires to honor the American flag, a sovereign foreign leader, and our past and present presidents. Our "national salute" it is also fired on federal holidays such as the 4th of July, Memorial Day, and President's Day.

I am the future. (*Photo courtesy of KaLea Lehman*)

The sound of 21 guns that is familiar to most, is the "three-volley salute" fired at military funerals. Seven service members simultaneously fire their rifles three times to honor the life and service of those who gave so much in service to the United States. Somehow the sound of those guns leaves a permanent imprint on the souls of those attending and replaces a need for words. This custom began long ago as a signal to halt fighting on the battlefield to remove the fallen.[28]

---

28. *21 Gun Salute*. Arlington National Cemetery. (n.d.). Accessed from https://www.arlingtoncemetery.mil/Visit/Events-and-Ceremonies/Ceremonies/21-Gun-Salute

Last Ride **Lemon Blossom Cupcakes**

TIME: 12 MIN (PREP), 1.5 HOURS MIN (COOK)
MAKES: 5 DOZEN

Ingredients

1 (18.5-ounce) package yellow cake mix
1 (3.5-ounce) package instant lemon
   pudding mix
4 large eggs
¾ cup vegetable oil

Glaze

4 cups confectioners' sugar
⅓ cup fresh lemon juice
1 lemon, zested
3 tablespoons vegetable oil
3 tablespoons water

(Photo courtesy of Bridget Orr)

Steps

1. Preheat the oven to 350°F.
2. Spray miniature muffin tins with vegetable oil cooking spray.
3. Combine the cake mix, pudding mix, eggs and oil and blend well with an electric mixer until smooth, about 2 minutes.
4. Pour a small amount of batter, filling each muffin tin half way.
5. Bake for 12 minutes. Turn out onto a tea towel
6. To make the glaze, sift the sugar into a mixing bowl. Add the lemon juice, zest, oil, and water. Mix with a spoon until smooth.
7. Dip the cupcakes into the glaze while they're still warm, covering as much of the cake as possible, or spoon the glaze over the warm cupcakes, turning them to completely coat.
8. Place on wire racks with waxed paper underneath to catch any drips.
9. Let the glaze set thoroughly, about 1 hour, before storing in containers with tight-fitting lids.

VARIATION: Change it up with lime, orange, or any preferred citrus.

Together with New Adventures

LOOKING BACK ON IT ALL, THOSE DEPLOYMENTS AND TIME APART, it seems like it was all a dream. It is part of our story, our history, of who we are now, and the path we are charting. Thank goodness for the family table. It held all the dishes of adventure, uncertainty, and surprise—though by the end of our time in special operations, it certainly needed to be sanded and re-stained. It's more beautiful now, set with new and unique challenges. Somehow it better tells our story from a wild and romantic beginning to our current place.

Sunset on the East Coast (*Photo courtesy of KaLea Lehman*)

The kids laugh at how we all squeeze around our old table. They hardly know our real journey because all that intensity happened in their early years. Our kids relive our tales because, thankfully, we realized the need to be deliberate. We took pictures of the family jump day. We attended the ceremonies and now the reunions. We tried hard never to take for granted what could be the last time because eventually, we knew there was always a last time. When you are new, the idea of a last time seems like a nightmare scenario, but as a sage spouse once pointed out, there is always a last time. Everyone's military journey will culminate and end, and few are aware of the last times until they pass.

It doesn't look the same for everyone, but those lasts sure came. We are glad we were deliberate about embracing the moments all those years. It helped us prepare for this transition that many days feels too big. The intensity is part of who we are and how we know how to live. Now, it just plays out in a different theater with a less dangerous and risky set. Our families have new routines and rituals, though admittedly we struggled to find them. What revs us up is different, but the bonus is we craft the future together. We don't have to be tenacious about celebrating a birthday or an accomplishment, and we can plan bucket list vacations without the fear of a last minute cancellation. We make time for dreamy or necessary but challenging conversations we had tabled before. We are in a new season, and it has a unique flavor. The slower pace and view from this other side of life presents new challenges, but we continue the ride and continue to celebrate big dates and new firsts.

Wrestling coach and wrestling sons. *(Photo courtesy of Cher and Jay Powers)*

Got Your Six **Sausage and Pepper Pasta Pan**

TIME: 10 MIN (PREP), 20 MIN (COOK)
MAKES: 6 SERVINGS

- -

Ingredients

12 ounces penne or rigatoni pasta

6 diced green onions or 1 diced onion

5-6 Italian sausage links

6 tablespoon cream cheese

1¼ cup sour cream

¾ cup shredded Parmesan cheese

3 sliced bell peppers (red, yellow, and orange)

2 diced tomatoes or 1 can of diced tomatoes

Steps

1. Boil a large pot of water and cook the pasta.
2. In a separate pan, cook the sausage until it is almost fully cooked.
3. Drain the grease from the pan, and add the diced onion and sliced bell peppers.
4. Sauté them in the sausage mixture.
5. When the pasta is ready, drain the water and move the pasta into the pan with the sausage and peppers.
6. Stir in the cream cheese, sour cream, and Parmesan cheese.
7. Once mixed, serve.

A special operations princess cutting peppers for dinner. (*Photo courtesy of Samantha Gomolka*)

SOF STORIES
Finding Ourselves and a New Normal — Andrea

Ah, retired life. We were looking forward to this time so much. My husband decided to take extra time off to spend time with our family. It started out great, and now I keep wondering when his next deployment will be! It sounded like a dream, but I didn't realize how much of a transition it would be for all of us. Every routine changes, and it took some adjusting.

In all seriousness, it's so great to have him around for more time with the kids, more time to help with homework, more time to coach the kids' sports teams, more family meal time, and more time with me, but transition doesn't have an end date. It can be just a phase of life. So comfort food has been our go-to! This "more time" togetherness has its pros and cons. Like every change in life, military transition makes us aware of things we pushed aside and ignored. It opens up new opportunities and presents new challenges, and it takes all of us to rise to the occasion to make it good.

We each had to find our own stride. What did I want to do? What did he want to do? What do our kids need? In what ways do we need each other? Each of these questions was its own set of hurdles, hard conversations, and the realization that comes with finding a new way and new normal. It was all an acquired taste, and it took a while to appreciate it.

Colonel Bank BLT Chopped Salad (*Photo courtesy of Lynnsy Snook*)

Colonel Bank **BLT Chopped Salad**

TIME: 10 MIN (PREP), 10 MIN (COOK)
MAKES: 4 SERVINGS

Ingredients

¼ cup olive oil

¼ cup apple cider vinegar

Zest of 1 lime

2 tablespoons freshly squeezed lime juice

2 teaspoons sugar, or more to taste

4 slices bacon, diced

4 cups chopped romaine lettuce

1 avocado, halved, pitted, peeled and diced

1 cup cherry tomatoes, halved

½ cup corn kernels

¼ cup crumbled goat cheese

Steps

1. To make the vinaigrette, whisk together olive oil, apple cider vinegar, lime zest and juice, and sugar in a small bowl. Set aside.

2. Heat a large skillet over medium-high heat.

3. Add bacon and cook until brown and crispy, about 6-8 minutes. Transfer to a paper towel-lined plate.

4. In a large bowl, combine romaine lettuce, avocado, tomatoes, corn, goat cheese and bacon.

5. Stir in lime vinaigrette. Serve immediately.

VARIATION: Skip the vinaigrette and serve with your favorite bottled dressing. Substitute your favorite cheese for the goat cheese.

TACTICAL TOPICS

Best Tip, Worst Tip

What is the one piece of advice you keep hearing over and over from families who transitioned from service? What is the most insightful tip you've heard? Have you heard any tips that you plan not to take?

A group of four special operations guys participate in a relay to support the 75th Ranger Regiment. *(Photo courtesy of KaLea Lehman)*

Sheepdog **Shepherd's Pie**

TIME: 15 MIN (PREP), 1.5 HOURS (COOK)
MAKES: 4 SERVINGS

- -

Ingredients

Shepherd's Pie Filling

1 pound ground beef or lamb

2 medium carrots, peeled and diced

1 small green pepper, diced

1 small yellow onion, diced

1 cup mushrooms, cleaned and stemmed, diced

4 garlic cloves, minced

3 ounces tomato paste

1 teaspoon chili powder

½ teaspoon dried rosemary or dried herb of choice

½ teaspoon salt, or to taste

¼ teaspoon black pepper

¼ cup water

Sweet Potato Topping

2 large sweet potatoes (about 12 ounces each), peeled and cubed (~6 cups cubed)

1 tablespoons butter

½ teaspoon chili powder

¼ teaspoon salt

Steps

1. Preheat the oven to 375°F.
2. Bake the sweet potatoes until fork tender, 45 to 60 minutes. Alternatively, you can steam peeled and diced sweet potatoes until tender.
3. In a medium skillet over medium-high heat, sauté the ground beef, chopped carrots, green pepper, onion, mushrooms, and garlic.
4. Continue cooking until the carrots are soft, about 12-15 minutes.
5. Begin making the sweet potato topping while the filling cooks. To make the topping, place the peeled and baked/steamed sweet potato with all of the topping ingredients in a food processor (or blender) and process until smooth.
6. Once the carrots from the filling are soft, stir in tomato paste, chili powder, rosemary, salt, black pepper, and water.
7. Top the meat filling with the sweet potato mash. If you're not using an oven-safe 10-inch cast-iron skillet, transfer the meat filling to a casserole dish or 9×9 inch baking dish and top the meat filling with the sweet potato mash.
8. Sprinkle the top with a little sea salt and chili powder.
9. Bake for 10 minutes.
10. Remove from the oven and serve.

TIP: We recommend making this in a 10-inch cast iron skillet so that you can cook everything in the skillet, top it with the mashed sweet potatoes and bake it right in the cast iron.

VARIATION: You can swap out sweet potatoes for white potatoes. We recommend mashing them by hand rather than blending to prevent them from getting pasty.

SOF STORIES
Dinnertime Tales — Cindy

Camels at Petra. *(Photo courtesy of Collin Moore)*

When our kids were young they didn't pick up on the things most people would think were cool, like the pictures of camels, Bedouin tents, tanks, fighter jets, or far away palaces and ancient ruins. To the kids, dad was "just at work." Their attention span was too narrow to really process the extraordinary moments captured in pictures and stories. I didn't have the energy to field their questions about where he was or why it had to be daddy that went. It was easier to dismiss his absence from our home with, "Dad's away at work." We were all too busy to slow down, and I guess I kept it that way. I followed the kids' lead and pushed the cool or worrisome moments to the back of my brain. Minimizing stressful events and narratives became our way of life. We didn't talk. We just did.

Our kids are older now, and his time in service comes up at dinnertime for random reasons—an event at school, homework, or something in the news. It always catches me by surprise. My husband is more comfortable telling old stories now that there is no next mission or identity to protect. He is more animated and fun. When they ask him questions at dinner, the stories seem unbelievable to retell. I drift into a sort of twilight zone picking at my roast beef and potatoes.

The new interest in his military adventures—our family journey—gives the stress, fear, and tense moments from our past a renewed meaning. Now, all the years feel more comfortable and familiar than hard. But, it is still hard to shake off those old habits rooted in a life we kept close-hold during the years of SOF home and away routines. I would still rather run a marathon than plan a birthday party.

A Final Farewell **Instant Pot Mac and Cheese**

TIME: 2 MIN (PREP), 10 MIN (COOK)
MAKES: 6 SERVINGS

- -

Ingredients

1 (16-ounce) box of noodles (elbows or shells recommended)

4 cups water

2 teaspoons salt

3 tablespoons butter

1 cup heavy cream (or 1 can evaporated milk)

2 cups shredded cheddar

Steps

1. Place uncooked noodles, water, salt, and butter in a multi-cooker appliance on the manual pressure cooker setting for 4 minutes (or according to manufacturer directions). When done, use the quick release and watch for release overflow.

2. Remove lid and set multi-cooker to sauté while stirring in the cream.

3. Slowly stir in the cheese until melted. Serve warm and top with extra cheese as desired.

(Photo courtesy of Bridget Orr)

CUSTOMS AND CAMARADERIE
SOF Legend Spotlight

Did You Know? Special Operations units conduct special missions with a spirit to tackle the impossible. A unit's legacy is almost always tied to the tenacity, courage, creativity, and bold spirit of its founding member. Can you match the unit that connects to each of these special operations legends?

1. Col. "Chargin' Charlie" Beckwith
2. Cmdr. Richard Marcinko
3. Col. Aaron Bank
4. Maj. Gen. Merritt Austin "Red Mike" Edson
5. Capt. Phil Bucklew
6. Gen. Henry "Hap" Arnold
7. Maj. Gen. Frank Merrill

A. Naval Special Warfare
B. NSW Development Group
C. Marine Raiders
D. Army Special Forces
E. 1st Special Forces Operational Detachment-Delta
F. Air Force Special Operations
G. 75th Ranger Regiment

1:E, 2:B, 3:D, 4:C, 5:A, 6:F, 7:G [29][30][31][32][33][34]

A Bataan Death March memorial run with old SOF friends. *(Photo courtesy of KaLea Lehman)*

29. United States Army John F. Kennedy Special Warfare Center and School. (n.d.). *Distinguished Member of the Special Forces Regiment: Colonel Charles A. Beckwith*. Accessed from https://www.swcs.mil/Portals/111/sf_beckwith.pdf

30. Hauptman, M. (2021, December 28). *How SEAL team 6 founder Richard Marcinko shaped America's modern-day special operations forces*. Task & Purpose. Accessed from https://taskandpurpose.com/news/richard-marcinko-seal-team-6-founder-obituary/

31. Office of the Command Historian . (n.d.). *Colonel Aaron Bank Commander, 10th Special Forces Group (1902-2004)*. ARSOF History. Accessed from https://arsof-history.org/icons/bank.html

32. Global SOF Foundation. (2021, April 20). *Hole 8 – Major General Merritt Edson*. Global SOF. Accessed from https://gsof.org/hole-8-major-general-merritt-edson/

33. Stilwell, B. (2022, April 1). *'The Father of Naval Special Warfare' Almost Changed the History of the Vietnam War*. Military.com. Accessed from https://www.military.com/history/father-of-naval-special-warfare-almost-changed-history-of-vietnam-war.html

34. Captain Nicholas Schade Whitlock Foundation. (n.d.). *About the heritage of the Special Operations Professionals*. WhitlockFoundation. Retrieved October 13, 2022, from https://whitlockfoundation.com/about-the-heritage-of-the-special-operations-professionals/

SOAR **Sweet and Salty Broccoli Salad**

TIME: 30 MIN (PREP), 1 HOUR (COOK)
MAKES: 6 SERVINGS

Ingredients

3 tablespoons apple cider vinegar
2 tablespoons honey
1 cup mayonnaise
6-8 cups of broccoli, chopped
½ cup red or white onion, diced
½ cup raisins or craisins
¼ cup cooked bacon crumbles, optional
¼ cup shredded carrot, optional
½ cup walnuts or sunflower seeds, optional

Steps

1. Mix the cider vinegar, honey, and mayonnaise together separately.
2. Combine remaining ingredients in a large bowl.
3. Stir in the dressing mixture and refrigerate 30 minutes to an hour before serving.

Exploring post retirement. *(Photo courtesy of Matt and Elin Pitts)*

Just Roll with it Cinnamon Roll Cake

TIME: 10 MIN (PREP), 30 MIN (COOK)
MAKES: 8 SERVINGS

Ingredients

½ cup flour
½ cup sugar
8 teaspoons salt
2 teaspoons baking powder
¾ cup milk
1 egg
1 teaspoons vanilla
4 tablespoons butter, melted, divided
½ cup butter, softened
½ cup brown sugar
2 teaspoons cinnamon
⅓ cups nuts, optional
1 teaspoon pumpkin spice, optional

Glaze

1 cup powdered sugar
2-3 tablespoons milk
1 teaspoon vanilla

Steps

1. Combine the flour, sugar, salt, baking powder, milk, egg, and vanilla, then slowly stir in 2 tablespoons melted butter. Pour the batter into a greased 9×9-inch pan.
2. In a medium sized bowl, mix the 2 tablespoons melted butter, brown sugar, cinnamon and optional ingredients. Drop evenly over the cake better in the pan.
3. Use a knife or spatula to swirl the mixture into the batter like a cinnamon roll.
4. Bake for 25-30 minutes at 350°F.
5. Make the glaze by adding the powdered sugar, milk and vanilla to a medium sized bowl. Whisk until smooth and drizzle over the warm cake.
6. Serve warm or at room temperature.

(Photo courtesy of KaLea Lehman)

TACTICAL TOPICS
Making New Memories

It can take time to uncover new hobbies, interests, and passions. Vacation, physical activity, acts of service, art, and time spent casually with our family and people we care about help us to discover these golden nuggets in life. The next mission doesn't typically just fall into your lap at transition. Name one thing you want to do in the next year? What is it, why is it important to you, and what are some steps you can take to make it happen?

Exploring the outdoors together. *(Photos courtesy of Chris and Robin VanSant)*

Special operations couple check-off a life bucket-list item climbing Mount Kilimanjaro. *(Photo courtesy of Jennifer Byrne)*

A Moment of Reflection

WRITING THIS BOOK has been a journey in itself. Our team started out on a mission to write a book to storytell the importance of family dinner in special operations—just one month before the pandemic shut the world down. We just got started, and then we basically paused for more than eight months as we all hunkered down and pivoted to homeschool, readjust, and find a new normal amid all the world changes. That tactical pause turned out to be a pivotal moment. When we returned to our outline, we threw it out and started unpacking the emotions that defined each of our spec ops family journeys.

The themes, struggles, and grounding passions we all shared, but we had to unpack them to make sense of it all as a team. We found that even though we shared similar tendencies or habits, getting to the "why" and talking about it helped us make sense of the moments. Many times we each had done similar things, things we felt guilt or insecurity about but laughed as we all experienced it. We realized that many of the ways we learned to cope with the day to day stressors were grounded in a greater why. Ultimately, this "why" is what kept us at the table. *The Warrior's Table* is a book that highlights the universal needs we all share and it weaves them into our recipes.

We hope that in reading this book, you find your footing and feel welcomed into our warrior community. If you are like us and nearing the end or past your time in service, we hope you find company in our experiences and enjoy the storytelling of a SOF life. If you are new to this lifestyle, we hope you find laughter and energy for your own journey forward. The special operations community is an extraordinary community. We hope you learn to love it as much as we still do.

Meet Our Partner, The Family Dinner Project and Dr. Anne Fishel

Founded in 2010, **The Family Dinner Project (TFDP)** is a non-profit initiative that champions family dinner as an opportunity for family members to connect with each other through food, fun, and conversation about things that matter. More than two decades of scientific research document the many physical, mental health, and academic benefits of family dinners. While most parents know that family dinner is a great idea, only about 40% of American families are actually having regular family dinners. The Family Dinner Project works to make shared mealtime more accessible, doable, and enjoyable so that more families can reap the many benefits of this important ritual.

TFDP designs online and community-based tools to support families to improve the quantity and quality of their meals together. We are the only organization with resources that focus on three key areas: food, fun and conversation about things that matter. We carry out our work through several online and community-based programs. Included among our programs are digital materials to support daily habit change, community events, and parent/health professional workshops. We have reached well over 2.5 million people with our online resources. Additionally, TFDP has cultivated a large community via social media (more than 80,000 followers).

The Family Dinner Project could not have achieved a deep impact over the years without support from our community- based partners across the country, including The Commission on the Status of Grandparents Raising Grandchildren, No Kid Hungry, Title 1 school districts in Atlanta, Boston Children's Museum, Blue Star Families, Idaho Office of Drug Policy, YMCAs, Home Base, MCEC. Our digital partnerships include content collaborations and digital campaigns with Common Sense Media, Making Caring Common, MGH Clay Center for Healthy Minds, Feed the Children, American Speech and Hearing Association, The Herren Foundation, #GivingTuesday, The Harry Potter Alliance, and On the Table.

Anne Fishel, Executive Director and co-founder of The Family Dinner Project is a family therapist, clinical psychologist and Associate Clinical Professor of Psychology at the Harvard Medical School. She is Director of the Family and Couples Therapy Program at Massachusetts General Hospital, where she trains child and adult psychiatry residents and psychology interns in family therapy. She has published numerous scholarly articles and chapters about family issues and has also written family-oriented articles for NPR, PBS, Washington Post, and other media outlets. She is the author of three books: *A Life-Cycle Approach to Treating Couples: From Dating to Death* (Momentum Press, 2018); *Home for Dinner: Mixing Food, Fun, and Conversation for a Happier Family and Healthier Kids* (Harper Collins, 2015); *Treating the Adolescent in Family Therapy: A Developmental and Narrative Approach* (Rowman and Littlefield, 1999) and the co-author with TFDP team of Eat, Laugh, Talk: The Family Dinner Playbook (Familius, 2019). She lectures widely at academic conferences, medical conferences, and to parent and teacher groups. She has been featured in media articles, radio shows, and TV appearances, including NYT, CNN, WSJ, Time Magazine, ABC news, Web MD, and NPR. She is the mother of two adult sons who are better and more adventurous cooks than their mother.

Meet The Cast Iron Crew, MSOFC's Family Dinner Team

KaLea Lehman is the Executive Director and Founder of the Military Special Operations Family Collaborative (MSOFC). KaLea grew up in rural Missouri, and learned to cook as a young child at home and more formally through required home economics classes in high school. She took this homegrown spirit to Washington, D.C., where she's been a longtime advocate for health education, research, and policy. KaLea earned her bachelor's degree in Sociology from The George Washington University in 2007, shortly after marrying her husband of nearly 20 years. In 2018, she earned her Master of Education from Vanderbilt University, and founded MSOFC to address the SOF wellness challenges that too often get lost in tempo and time or muddled by the unique aspects of the special operations lifestyle. KaLea and her husband have seven children. Her favorite pastimes are running with her family and friends and exploring coastal places.

Lynnsy Snook is an Air Force veteran and 20-year Special Operations spouse with a passion for supporting military families and connecting them with resources across all levels to meet their diverse needs. An advocate of continuous learning, she earned her undergraduate degree in Sociology from the University of California, Los Angeles, a Master of Arts in International Relations from the University of Oklahoma, and a Master of Business Administration from the University of Maryland Global Campus. Lynnsy brings experience in leadership, analysis, training, and volunteer management to achieve the MSOFC mission. In her personal time, she enjoys exploring new locales, sampling her husband's cooking, and leisurely bike rides with her two sons.

Wendy Jo Peterson, MS, RDN, has been a registered dietitian for over 20 years and has published eight culinary and nutrition-focused books, from *Born To Eat* to the *Instant Pot Cookbook For Dummies*. As an Army brat, her parents placed great emphasis on the family meal and she continues to carry on this tradition in her family. Wendy Jo has followed her husband's 30-year-career within Naval Special Warfare and given her best smile (and tears) during 13 deployments. She is excited to share some of her staple meals, and culinary tricks to make mealtimes more manageable and change the plate during deployments. Wendy Jo's specialties include Tex-Mex, Mediterranean (check out her book, *Mediterranean Diet Cookbook For Dummies*), and her German favorites, like spätzle.

Andrea Geraldi has a degree in Dietetics and Nutritional Science from the University of Vermont and a Masters in Public Health with a focus in Maternal and Child Health from the University of Hawai'i. She's traveled the world from Teman

Negara, Malaysia to the Tatras Mountains in Slovakia. What she's learned from her travels and life as a mom is what works for some families does not work for others. And that her science background has proved pointless when the tantrum is about a speck of green in a meatball. Andrea and her husband have three children and have been a part of the Special Operations community for over 20 years. Her business, Back At The Table, helps families unplug, laugh and reconnect at the table, where she and her family are happiest. Or so she tells everyone.

Christine Trax graduated from Austin Peay State University with a bachelor's degree in English and Ancient Literature. Her experience as a deputy sheriff, teacher, coach, and religious facilitator has given her a whole-person approach to supporting military families. She places a particular emphasis on the needs of families with deployed spouses and Gold Star families. She has served as coordinator, committee chair, and readiness leader in a special operations unit for the last 15 years. Currently, Christine acts as the care coalition leader for over 500 Soldiers and their families. As an amateur chef, she channels her love for cooking into editing cookbooks and freelance writing. Her research interests focus on families enrolled in the exceptional family member program, nurturing family communication dynamics, and reducing stressors for the military child. Christine and her husband have been part of the special operations community for nearly 20 years and have three spirited children.

Heather Campbell MS, RDN, registered dietitian and mom of 3, is a lifelong Air Force dependent turned Air Force wife who currently lives near Fairbanks, Alaska. She believes that the foundation of a resilient military family begins with intentional relationship building around shared meals together. As a volunteer, Heather serves with multiple military connected non-profits, her local base, and as a subject matter expert and advocate for military families facing food insecurity. She lends her expertise to multiple speaking and writing commitments as well. Heather was most impacted by a challenging season as a military family when they had three children under the age of four, a high TDY tempo, and only one income in one of the most austere and expensive locations in the country. Heather has received national recognition for her advocacy, including being named as the 2022 Armed Forces Insurance Eielson AFB Spouse of the Year and as a "Spouse in the Fight," a feature by Mrs. Sharene Brown, Spouse of the Chief of Staff of the Air Force. Heather's mission is to help busy parents overcome obstacles to bring their families back to the table for intentional relationships with one another.

Translation Please: A Glossary Guide for the Warrior's Table

★ ★ ★

WE COULDN'T WRITE AN AUTHENTIC family dinner book without weaving the language, meaning, and unit history of our community into the writing. This Glossary Guide will help you decode our "easter eggs" and hopefully help families see their special operations unit isn't alone. Our stories are colored with acronyms, special ops slang, and military life talk-isms. Army, Navy, Air Force, Marine, and National Guard special operations families share a unique warrior lifestyle that is sprinkled with a slightly different spice. While we could not cover every unit or common term—official or slang—we tried to cover common terms used across the Special Operations community in a wide variety of units.

Terms, Jobs, Organizations, People, and Equipment commonly used among special operations units:

21 Guns: 21 Guns is a reference to the "three-volley salute" that is fired at military funerals. Seven service members fire their rifles three times to honor the life and service of those who served in the United States military.

A-Team: An elite or expert group; a U.S. Special Forces unit of 12 soldiers trained for a wide range of combat and counterinsurgency operations.

Adaptive Strike: Strategic attack with a characteristic ability to change or shift in order to best meet the needs of the particular situation at hand.

Advise, Support, and Stabilize: Motto of 95th Civil Affairs Brigade in U.S. Army Special Operations Command.

AFSOC: Air Force Special Operations Command; all United States Air Force special operations fall under AFSOC. It constitutes the Air Force component of the unified USSOCOM (United States Special Operations Command).

Air Commando: Operators of AFSOC (see above). The term was coined by General Henry "Hap" Arnold, a World War II general and father of the modern Air Force.

Airborne: Ground combat units and service members qualified to airdrop into battle zones.

Alpha: Part of Military Phonetic Alphabet; acronym for letter "A" to ensure accurate communication of language. Alpha is also military slang for "officer."

Any Place, Any Time, Anywhere: Part of the AFSOC mission to "provide our nation's specialized airpower, capable across the spectrum of conflict . . . Any place, any time, anywhere"

Army Ranger: The 75th Ranger Regiment is an Army special operations unit. Rangers are expert soldiers that are highly mobile and often deployed on short notice missions.

Austere Environment: A plain location that is an uninviting or challenging environment. In military slang it can often refer to an area that regularly experiences environmental hazards such as extreme heat, cold, or altitude.

Battle Buddy: A partner assigned to a soldier in the United States Army; another service member assigned to mutually help another under the battle buddy system

Black Daggers: The U.S. Army Special Operations Command Parachute Demonstration Team. They jump from 12,500 feet and freefall at 120 MPH.[35]

Black Hawk: A front-line utility helicopter of the Army, commonly used in air assault, air cavalry, and aeromedical evacuation units

Boat Guys: United States Navy Special Warfare Combatant-Craft Crewmen (SWCC).

Boom: An aircrew member aboard tanker aircraft who is responsible for safely and effectively transferring aviation fuel from one military aircraft to another during flight.

Boots on the ground: Active ground troops—physically present and fighting in a war zone; direct physical presence.

Bravo: 1. B in the Military Phonetic Alphabet. 2. In Army Special Forces, a 18 Bravo MOS is the weapons sergeant. 3. An Operational Detachment Bravo is the headquarters detachment for a Special Forces company, which is the command between a Special Forces battalion and a Special Forces team.

Breacher: In special operations a breacher is the expert on explosive entry.

35. USASOC. (2009, October 26). *The Black Daggers - Global Warriors*. www.army.mil. Accessed from https://www.army.mil/article/29318/the_black_daggers_global_warriors

BUDS: Basic Underwater Demolition/SEAL training; designed to find and develop men of the strongest character who give everything they have to accomplish their mission and support the men on their team. *Also see Selection.*

Build rapport: The process of creating connection with a person and building a trusting relationship. This is an invaluable skill for both special operators and the strategic success of Special Operations.

Camp Lejeune: Home of Marine Raiders and USMC training base that promotes the combat readiness of the operating forces and missions of other tenant commands by providing training venues, facilities, services, and support.

Cannon AFB: Air Force Base in Curry County, New Mexico; one of four Air Force active duty Special Operations wings within Air Force Special Operations Command.

Casualty Assistance Officer: The Casualty Assistance representative is responsible for notifying family members when a service member has died, providing as much information as available regarding the circumstances of the death, responding to survivors immediate needs, and providing assistance in making funeral or memorial arrangements, as appropriate. The Army uses the term "Officer," while the Navy and Marines use "Calls Officer," and the Air Force uses the term "Representative."

Charlie: 1. In Army Special Forces, Charlie is a common reference for the MOS 18C which is the designation for a Special Forces Engineer Sergeant. 2. Represents the letter "C" in the military phonetic alphabet to ensure accurate communication of language.

Chief: 1. The person who exercises supreme command and control over armed forces or a military branch. This term is also used to reference a leader in some special operations units at various levels. 2. In special operations a warrant officer is sometimes called a chief. Warrant officers are senior technical experts.

Chinook: The CH-47 "Chinook" is a multi-mission helicopter used by special operations forces to transport troops and supplies.

Chow: Food.

Chow hall: A military's version of the cafeteria, where everyone gathers for food, often served at a counter and meals are carried on trays to tables.

Civil Affairs: A branch of the Army; all Active Component Army Civil Affairs personnel are SOF-qualified and as such undergo rigorous assessment and selection, followed by extensive training in foreign languages, advanced survivability skills, and negotiations techniques in order to operate autonomously as a small team.

Civil Affairs Operations: These operations enhance the relationship between military forces and civilian authorities in localities where military forces are present.

Clandestine: To plan or act with secrecy or concealment; covert or stealth missions.

Cold, wet, tired: Phrase used by all in the NSW community.

Col. Maggie Raye: Honorary Colonel and popular entertainer during World War II through the Vietnam War. She was honored for her dedication to the troops and her services during a major battle in Soc Trang when she donned fatigues and provided medical assistance at the dispensary for over 30 hours.

Combat Talon: The MC-130 "Combat Talon" is an Air Force special operations transport and tanker aircraft used for infiltration, exfiltration, and resupply.

Combatives: Hand-to-hand combat training and techniques in the Army branch.

Coronado: Naval Base Coronado is a consolidated Navy installation encompassing eight military facilities stretching from San Clemente Island, located 70 miles west of San Diego, California, to the Mountain Warfare Training Camp Michael Monsoor and Camp Morena, located 60 miles east of San Diego.

Counterinsurgency: The blend of civilian and military efforts designed to end insurgent violence and facilitate a return to peaceful political processes.

Counter-proliferation of Weapons of Mass Destruction: Activities to support U.S. efforts to curtail the conceptualization, development, possession, proliferation, use, and effects of weapons of mass destruction, related expertise, materials, technologies, and means of delivery by state and non-state actors.

Counterterrorism: 1. Measures designed to combat or prevent terrorism. 2. Actions taken directly against terrorist networks and indirectly to influence and render global and regional environments inhospitable to terrorist networks.

Covert: A military operation intended to conceal the identity of the party that instigated the operation.

"Cross a red line": Phrase used worldwide to mean a figurative point of no return or line in the sand; a limit past which safety can no longer be guaranteed; historical Obama Administration reference.

Customs and Courtesies: Customs are rules and behaviors to adhere to in military culture, and courtesies is the following of those actions, including good manners and politeness while interacting with others.

Dam Neck Annex: Established in 1941 as an anti-aircraft gunnery range to train fleet personnel in the operation of 20 mm and 40 mm anti-aircraft guns. Today, Dam Neck Annex houses 20 tenant commands primarily focused on Navy fleet training and support activities, to include Naval special operations units.

Dark Horse: A reference to the 2nd Battalion, 160th Special Operations Aviation Regiment, equipped with the MH-47 Chinook and the MH-60 Black Hawk helicopters and the 1C Gray Eagle unmanned aircraft system.

Death waits in the dark: A reference to the Night Stalkers, officially known as the 160th Special Operations Aviation Regiment. These are the crews who fly America's top special operations units to combat.

Decisive influence: Motto on the insignia of 8th Psychological Operations Group in U.S. Army Special Operations Command.

Delta: 1. In Army Special Forces, Delta is a common reference for the MOS 18D, which is the designation for a Special Forces Medical Sergeant. 2. "D" in the Military Phonetic Alphabet.

Demo: Short for demolition, the use of explosives.

Deployment: The movement of armed forces. Deployment includes any movement from a military Service Member's home station to somewhere outside the continental U.S. and its territories.

Direct Action: Short-duration strikes and other small-scale offensive actions employing specialized military capabilities to seize, destroy, capture, exploit, recover, or damage designated targets.

Dive Team: Military diving unit. In Army Special Forces, some A teams are dedicated dive teams.

DOL: The Army Special Forces motto: de oppresso liber, "Free the Oppressed."

Down range: In a direction away from the launch site and along the flight line of a missile test range. This term is also commonly used to mean a deployed setting which is typically a more dangerous or combat setting.

Dress Blues: Military dress uniforms. Each branch has a different form of dress blues, but all the uniforms are the most formal uniforms reserved for special occasions and looking the best of the best.

Drop Zone: The area where troops, supplies, or equipment should be dropped and land in an airborne operation.

Eagle, Globe and Anchor: The official emblem and insignia used to represent the Marine Corps. The eagle represents aviation and the Marines' commitment to support and defend the Constitution. The globe represents the global reach of the Western hemisphere. The anchor represents the Marines' ties to the Navy.

Eat crow: Admitting to being wrong after taking a strong position; presumably because crows are scavenger birds and thus distasteful to eat.

Elite military: A unit of soldiers or recruits picked for their competence and put in a special elite unit.

Enterprise: In defense military terms, military enterprise represents activities/ventures (commercial and non-commercial) by the military and defense authorities. This term is often used to describe the whole of units within U.S. Special Operations Command.

Eyes on the ground: 1. Observers in the area, 2. Witnesses in the target zone.

Foreign Humanitarian Assistance: The range of DoD humanitarian activities conducted outside the U.S. and its territories to relieve or reduce human suffering, disease, hunger, or privation.

Foreign Internal Defense (FID): 1. Activities that support an Host Nation's internal defense and development (IDAD) strategy and program designed to protect against subversion, lawlessness, insurgency, terrorism, and other threats to their internal security, and stability, and legitimacy. 2. Term used to describe an integrated and synchronized, multi-disciplinary approach to combating actual or threatened insurgency in a foreign state.

Fort Bragg: Located in North Carolina, it is the largest Army base in the U.S. and home to U.S. Army Special Operations Command, 1st Special Forces Command, and several airborne and special operations units. Fort Bragg will soon be renamed Fort Liberty.

Fort Campbell: An Army base located in Fort Campbell, Kentucky. Home of the 5th Special Forces Group and 160th Special Operations Aviation Regiment.

Fort Carson: An Army base located near Colorado Springs, Colorado. Home of the 10th Special Forces Group.

Fox: 1. In Army Special Forces, Fox is a common reference for the MOS 18F, which is the designation for a Special Forces Intelligence Sergeant. 2. Short for "foxtrot"; "F" in the Military Phonetic Alphabet.

Freefall: Tactical form of skydiving employed by Armed Forces personnel. This is a high altitude low opening airborne jump that requires special training. It is often called a HALO jump. *See HALO.*

Frogmen: 1. This is a common nickname for Navy SEALs. 2. Combat divers who are trained in scuba diving or swimming underwater in a tactical capacity.

Ghoststrider: AC-130J "Ghostrider" is an AFSOC aircraft used for close air support, air interdiction, and armed reconnaissance.

Go Bag: Your bag of emergency supplies and essentials, always loaded and ready to go at a moment's notice when it's "go time."

Go-Time: When it's time for action.

Got Your Six: Slang phrase meaning "I have your back"; the saying originated with World War I fighter pilots referencing a pilot's rear as the six o'clock position.

Gray Eagle: Long-endurance unmanned aircraft system used by Army special operations for surveillance, communications relay, and electronic warfare.

Green Beret: A U.S. military special operations soldier that focuses on Unconventional Warfare; (UW is the art of organizing resistance forces to overthrow governments or terrorist groups). Green berets serve in Special Forces units and are authorized to wear a green beret. The green beret was given to Army Special Forces by President John F. Kennedy. Also see Quiet Professionals and Special Forces.

Green Platoon: Green Platoon is the initial training program all Soldiers must attend prior to becoming a member of the 160th (160th Special Operations Aviation Regiment (Airborne, AKA Nightstalkers).

Grub: Food.

Guerrilla Force: An irregular military force fighting small-scale, limited actions, in concert with an overall political-military strategy, against conventional military forces. G Force is a slang reference for Guerrilla Force, and it may be commonly used within Special Forces.

Guidon: A small military flag that units carry to signify their unit designation and affiliation

Hail and Farewell: A traditional military event whereby those coming to and departing from an organization are celebrated. This may include a change in command, be scheduled on an annual basis, or be prompted by any momentous change.

HALO: Tactical form of skydiving employed by Armed Forces personnel. This is a high altitude low opening airborne jump that requires special training. *See Freefall.*

Hand to Hand: Face to face combat without the use of long-range weapons.

Hard landing: 1. Any landing that may have resulted in an exceeding of limit load on the airframe or landing gear, with a sink rate of 10 feet per second with a zero roll touchdown. 2. Slang term for crash landing.

High Altitude: In high altitude military parachuting, generally 30 to 40 thousand feet.

High Value: Referring to high value target (HVT), a person or resource that an enemy commander requires to complete a mission.

Homecoming: Returning home after deployment.

"honor and heritage:" An excerpt from the SEAL creed.

Horse Soldier: U.S. Special Forces soldiers from 5th Special Forces Group who rode on horseback and fought against the Taliban. The Special Forces teams were deployed in support of Operation Task Force Dagger during the Afghanistan Invasion in 2001, immediately following the terrorist attacks on 9/11.

Hostage Rescue: Retrieval mission to locate and bring to safety someone who has been taken.

Hot Range: Live range with active munitions of various types. *See live fire.*

Household 6: Term used by many service members to refer to their spouse as the numerical designation of 6 is often reserved for commanders. Slang for home commander or commander of the homefront.

Hurlburt Field: A U.S. Air Force installation located in Okaloosa County, Florida; named for First Lieutenant Donald Wilson Hurlburt; home to Air Forces special Operations Command and Joint Special Operations University.

Invisible Wounds of War: Non visible wounds such as Post-traumatic stress disorder (PTSD) and chronic issues resulting from traumatic brain injuries (TBI).

Irregular Warfare: A struggle between state and nonstate actors to influence populations and affect political legitimacy.

Islamic State: A militant Islamic fundamentalist group active particularly in Syria and Iraq.

ITC: Abbreviation for Individual Training Course. ITC is a physically and mentally challenging 7-month course designed to produce MARSOC Special Operations Officers (SOOs) and Critical Skills Operators (CSOs) who can operate across the spectrum of special operations in small teams under spartan conditions.

JEB Little Creek: Joint Expeditionary Base Little Creek is a major Naval operating base for Amphibious Forces near Virginia Beach, Virginia. Little Creek is home to Naval Special Warfare units to include Naval Special Warfare Groups 2 and 4.

Jedburghs: During World War II, the OSS (Office of Strategic Services), Special Operations Branch had recruited foreign language speakers who would volunteer for hazardous duty behind enemy lines and parachute into denied territory. These were known as the Jedburgh teams.

JCET: Abbreviation for Joint Combined Exchange Training. These training missions are designed to provide special operations units specific training that can only be accomplished in friendly foreign countries. JCETs often enhance U.S. relationships with partner nations by developing and maintaining critical military-to-military connections and improving partner force readiness and interoperability.

JSOC: Abbreviation for Joint Special Operations Command. This special operations command overseas operations of Special Mission Units.

JTAC: Abbreviation for Joint Terminal Attack Controller, a term used in the U.S. Armed Forces and some other military forces for a qualified service member who directs the action of combat aircraft engaged in close air support and other offensive air operations from a forward position.

Key Spouse: Spouse volunteers appointed by the unit Commander to serve as a conduit of information providing resources to Air Force families. Key Spouse Mentors are volunteers who have experience in a spouse leadership role and in many cases are the spouse of an active duty leader.

Land Navigation: A basic skill for service members. It is the discipline of following a route through unfamiliar and often rough terrain on foot or by vehicle. Historically, service members had to learn how to navigate the terrain with only a map and compass. It is often spoken of as "land nav." U.S. Special Forces selection has a land navigation course known as the "Star Course" that service members must pass.

Legion: Reference to 5th Special Forces Group at Fort Campbell, Kentucky, known as "the legion".

Little Bird: The AH-6M/MH-6M "Little Bird" are light attack/assault helicopters operated by the 160th Special Operations Aviation Regiment (Night Stalkers).

Live Fire: Range or area with active munitions of various types. See hot range.

Low Intensity Conflict: A usually localized conflict between two or more state or non-state groups which is below the intensity of conventional war.

LT: Abbreviation for Lieutenant, typically the most senior of junior officer rank in the Navy. For the Army, Marine Corps, and Air Force, LT is the most junior rank of junior officers.

MacDill AFB: An Air Force base located in Tampa, Florida. MacDill is the home of U.S. Special Operations Command, Special Operations Command Central, Central Command, and other Air Force units.

Mandatory Fun: An unofficial term that is used to describe customary functions and other social activities supported by military units. Attendance of service members (and unofficially their families) is often required by the commander. Presence was historically interpreted as a sign of commitment or dedication to service in the unit/profession/community.

Marine Raider: Units established by the United States Marine Corps to conduct amphibious light infantry warfare, particularly landing in rubber boats and operating behind the lines

MARSOC: Abbreviation for Marine Special Operations Command.

Master of Influence: A reference to Psychological Operations, the units dedicated to information warfare. PSYOP units conduct activities of influence to create or intensify fissures, confusion or doubt among the enemy or adversary.

Master Sergeant: High ranking, non-commissioned officers in the U.S. Army, Air Force, and Marine Corps. In the Navy, the equivalent rank is known as a senior Chief Petty officer. Their pay grade is E-8.

Meals Ready to Eat (MRE): self-contained, individual field ration in lightweight packaging bought by the United States military for its service members for use in combat or other field conditions where organized food facilities are not available. MREs are nutritious and not always delicious.

Med Kit: Short for Medial Kit. This is the bag of medical supplies carried by special operations forces on missions and often in their go-bag at home.

Military Information Support Operations (MISO): The abbreviated term is pronounced Me-so. These operations are planned to convey selected information and indicators to foreign audiences to influence their emotions, motives, objective reasoning, and ultimately the behavior of foreign governments, organizations, groups, and individuals in a manner favorable to the originator's objectives.

Missing Man: Reference to a fallen, missing, or imprisoned service member. The Table of the Missing Man is often present at military functions as a symbol of honor and respect. It is also known informally as the POW/MIA table.

Mission Planning: The process in which teams, at any level, plan for a military mission or action. This is typically a formal process that can be time intensive and may require the isolation of small teams.

Mission Success: Accomplishment of assigned mission.

Naked Warrior: A reference to the two Navy combat divers who conducted a reconnaissance mission in World War II. The two "frogmen" are recognized as forerunners of the Navy SEALs.

NAB: Abbreviation for Naval Air Base.

Navy SEAL: Naval Special Warfare unit trained in unconventional warfare; SEAL is an acronym for Sea Air and Land.

Not Forgotten: Reference to the POW/MIA flag which states "You Are Not Forgotten."

NSW: Abbreviation for Navy Special Warfare Command, which is the naval component of the US Special Operations Command.

Office of Strategic Services (OSS): Wartime intelligence agency of the United States during World War II, and a predecessor to the Department of State's Bureau of Intelligence and Research (INR), and the independent Central Intelligence Agency (CIA).

One Man: Stands for "one-man army," someone who can do, or thinks they can do, everything by themselves and without assistance. Some special operations missions call for only one "man."

Only easy day was yesterday: A well-known motto and common saying of U.S. Navy SEALs.

On Time, On Target, Never Quit: The final line of the Special Warfare Combatant-craft Crewmen (SWCC) creed, which are often called the boat teams.

Operation Eagle Claw: A failed mission of multiple special operations units in 1980 to rescue Americans held hostage in the Iran hostage crisis. This failed mission was a major catalyst to the creation of U.S. Special Operations Command.

Operational Detachment Alpha (ODA): Formal military reference for an A-Team. This is the smallest tactical unit in Army Special Forces. *See A-team.*

Operator: It's a term used to refer to a member of special operations forces (SOF)—particularly a trained shooter, medic, forward observer, or other combat arms position. Modern use of the term operator often includes a broader subset of special operations personnel.

Osprey: The CV-22 "Osprey" is a tiltrotor aircraft that combines the vertical take-off, hover and vertical landing qualities of a helicopter with the long-range, fuel efficiency and speed characteristics of a turboprop aircraft. The mission of the CV-22 is to conduct long-range infiltration, exfiltration and resupply missions for special operations forces.

Permanent Change of Station (PCS): An assignment of a new appointee to an official station or the transfer of an employee from one official station to another on a permanent basis.

Personnel Recovery: A core mission of Air Force Special Tactics. Personnel recovery capabilities include technical rescue, battlefield trauma care, SOF-tailored recovery, and mountaineering and high-angle rescues. *See also PJ.*

Peterson SFB: Peterson Space Force Base (formerly an Air Force Base) is home to Headquarters, Special Operations Command North.

Phantom Knights: 8th Psychological Operations Group in the U.S. Army Special Operations Command are known as the Phantom Knights.

PJ: Also known as Pararescue, are U.S. Air Force Special Operations Command (AFSOC) and Air Combat Command (ACC) operators tasked with recovery and medical treatment of personnel in humanitarian and combat environments. They provide emergency and life-saving services.

PJ Rodeo: A competition for active duty, reserve, and retired pararescue two man teams to determine the best PJ. This competition is hosted by the nonprofit the Pararescue Association.

POW: Acronym for Prisoner of War; a person who is held captive by a belligerent power during or immediately after an armed conflict.

Precision Strike: A strike conducted by coordinating with aircraft for a direct and accurate hit with little collateral damage. This is typically a kinetic strike, but non-kinetic strikes involve air drops of humanitarian supplies. The strikes are often coordinated by Air Force Special Tactics Precision Strike Teams in the 24th Special Operations Wing.

Proud Tradition: Excerpt from the SEAL Creed

Qualification Course (QC): Qualification training; this is the "field" phase of training. Also called the Course, or the Special Forces Qualification Course (SFQC).

Quiet Professionals: Army Special Forces service members are also known as both "Green Berets" and "Quiet Professionals." They earned this nickname for a quiet attitude and demeanor and expertise of particular unconventional warfare skills. Special Forces units value a quiet and humble professionalism. Many of their missions demand service members go unnoticed and unrecognized in secret locations. *Also see Green Beret and Special Forces.*

Raider: 1. Service member serving in or retired from the Marine Special Operations Command's Raider battalions. 2. Historical reference to service members on raider missions in World War II. 3. A military tactic or operational warfare mission which has a specific purpose. Raiders do not capture and hold a location, but quickly retreat to previously defended positions before enemy forces can respond in a coordinated manner.

Range: An area designated to train military service members their use and handling of military munitions.

Ranger: Rangers are expert soldiers that are highly mobile and often deployed on short notice missions. The 75th Ranger Regiment is an Army special operations unit.

Rangers Lead the Way: The final sentence/declaration of the Army Ranger Creed.

RASP: Abbreviation for Ranger Assessment and Selection Program.

Ratline: A ratline is an organized effort to move people or material by clandestine efforts across a denied area or border.

Reaper: The MQ-9 "Reaper" is an armed, multi-mission, medium-altitude, long-endurance remotely piloted aircraft. This aircraft is flown by Air Force Special Operations units for intelligence, surveillance, reconnaissance, close air support, combat search and rescue, precision strike, buddy-lase, convoy/raid overwatch, target development, and terminal air guidance.

Redeployment: The return home from a military deployment/mission.

Red Horse: RED HORSE stands for Rapid Engineer Deployable, Heavy Operational Repair Squadron, Engineer; these units are the civil engineering SWAT teams of the Air Force.

Rough Terrain: Ground that is hard to traverse through because it is covered by brush, boulders, or other natural obstacles and barriers.

Sabotage: 1. A special operations mission. 2. An act or acts with intent to injure, interfere with, or obstruct the national defense of a country by willfully injuring or destroying, or attempting to injure or destroy, any national defense or war materiel, premises, or utilities, to include human and natural resources.

Scouts and Raiders: Reference to service members in World War II who conducted special operations missions. Many special operations units connect their unit heritage to their WWII missions.

Scuba: 1. Special capability of some special operations service members. 2. Self-contained underwater breathing apparatus that allows divers to breathe underwater.

SEALs: Members of an elite force within the U.S. Navy, specializing in guerrilla warfare and counterinsurgency.

Search and Seizure: Select special operations units conduct search and seizure missions. Special operations service members in these units complete Visit, Board, Search, and Seizure (VBSS) training. Search and Seizure missions combat terrorism, piracy, and smuggling activities.

Security Force Assistance: Activities based on organizing, training, equipping, rebuilding, and advising various components of Foreign Security Forces.

Selection: Refers to a battery of special physical, mental, and intellectual tests that are designed to select service members capable of service in special operations units. Each unit designs and runs their own selection. Also see RASP and BUDS.

SERE: Abbreviation for Survival, Evasion, Resistance, and Escape. A training program best known by acronym that prepares U.S. military personnel, Department of Defense civilians, and private military contractors to survive and "return with honor" in survival scenarios.

Service branch: 1. A subdivision of the military. The U.S. military has six branches of service: Army, Navy, Air Force, Marine Corps, Space Force, and Coast Guard. 2. A subdivision within military service branches that distinguish their military occupation or role.

Service Dress Blue/White: Basic uniform options for Navy service members.

Sheep Dog: A warrior, walking the hero's path; someone that performs acts that most of us wouldn't.

Shield Maiden: A reference to an Army Special Forces spouse organization. They are the "women behind the Green Berets." It is a reference to viking lore and mythology.

Shots for the fallen: A salute to the fallen soldiers; reference to either shots of liquor or the three volley, riffle salute at military funerals.

Show of Force: An act intended to warn (such as a warning shot) or intimidate an opponent by showcasing a capability or will to act if one is provoked.

Short fuse: A tendency to lose one's temper.

Sling Load: A cargo carried beneath a helicopter and attached by a lead line. "Cut or drop sling load" may be used as slang for "cut and run."

Small Team: A reference to teams operating at the tactical level such as an A-Team.

Snake eater: A reference/nickname for Army Special Forces, also known as Green Berets.

Sniper: A military/paramilitary marksman who engages targets from positions of concealment or at distances exceeding the target's detection capabilities.

SOAR: Abbreviation for Special Operations Aviation Regiment. The 160th SOAR is also known as the Nightstalkers.

SOCAFRICA: Abbreviation for Special Operations Command Africa. The command responsible for special operations in the African Theater.

SOCCENT: Abbreviation for Special Operations Command Central. The command responsible for special operations in the Central Theater.

SOCEUR: Abbreviation for Special Operations Command Europe. The command responsible for special operations in the European Theater.

SOCKOR: Abbreviation for Special Operations Command Korea. The command responsible for special operations in the European Theater.

SOCNORTH: Abbreviation for Special Operations Command North. The command responsible for special operations in the Northern Theater.

SOCOM: Abbreviation for short for U.S. Special Operations Command or US-SOCOM. The command responsible for the training and readiness of all special operations forces.

SOCPAC: Abbreviation for Special Operations Pacific. The command responsible for special operations in the Pacific Theater.

SOCSOUTH: Abbreviation for Special Operations South. The command responsible for special operations in the Southern Theater.

SOF: Abbreviation for special operations forces.

SOW: Abbreviation for Special Operations Wing, an Air Force organizational level roughly equivalent to a Battalion in the Army.

Spartan Spouse: A strong spouse who is independent enough to stoically manage anything.

Special activity: Generally refers to a special skill or mission.

Special Missions Aviator: An Air Force special operations career field that covers everything from pre-flight inspection of aircraft systems to the placement and delivery of all cargo on board.

Special Forces: A branch of the U.S. Army composed of soldiers trained in special operations; also known as Green Berets or Quiet Professionals.

Spec ops or special operations: A military or paramilitary unit trained to carry out special operations.

Special Reconnaissance (SR): 1. Special Reconnaissance is a form of human intelligence collection. It may include covert direction of airstrikes or indirect fires from behind enemy lines, placement of remotely monitored sensors, and preparations for other special operators for direct action and unconventional warfare missions. 2. Special Reconnaissance airmen conduct multi-domain reconnaissance and surveillance across the spectrum of conflict with a focus on lethal and non-lethal air-to-ground integration of air power.

Special Tactics: Special Tactics constitutes the Air Force's ground force within U.S. Special Operations Command, conducting special operations core activities with expertise in air, space and cyber application. Special Tactics forces plan, lead and execute global access, precision strike, personnel recovery and other missions.

Spiritus Invictus: The motto on the Marine Raider insignia. It means "unconquerable spirit."

Stone Bay: A satellite facility of USMC Base, Camp Lejeune. MARSOC officially re-designated its subordinate commands as Marine Raiders at a ceremony in Stone Bay in 2015.

STRAY 59: Callsign of the MC-130 E Combat Talon that went down with eight air crew and 15 special operators during Special Warfare Exercise 81 on Feb. 26, 1981.

Steel Magnolias: A nonprofit group, associated with the Green Beret Foundation, for spouses of Special Forces service members. Steel Magnolias are also called "Steel Mags."

Tab: Tabs are cloth and/or metal arches displaying a word or words signifying a special skill that are worn in the U.S. Army uniforms.

Tampa: Location of MacDill AFB, home of U.S. Special Operations Command, Special Operations Command Central, and Central Command. *Also see MacDill AFB.*

Tan beret: The Army beret worn only by service members in the 75th Ranger Regiment.

Teams: Small groups of a military branch that are sent together on missions and deployments, such as the Marine fire teams, SEAL teams, or Air Force Special Tactics teams. *Also see small team.*

Tempo: The rate of military activity. Families talk about tempo in regard to how much time the service member is home or away from home.

TDY: The military acronym for Temporary Duty Travel. Many special operations deployments, official working trips, and training are classified as TDY.

"The Army Goes Rolling Along": The official song of the United States Army; played at the conclusion of every U.S. Army ceremony and all Soldiers are expected to stand and sing.

The Bridge Between: The motto of the 98th Civil Affairs Battalion of the U.S. Army Special Operations Command.

Tier 1: Term often used to reference Special Mission Units in Joint Special Operations Command. These units deploy to conduct classified missions in reconnaissance, black operations, counter-terrorism, and unconventional warfare.

Tip of the spear: The first line of defense. The most elite warfighters of all military units. This phrase is often used to describe units within special operations.

Torii Station: US Army post in Okinawa, Japan. Torii Station is the home of 1st Battalion of 1st Special Forces Group.

To the ladies: A reference to official Toasts, a traditional element at military balls and other events such as a dining in or dining out. Toasts recognize important parties or ideas connected to the unit and mission. Spouses and significant others are typically toasted and historically the response to this toast was "to the ladies."

Tower of Power: A reference to someone who earned the right to wear the three, Army special qualification tabs: Special Forces tab, Ranger tab, Airborne tab.

Trident: Special Warfare Insignia of the Navy SEALs; The trident symbolizes the connection a SEAL has with the sea. The origin of the trident symbol comes from Neptune, the Roman god of the sea, and Poseidon, the Greek god counterpart

TSOC: Abbreviation for Theater Special Operations Command. TSOC is the primary theater SOF organization capable of performing broad continuous missions uniquely suited to SOF capabilities.

TTPs: Abbreviation for Tactics, Techniques, and Procedures. Lessons learned or best practices that have become enshrined in official military doctrine.

Unconventional Warfare: Actions to enable a resistance movement or insurgency to coerce, disrupt, or overthrow a government or occupying power. Note: If you are a Special Forces family, think about the Qualification Course and Robin Sage.

Underwater demolition: Making hydrographic reconnaissance of approaches to prospective landing beaches; clear mines in certain areas, locate, improve, and mark usable channels; channel and harbor clearance.

Unit: A group having a prescribed size and a specific combat or support role within a larger military organization. This is often how special operations service members talk about their own service unit.

Valhalla: In Norse mythology (Viking culture) the brave live forever in Valhalla. Those selected for Valhalla lived a life of valor, bravery, courage and an unyielding devotion to your fellow man in combat.

Wolfhound: The C-146A "Wolfhound" is a tactical transport aircraft used to provide U.S. Special Operations Command flexible and responsive operational movement of small teams and cargo in support of Theater Special Operations Commands.

Work trip: A casual term for any type of obligated duty that includes travel, such as a deployment. A tour of duty, or temporary duty travel (TDT) is another proper term describing a work assignment at a location other than the service member's permanent duty station.

Yarborough Knife: A combat field knife with a blade length of 7 inches designed by renowned knife maker William Harse, which serves as a link to the brotherhood of unconventional warriors.

A Simple Resource List

★ ★ ★

LIST OF CAST IRON CREW FAVORITE resources to uncover more on the topics that go beyond The Warrior's Table.

Family Life Resources:

All Secure Foundation: allsecurefoundation.org

All Secure Foundation assists special operations warriors and their families heal from the trauma of war. All Secure Foundation retrains your brain from Post Traumatic Stress (PTS) to Post Traumatic Growth (PTG) through programs and workshops, individuals and couples coaching, and online courses.

Blue Star Families: bluestarfam.org

We empower families to thrive as they serve. We are committed to strengthening military families by connecting them with their neighbors to create vibrant communities of mutual support.

Boulder Crest Foundation: bouldercrest.org

Our mission is to help struggling veterans, first responders, and their families, rediscover hope, purpose, and a belief in the future that is truly worth living. Our team at Boulder Crest uses the science of Post Traumatic growth to train participants through a proven process of transformation.

InDependent: in-dependent.org/about

InDependent makes wellness accessible and creates opportunities for all military spouses to connect for friendship, accountability, and inspiration.

Military Family Advisory Network: mfan.org

Connecting military families to the resources, people, and information they depend on to successfully navigate all phases of military life.

Military Family Building Coalition: militaryfamilybuilding.org

Our vision is for an America that supports all active duty military service members and their families to build the families they want regardless of deployment schedules, gender, fertility challenges or financial situation.

Military Special Operations Family Collaborative: msofc.org

We enable the sustained success of SOF Warriors and Families through collaborative health and well-being research and programs.

National Military Family Association: militaryfamily.org

We are on a mission to stand up for, support, and enhance the quality of life for every military family through bold advocacy, innovative programming, and dynamic and responsive solutions.

Operation Healing Forces: operationhealingforces.org

Operation Healing Forces is a nonprofit 501(c)(3) corporation dedicated to America's special operations forces who have served at the tip of the spear in our Nation's battle to defeat violent extremists around the world. Our work focuses on helping to restore the relationships wounded by the call of duty faced by Special Operators and their families.

Special Operations Care Fund: soc-f.org

We created SOC-F in 2013 for one purpose: to make a positive and meaningful difference in the lives of SOF families who have given so much for our country and our freedom. We do this by raising money for one incredibly worthwhile purpose: to provide medical, financial, and other support to SOF members and their families in ways that are often not met through other sources–what we call the "gaps."

The Family Dinner Project: thefamilydinnerproject.org

The Family Dinner Project, a nonprofit initiative started in 2010, champions family dinner as an opportunity for family members to connect with each other through food, fun and conversation about things that matter.

The Robert Irvine Foundation: https://robertirvinefoundation.org

The Robert Irvine Foundation supports and strengthens the physical and mental well-being of our service members, veterans, first responders, and their families. We provide these heroes with life-changing opportunities that unlock the potential in their personal and professional lives through food, wellness, community, and financial support.

The Station Foundation: thestationfoundation.org

The Station team is comprised of members of the Special Operations Community and amazing professionals fully dedicated to the SOF community. Helping participants navigate the rough terrain of transition and reintegration back to civilian life. Offering experience, strength and hope to individuals as they identify and translate strengths to new arenas.

Warrior Angels Foundation: warriorangelsfoundation.org

WAF sponsors individualized assessments and personalized treatment protocols that pinpoint – and, more importantly, treat – the underlying condition for U.S. Service Members and Veterans who have sustained a Traumatic Brain Injury (TBI) while in the line of duty.

Warriors Heart: warriorsheart.com

Our mission is to heal our nation's warriors through our private, licensed, and accredited resort-style healing centers. We do this by specializing in substance abuse treatment and co-occurring psychological disorders, with special attention to post-traumatic stress, unresolved grief/loss, and moral injury. Our treatment courses provide the full continuum of care, from detox, inpatient (residential), day treatment, outpatient, sober living, and 1-on-1 counseling.

Also see: Organizations such as SOF Missions, Special Operations Warrior Foundation, Task Force Dagger Special Operations Foundation, Hunterseven Foundation, Donovan and Bank Foundation, Gary Sinise Foundation, and The Charlie Daniels Journey Home Project have a missions that include support to all special operations units or support the military community. Family programs of official military units and nonprofit organizations that care for service members, veterans, and families of special operations units such as Navy SEALs, Green Berets, PJs, and other units/specialties such as the Special Forces Charitable Trust, Green Beret Foundation, Navy SEAL Foundation, SEAL Future Foundation, Marine Raider Foundation, Pararescue Foundation, C4 Foundation, The Pillar Foundation, EOD Warrior Foundation, and many others.

Additional resources can be found in MSOFC's online, searchable, resource directory, Connecting SOF. The directory is regularly updated and can be found at: https://msofc.org/connecting-sof/

Transition Resources:

DOD Skillbridge: skillbridge.osd.mil/military-members.htm; For Spouses: skillbridge.osd.mil/spouses.htm

SkillBridge is an excellent opportunity as you plan for your life after the military. SkillBridge matches civilian opportunities to your job training and work experience at the end of your military duty. In addition to opportunities such as Tuition Assistance and the GI Bill program, you can enhance your marketability and career prospects by participating in a SkillBridge opportunity.

Elite Meet: elitemeetus.org

Elite Meet, founded in 2017, is a network-focused 501(c)3 organization that provides support to transitioning elite Veterans and an unmatched talent pool to corporate partners.

Operation Socrates: operationsocrates.org

Our mission is to provide a pipeline for military veterans to become teachers, create a guided pathway all the way from the military to employment in a K-12 School, and increase the diversity of teachers in the United States.

SOF for Life: sofforlife.org

A platform of mutually supporting and networked non-governmental programs that enable special operations personnel transitioning from military service to civilian employment. *SOF for Life* programs help prepare transitioning personnel above what the government provides.

Special Operators Transition Foundation: sotf.org

Special Operators Transition Foundation (SOTF) is a 501(c)(3) non-profit organization committed to helping SOF veterans transition from the military into their next successful career.

The COMMIT Foundation: commitfoundation.org

The COMMIT Foundation empowers service members, veterans, and their families through personalized programs, resources, and the support of our community to create purposeful and fulfilling transitions.

The Honor Foundation: honor.org

The Honor Foundation (THF) is a career transition program for U.S. Special Operations Forces that effectively translates their elite military service to the private sector and helps create the next generation of corporate and community leaders.

We provide a clear process for professional development and a diverse ecosystem of world class support and technology. Every step is dedicated to preparing these outstanding men and women to continue to realize their maximum potential during and after their service career.

The Transition Mission by Herb Thompson

Following a successful career in Special Forces, Herb Thompson wrote The Transition Mission. Herb lays out a different approach and way of thinking for transition. Instead of teaching you what to think, he opens your eyes with how to think about the transition process. Every service member's situation is unique, and there is no one checklist to follow. You won't find many of the skills needed in transition on any checklist because they are tied to developing new skills and a healthy post-service mindset. Every service member should read this well before (5-7 years) they begin their transition from service.

Podcasts: SOFcast, USSOCOM's official podcast, Pineland Underground, the official podcast of the U.S. Army John F. Kennedy Special Warfare Center and School, AfterSOF, Mind of the Warrior with Mike Simpson, The Jedburgh Podcast with Fran Racioppi, and MCTI Teamcast are a few podcasts that routinely cover topics needed after service.

For more resources, visit MSOFC.org where you can access or provide information about resources fit for the special operations community in our online, searchable resource directory, *Connecting SOF*.

Works Cited

★ ★ ★

21 Gun Salute. Arlington National Cemetery. (n.d.). Accessed from https://www. arlingtoncemetery.mil/Visit/Events-and-Ceremonies/Ceremonies/21-GunSalute

Aguirre, V. (2016, October 24). *1st Special Forces Command celebrates Col. Maggie Raye Volunteer Award recipients*. www.army.mil. Accessed from https://www.army. mil/article/177189/1st_special_forces_command_celebrates_col_maggie_raye_ volunteer_award_recipients

Briscoe, C. H. (2012, November 1). *Born of Desperation: Early Special Operations in the Korean War*. Accessed from https://arsofhistory.org/articles/v6n1_born_of_ desperation_page_1.html

Burke, M. M. (2019, August 9). *One year after Thai Cave Rescue, US airman recalls harrowing effort to save youth soccer team*. Stars and Stripes. Accessed from https://www.stripes.com/theaters/asia_pacific/one-year-after-thai-cave-rescu e-us-airman-recalls-harrowing-effort-to-save-youth-soccer-team-1.593762

Cline, P. B. (2020, April 20). *Residue*. Accessed from https://missioncti.com/wp -content/uploads/2020/06/RESIDUE-V.4-PUBLIC-DISTRIBUTION-4.20.20-1 .pdf

Collins, E. (2015, May 6). *Experts explain mental state of military children*. www .army.mil. Accessed from https://www.army.mil/article/147786/experts_explain_ mental_state_of_military_children

Correll, D. (2022, August 18). *How the 'horse soldiers' helped liberate Afghanistan from the Taliban 18 years ago*. Military Times. Accessed from https://www.militarytimes .com/news/your-military/2019/10/18/how-the-horse-soldiers-helped-liberat e-afghanistan-from-the-taliban-18-years-ago/

Correll, D. (2022, August 19). *40 years later: How the Iran hostage crisis shaped the future of Special Operations*. Military Times. Accessed from https://www.military times.com/flashpoints/2019/11/04/40-years-later-how-the-iran-hostage-crisis -shaped-the-future-of-special-operations/

Darack, E. (2015, March). *The Final Flight of Extortion 17*. Smithsonian.com. Accessed from https://www.smithsonianmag.com/air-space-magazine/final-flight-extortion-17-180953947/

Defense Logistics Agency. (n.d.). *Reveille, retreat, and Taps - Defense Logistics Agency*. Accessed from https://www.dla.mil/Portals/104/Documents/Distribution/Reveille.pdf

Defense Media Network. *The Son Tay Raid*. Accessed from https://www.defensemedianetwork.com/stories/son-tay-raid-50-years-november-21-1970-special-operations-vietnam-war/

Duke, M.P. Lazarus, A., & Fivush, R. 2008. Knowledge of family history as a clinically useful index of psychological well-being and prognosis: a brief report. Psychotherapy Theory, Research Practice, Training, 45:268-272.

Eckert , R. A. (n.d.). *Remembering Martha Raye WW II, Korea, Vietnam*. American Legion. Accessed from https://www.legion.org/yourwords/personalexperiences/252896/remembering-martha-raye-ww-ii-korea-vietnam

Fishel, Anne. *The Benefits of Family Dinner for Adults*. Blog Post May 11, 2021. Accessed from https://thefamilydinnerproject.org/food-for-thought/benefits-family-dinner-adults/

Fishel, Anne. 2022. FAQ. The Family Dinner Project. Accessed from https://thefamilydinnerproject.org/resources/faq/

Fratus, M. (2022, September 2). *Killer Vampires, demon dolls, and Sauerkraut: A brief history of American psyops*. Coffee or Die.Accessed from https://www.coffeeordie.com/craziest- american-psyops

HISTORY OF MACV-SOG. (n.d.). *About SOG*. Accessed from https://sogsite.com/about-sog/

KA-BAR. (n.d.). *About*. Kabar. Accessed from https://www.kabar.com/customer/aboutUs.jsp

Kniffin, Kevin M., Wansink, Brian, Devine, Carol M. & Sobal, Jeffery (2015). Eating Together at the Firehouse: How Workplace Commensality Relates to the Performance of Firefighters, Human Performance, 28:4, 281-306, DOI: 10.1080/08959285.2015.1021049

Krivdo, M. E. (2018, November 2). *Rescue at Cabanatuan*. U.S. Army Special Operations History. Accessed from https://arsof-history.org/articles/v14n2_cabanatuan_page_1.html

LT Michael P. Murphy Navy SEAL Museum. (n.d.). *Operation Red Wings*. MurphySeal Museum. Accessed from https://murphsealmuseum.org/operation-red-wings/

Marine Forces Special Operations Command. (2020, September 4). *Who we are*. Marine Raider Recruiting. Accessed from https://www.marsoc.com/who-we-are/

Markowitz, M. (2013, June 3). *Urgent fury: U.S. Special Operations Forces in Grenada, 1983*. Defense Media Network. Accessed from

https://www.defensemedianetwork.com/stories/urgent-fury-u-s-special-operations-forces-in-grenada-1983/

Mayo Clinic Health System. March 22, 2019. Family Meals: Building Relationships. Speaking of Health blog. Accessed from https://www.mayoclinichealthsystem.org/hometown- health/speaking-of-health/family-meals-building-relationships

Military.com. (n.d.). *The Army Rangers: Missions and History*. Accessed from https://www.military.com/special-operations/army-ranger-missions-and- history.html

National Museum of the United States Air Force. (n.d.). *Special Operations: In the Enemy's Backyard*. Accessed from https://www.nationalmuseum.af.mil/Visit/Museum-Exhibits/Fact-Sheets/Display/Article/196083/special-operations-in-the-enemys-backyard/Isby, D. C. (2021, November 23).

National Navy UDT-SEAL Museum. (n.d.). *The History of the Naked Warrior*. Navy Seal Museum. Accessed from https://www.navysealmuseum.org/nakedwarrior

Navy and Marine Corps WWII Commemorative Committee. (n.d.). *Marine Corps Raiders*. United States Marine Corps University. Accessed from https://www.usmcu.edu/Research/Marine-Corps-History-Division/Brief-Histories/Marines-in-World-War-II/Marine-Corps-Raiders/

Osborn, K., & Lin, H. (2022, April 6). *The operation that took out Osama bin Laden*. Military.com. Accessed from https://www.military.com/history/osama-bin-laden-operation-neptune- spear

Sof, E. (2022, April 4). *Task Force 121: The Capture of Saddam Hussein*. Accessed from https://special-ops.org/task-force-121-saddam-hussein-capture/

Ryan, Tom.(2022, April 19). *Sleep in the Military*. Sleep Foundation. Accessed from https://www.sleepfoundation.org/sleep-in-the-military

Sacquety, T. J. (2009, November 4). *Over the Hills and Far Away: The MARS Task Force, the Ultimate Model for Long Range Penetration Warfare*. Accessed from https://arsofhistory.org/articles/v5n4_over_the_hills_page_1.html

Schaeffer, K. (2021, April 5). *The changing face of America's veteran population*. Pew Research Center. Accessed from https://www.pewresearch.org/fact-tank/2021/04/05/the- changing-face-of-americas-veteran-population/

Seals, R. (2019, January 25). *MACV-SOG history*. Accessed from https://www.army.mil/article/216498/macv_sog_history

Searcey, Dionne. (2016). A General's New Mission: Leading a Charge Against PTSD. *New York Times*. Retrieved from https://nyti.ms/2dElkYT

Sisk, R. (2019, October 27). *ISIS Leader Baghdadi Killed In Daring Special Ops Nighttime Raid In Syria*. Military.com. Accessed from https://www.military.com/daily-news/2019/10/27/isis-leader-baghdadi-killed-daring-special-ops-nighttime-raid- syria.html

Smith, S. (2021, September 29). *What Are You Doing This Memorial Day? Try the Murph*. Military.com. Accessed from https://www.military.com/military-fitness/workouts/what-are-you-doing-this-memorial-day-try-the-murph

Snow, C.E., Beals, D.E. 2006 Mealtime talk that supports literacy development. New Directions in Child and Adolescent Behavior, 111:51-66.

South, T. (2018, October 2). *The battle of Mogadishu 25 years later: How The fateful fight changed combat operations*. Accessed from https://www.armytimes.com/news/your-army/2018/10/02/the-battle-of-mogadishu-25-years-later-how-the-fateful-fight-changed-combat-operations/

Special Operations Command South. (n.d.). *Special Operations Command South (SOCSOUTH)*. Accessed from https://www.socom.mil/socsouth

Special Operations Command North. (n.d.). *Special Operations Command North (SOCNORTH)*. Accessed from https://www.socom.mil/socnorth/Pages/default.aspx

The American Legion. (n.d.). *Blue Star Banner*. American Legion. Accessed from https://www.legion.org/troops/bluestar

The Family Dinner Project. 2019. Eat, Laugh, Talk: The Family Dinner Playbook. Familius LLC.

The Family Dinner Project Team. Research Shows Family Dinner Improves Literacy. Blog Post August 31, 2020. Accessed from https://thefamilydinnerproject.org/blog/research- shows-family-dinner-improves-literacy/

The Yarborough Knife: Symbol of a legacy. Professional soldiers. (2010, March 28). Accessed from https://www.professionalsoldiers.com/forums/showthread.php?t=28311

United States Special Operations Command Pacific. (n.d.). *Special Operations Command Pacific (SOCPAC)*. Accessed from https://www.socom.mil/socpac/

USAICoE Command History Office. (2013, December 6). *Operation RED DAWN nets Saddam Hussein*. www.army.mil. Accessed from https://www.army.mil/article/116559/operation_red_dawn_nets_saddam_hussein

U.S. Army. (n.d.). *Gold Star Survivors*. www.army.mil. Accessed from https://www.army.mil/goldstar/

U.S. Army Rangers. (n.d.). *History & Heritage*. Heritage - United States Army Rangers - The United States Army. Accessed from https://www.army.mil/ranger/heritage.html

U.S. Department of Defense. (2021, September 15). *The POW/MIA or Missing Man Table*. Accessed from https://www.defense.gov/external-content/story/Article/2776327/the- powmia-or-missing-man-table/

U.S. Special Operations Command Africa. (n.d.). *Welcome*. Accessed from https://www.socom.mil/socaf/

U.S. Special Operations Command Central . (n.d.). *Welcome*. Accessed from https://www.socom.mil/soccent/Pages/Home.aspx

Utter J, Larson N, Laska MN, Winkler M, Neumark-Sztainer D. Self-Perceived Cooking Skills in Emerging Adulthood Predict Better Dietary Behaviors and Intake 10 Years Later: A Longitudinal Study. J Nutr Educ Behav. 2018 May;50(5):494-500. doi: 10.1016/j.jneb.2018.01.021. Epub 2018 Mar 7. PMID: 29525525; PMCID: PMC6086120.

Warner, M. (2000, May). *Office of Strategic Services - Central Intelligence Agency*. Accessed from https://www.cia.gov/static/7851e16f9e100b6f9cc4ef002028ce2f/Office-of- Strategic-Services.pdf

WebMD Editorial Contributors. (n.d.). *Psychological Benefits of Routines*. WebMD. Accessed from https://www.webmd.com/mental-health/psychological-benefits-of-routine

Yaribeygi H, Panahi Y, Sahraei H, Johnston TP, Sahebkar A. The impact of stress on body function: A review. EXCLI J. 2017 Jul 21;16:1057-1072. doi: 10.17179/excli2017-480. PMID: 28900385; PMCID: PMC5579396.

VeteranLife. (2022, February 4). *U.S. Military Dress Uniforms: What Each Branch Wears To Look Their Best*. VeteranLife. Accessed from https://veteranlife.com/lifestyle/military-dress- uniforms/

Virginia War Memorial Foundation. (n.d.). *The Missing Man Table*. Virginia War Memorial. Accessed from https://vawarmemorial.org/the-missing-man-table/

Dinner time can only hold a toddler for a short while. *(Photo courtesy of Jussley Filcik)*

Recipe Index

★ ★ ★

Side Dishes

Desserts

CAKES & PIES

Book Features